# THE HEALER'S VOCATION

"Now, suppose we find out just how much you know already," Dom Kilian said to the student. "Can you hold pain and bleeding? Do you want to see what the inside of your hand looks like?"

"Aye, Domine," Simonn murmured.

Without further preamble, and watching the boy very closely, Kilian jabbed a knife blade into the flesh of Simonn's hand, to half the depth of his little finger nail. Simonn's gaze flicked away, but he neither flinched nor bled. The Healer turned the wounded hand and pressed at the sides to make the wound open.

Simonn admitted, "I—when you move the wound, so that it gapes, it feels like a—a mouth, where no mouth should be. I can feel the coolness of the air in the wound, which should be warm."

"We'll examine those perceptions in our next session," Kilian promised. "For now, it's time to heal this wound."

By Katherine Kurtz
*Published by Ballantine Books:*

# DERYNI MAGIC

## Katherine Kurtz

A DEL REY BOOK

BALLANTINE BOOKS • NEW YORK

A Del Rey Book
Published by Ballantine Books

Library of Congress Catalog Card Number: 90–93285

ISBN 0-345-36117-2

Manufactured in the United States of America

First Edition: January 1991

Cover Art by Michael Herring

for
John and Caitlín Matthews
Companions on the Quest

# CONTENTS

# Foreword

A grimoire is a book about magic. Depending on the variety of magic, a grimoire may be a collection of spells and recipes, a more formal book of ritual procedures, a book of magical instruction, or sometimes a combination of all three.

This grimoire is mostly akin to the latter, though it is not so much a book of instruction as a book of exposition and a companion book to the ten novels and the collection of short stories that currently make up the canon of work in the universe of the Deryni. In chronological order of their occurrence (not the order in which they were written and published), the books comprising the Deryni Canon are:

> *Camber of Culdi*
> *Saint Camber*
> *Camber the Heretic*
> *The Harrowing of Gwynedd*
> *Deryni Rising*
> *Deryni Checkmate*
> *High Deryni*
> *The Bishop's Heir*
> *The King's Justice*
> *The Quest for Saint Camber*

In addition, the short stories collected in *The Deryni Archives* cover the entire time span of the novels. All page citations refer to the standard Del Rey paperback editions.

# INTRODUCTION

# Deryni Magic:
# A Few Definitions

Deryni magic. It began as a fictional concept, based on real-world theories of magical practice and mystical thought and a generous sprinkling of speculation. Over the years (and through ten novels and a collection of short stories, to date), it has assumed almost mythic proportions for the many readers who enjoy exploring Gwynedd and its environs. What is the allure? What is it about the Eleven Kingdoms that inspires such fascination and, indeed, devotion?

Well, familiarity, for one thing. For Gwynedd and its neighboring kingdoms are roughly parallel to our own tenth-, eleventh-, and twelfth-century England, Wales, and Scotland in terms of culture, level of technology, similarity of social structure, and influence of a powerful medieval Church that extends its machinations into the lives of nearly everyone, highborn or low. The major difference, aside from historical personalities and places, is that magic works. Those who can make that magic work are called Deryni.

So. If familiarity is one side of Gwynedd's coin, the other might be the mystery of the Deryni and their magic. Who are the Deryni, *really*? Where do they come from? How do they do what they do? What *can* they do? What can they *not* do? What *are* Deryni?

In the broadest sense, and by the most convenient phraseology of their detractors, the Deryni are a race of sorcerers and magicians. In fact, neither term is particularly accurate, for a "sor-

1

cerer'' supposedly employs power gained from the assistance or control of evil spirits—which no self-respecting Deryni would espouse—and ''magician,'' in our modern world, more often conjures the illusions and legerdemain of stage magic than any real harnessing of extraordinary power and ability. (Indeed, the Deryni *are* masters of illusion and *may* even have some modest accomplishments in sleight-of-hand, but they are not magicians of the Harry Houdini or David Copperfield school.)

No, the magic that concerns the Deryni is akin to the magic of Merlin and King Arthur, or perhaps the Force taught by Ben (Obi-Wan) Kenobi, in terms of more modern mythology. Dictionaries define magic as ''using the secret forces of nature,'' ''the art of producing illusions,'' and ''mysterious power over the imagination or will.'' These all are aspects of magic as the Deryni see it. Modern practitioners of magic might call it ''the art of causing change in conformity with will.'' No Deryni would disagree.

So, the harnessing and focusing of the will is one of the most important things any practitioner of magic must learn. But what are these secret forces of nature that the magician uses to produce his or her illusions, or to exert a mysterious power over the imagination or will? The Deryni call it magic, but much of what they can do falls into the general category of what we today might call ''paranormal'' phenomena—extrasensory perception or ESP-type functions such as telepathy, telekinesis, teleportation, and the like—functions we now are beginning to suspect may be far more normal than we had dreamed, as science on the brink of the twenty-first century continues to expand our understanding of human potential. If parapsychology is not yet quite a science, it is certainly a protoscience. And what *is* science, after all, but an understanding of how and why things work? If we do not have this understanding, as our medieval forebears did not, then we tend to call unexplainable phenomena ''magic.'' The medieval perspective might, indeed, have considered paranormal phenomena to be one aspect of ''magic.''

In fact, much of what we call science today would have been regarded as magic to the feudal, superstitious, nontechnological folk of the Middle Ages. Copernicus was regarded as a heretic for asserting that the earth went around the sun. Electricity surely was magic, until pioneers like Benjamin Franklin began discovering otherwise. Boxes that show moving pictures? Obviously akin to the "magic mirror" by which Sir Francis Drake was believed to have spied on the Spanish fleet. And diseases caused by invisible animalcules called "germs"? Nonsense! Why, everyone knew that "evil humours" made people get sick—or perhaps the wrath of God.

Of course, not all "magical" phenomena can be explained, even by modern science. Complicating matters in Gwynedd is the fact that even the Deryni themselves cannot always distinguish between *natural* Deryni abilities (paranormal-type functions, arising from and directed by an act of will); the grey area of ritual procedures that, when performed with suitable mental intent and focus, concentrate the operator's own power to produce certain predictable results; and *super*natural connections that even the Deryni cannot begin to explain, which tap into unknown power sources in unknown ways, at unknown cost to the well-being of one's immortal soul, the certain existence of which is also unknown. The latter is a realm that has always been of profound interest to those engaged in philosophical pursuits, whether those of science, organized religion, or the more esoteric disciplines that lie between and beyond.

The Deryni, then, have abilities and power connections that are not accessible to most people—though even Deryni are not omnipotent. At their best, the Deryni might represent the ideal of perfected humankind—the mastery of self and surroundings that all of us *might* attain, if we could learn to rise above our earthbound limitations and fulfill our highest destinies. In that respect, one would like to think there is at least a little Deryni in all of us.

Such attainment does not come easily or cheaply, however. With few exceptions, the use of one's Deryni abilities must be learned, like any other skill—and some Deryni are more skilled and stronger than others. Primary proficiencies have to do with balances—physical, psychic, and spiritual—and mastering one's own body and perceptions. All such control requires the ability to enter an "altered state" of consciousness, usually achieved by some form of meditation. Even without formal instruction, most Deryni can learn to banish fatigue (at least for a while), to block physical pain, and to induce sleep—skills that can be applied to oneself or to others, Deryni or not, with or often without the conscious cooperation of the subject, especially a human one. Some Deryni also have the power to heal—a greatly prized talent, though relatively rare even among Deryni, and requiring very specialized training for optimum use. A fully qualified Healer, provided he has time to engage healing rapport before his patient expires, can deal successfully with just about any physical injury.

Few would take serious exception to the abilities we have just outlined—other than sleep induction, perhaps, if it were used to the detriment of a subject unable to resist. What is far more threatening to non-Deryni is the potential use of Deryni powers outside a healing context. For Deryni can also read minds, often without the knowledge or consent of a human subject; and they can impose their will on others. Some extremely competent Deryni have even been known to take on the shape of another person.

In actual practice, there are definite limitations to the extent of all these abilities, of course, though most non-Deryni have wildly exaggerated notions of what those limitations might be, if they even acknowledge their existence. Nor are human fears reassured by the fact that some Deryni can tap into energies outside even their own understanding, consorting with powers that appear to defy or even challenge God's will.

Fear of what is not understood becomes a major theme, then, as the human and Deryni characters interact within the framework of the Deryni universe. For *us* to understand that interaction, we should begin by taking a brief, historical look at the Deryni in Gwynedd.

# CHAPTER ONE

# The Deryni:
# Origins and Historical Background

Nowhere have we yet been told just where the Deryni originated. We may surmise that they were not indigenous to Gwynedd, or at least not present in any great numbers, else the Deryni Prince Festil's invasion from Torenth in 822 would not have made such an impact. That Festil of Furstan was a younger son of a well-established Deryni ruling house tells us that they must have gained a strong toehold in Torenth (and perhaps other kingdoms to the east) at quite an early date—yet not so early that the western European and Mediterranean cultural imperatives associated with that part of the world in our own universe could be much influenced by the Deryni presence. Moorish-Islamic expansion over the previous two centuries would have had far more cultural impact; over the *next* two centuries, Moorish influence would have become even more marked, with the faintly Byzantine feel of King Imre's basically Torenthi court shifting to a more blatantly eastern flavor by the time of Wencit of Torenth, complete with an eastern orthodox-type religious structure and Moorish vassals. Whatever the origins of Gwynedd's Torenthi invaders, however, the followers of Prince Festil must have wielded powerful magic, for sheer force of arms alone can hardly account for the stranglehold they exerted over Gwynedd for the next eighty-three years.

Far stronger in Gwynedd than the influence of Torenth and

5

other neighbors to the east are the Celtic roots of the land itself. Very early on, isolated references to individual Deryni adepts begin to appear in written and oral sources, with several mostly Deryni colonies well ensconced in the central and northern plains areas by the beginning of the sixth century. Some of them claimed descent from refugees who fled the destruction of Caeriesse, said to have disappeared beneath the sea in the first quarter of the sixth century. Scholarly debate continues on the precise location of the doomed kingdom—as well as its literal existence—but most authorities suppose it to have been somewhere off the coast of what later became known as Kierney, where reefs and shoals abound and ghostly underwater bells sometimes are heard during storms. Local tradition would have it that Caeriesse's doom was foretold by a Deryni seeress called Nesta, in a series of prophecies later collected as the *Liber Fati Caeriesse*, but most historians of this period hold that the work was written after the fact, and some regard it as purely a work of fiction.

Whether or not Caeriesse existed as an actual place, by the mid-sixth century it had become a symbolic focus for much that the Deryni came to revere, a magical wellhead for the quasi-Druidic, Celto-Christian mysticism that was to become the hallmark of Deryni esotericism. The best known and most important group to claim Caeriessan antecedents was the Varnarite School, its founder said to have been a nephew of the legendary Nesta.

That the proto-Varnarites did come from outside Gwynedd is probably true, but whether from west or east may never be known. Whatever their origin, by the beginning of the seventh century the Varnarite School was part of the great university complex that had sprung up under the auspices of Canons Regular of the Cathedral Chapter at Grecotha. (The ledger stone that Camber and Joram read in the *templum* underneath the bishop's palace there reads either 603 or 503.) A charter granted in 651 by Augarin Haldane, ratified by the Archbishop of Valoret, and still held in the archives of All Saint's Cathedral, Valoret, confirms the institution of a seminary for the training of priests for the Province of the Purple March and further extends the mandate of the university to instruct young laymen of the nobility in reading and writing, mathematics, theology, philosophy, and medicine, the latter available both for human physician-trainees and for Healers—for Healer's training was only just becoming standardized for Deryni with that particular gift.

Unfortunately, the very process of setting up the university exacerbated philosophical differences already stirred by the amalgamation of the mostly Deryni Varnarite School, the mostly human Grecotha Chapter, and the associated smaller collegia and scholae, with the result that, in the early 700s, archconservative clergy among the Varnarites began quietly leaving the university, eventually to surface in 745 as the Order of Saint Gabriel, of which more later. Around the same time, we encounter vague references to an elite esoteric fraternity of Deryni called the Airsid, apparently in disagreement both with the Chapter and the proto-Gabrilites, who also split off and went underground. Beyond their name, little more is known about the Airsid except that they were involved in the construction of a stronghold and working lodge complex (never finished) that eventually became the headquarters for the Camberian Council, now believed to be located somewhere in coastal Rhendall.

As for the remaining Varnarites and their school, the departure of their more conservative brethren had only eased but not resolved the ongoing friction with the Cathedral Chapter. Rather than allow their ongoing differences to diminish the effectiveness of the university, it was mutually agreed that the Varnarites should separate from the chapter and move their facilities to a new site outside the city walls. In exchange for that site and for signing over their old properties to the Bishops of Grecotha— which is how the diocese came to own the manor house being converted to a bishop's palace at the time of Camber-Alister's incumbency—the Varnarites were permitted to take with them a fair share of the great library accumulated jointly over the years of association, mainly volumes pertaining specifically to Deryni, the only stipulation being that the Varnarite Library must remain accessible to researchers at the university. Whatever the precise cause of the separation, it presumably was of an amicable and nondoctrinal nature, for the Bishops of Grecotha permitted a mostly Deryni rival school to flourish in peace, just outside the city walls, for nearly two hundred years—until the Restoration, when all Deryni institutions faced the opprobrium of the ecclesiastical hierarchy.

These were days of relative human-Deryni amity, as the comparatively few Deryni in Gwynedd assimilated into the community and human warlords worked at consolidating the central lands of the Eleven Kingdoms. We know from documents that Evaine has read into the canon that very powerful Deryni like the great Orin and Jodotha, his disciple, were deeply involved in the affairs of the early Haldane kings. Nor can they have been perceived as any particular threat by the reigning human House, for Deryni were among the desert-bred knights who helped King Bearand push back the Moorish incursions of the mid-700s and who stayed at his invitation to found what became the Order of Saint Michael.

Certainly humans in general did not fear the Deryni as a race, though individual humans may have come to fear certain individual Deryni. For centuries before the Deryni Interregnum, especially under the consolidating rule of a succession of mostly benevolent Haldane kings, Deryni were few enough and circumspect enough in their dealings with humans that the two races lived more or less in harmony. The Deryni founded schools, hospices, and religious institutions and orders and shared their knowledge and healing talents with anyone in need, their own internal disciplines discouraging any gross abuse of the vast powers at their command. Certainly there must have been occasional incidents, for the greater powers of the Deryni surely subjected them to greater temptations. Exclusively Deryni outrages must have been rare, for we find no evidence of general hostility toward Deryni before 822, when Prince Festil, youngest son of the King of Torenth, invaded from the east and accomplished a sudden coup, massacring all the Haldane royal family except for the two-year-old Prince Aidan, who escaped.

We can blame the ensuing Festillic regime for much of the deterioration of human-Deryni relations after the invasion, for the Deryni followers of Festil I were largely landless younger sons like himself and quickly recognized the material gains to be had in the conquered kingdom by exploiting their Deryni advantages. Much was shrugged off or overlooked in the early years of the new dynasty, for any conqueror takes a while to consolidate his power and set up the apparatus for ruling his new kingdom. But Deryni excesses and abuse of power in high places became increasingly blatant, eventually leading, in 904, to the ouster of Imre, the last Festillic king, by fellow Deryni and the restoration of the old human line in the person of Cinhil Haldane, grandson of the Prince Aidan who had escaped the first Festil's butchers. The instrument of Imre's downfall and Cinhil's restoration was Camber MacRorie, Earl of Culdi, whose great-grandfather had come with the conqueror seeking lands and fame.

Unfortunately, Deryni magic itself, and not the ill judgment and avarice of a few individuals, came to be blamed for the evils of the Interregnum. Nor, once the Restoration was accomplished, did the new regime waste overmuch time adopting the aims, if not the methods, of their former masters. After the death of the restored King Cinhil Haldane in 917, regency councils dominated successive Haldane kings for more than twenty years—for Cinhil's sons were young and died young, within a decade, and the next heir was Cinhil's grandson Owain, but four years old when he came to the throne.

Such an enticing opportunity to redistribute the spoils of the Restoration to their own benefit could hardly be overlooked by regents nursing memories of past injustices. With lands, titles, and offices in the reckoning, the Deryni role in the Restoration soon became eclipsed by more emotion-charged recollections of the abuses that had triggered the overthrow of Deryni overlords. In the space of only a few years, Deryni remaining in Gwynedd found themselves politically, socially, and religiously disenfranchised, the new masters using any conceivable pretext to seize the wealth and influence of the former rulers.

The religious hierarchy played its part as well. In the hands of a now human-dominated Church, political expedience took on a veneer of philosophical justification in less than a generation, so that the Deryni soon came to be regarded as evil in and of themselves, the Devil's brood, possibly beyond the salvation even of the Church—for surely no righteous and God-fearing person could do the things the Deryni did. Therefore, the Deryni *must* be the agents of Satan. Only total renunciation of one's powers might permit a Deryni to survive, and then only under the most rigid of supervision. The slightest transgression against a rigid code of permissible behavior could lead to death.

None of this happened overnight, of course. But the Deryni had never been many; with the great Deryni families gradually fallen from favor or destroyed, most individuals outside the immediate circles of political power, whether temporal or spiritual, failed to realize how the balance was shifting until it was too late. The great anti-Deryni persecutions that followed the death of Cinhil Haldane reduced the already small Deryni population of Gwynedd by fully two-thirds. Some fled to the safety of other lands, where being openly Deryni did not carry an automatic death sentence, but many more perished. Only a few managed to go underground, keeping their true identities secret, and many who did go underground simply suppressed what they were, never telling their descendants of their once-proud heritage.

This, then, is a very general background of the Deryni. It is told in far greater detail in the ten novels and eight short stories that currently comprise the Deryni canon. The Camber Trilogy—*Camber of Culdi*, *Saint Camber*, and *Camber the Heretic*—chronicles the overthrow of the last Festillic king by Camber MacRorie and his children, their restoration of King Cinhil Haldane, and what happened immediately after the death of King Cinhil, thirteen years later. The Heirs of Saint Camber Trilogy, beginning with *The Harrowing of Gwynedd* and continuing with the forthcoming *King Javan's Year* and *The Bastard Prince*, continues the immediate post-Camber saga. The Chronicles of the Deryni—*Deryni Rising*, *Deryni Checkmate*, and *High Deryni*—take place nearly two hundred years later, when anti-Deryni feeling has begun to abate somewhat among the common folk, but not yet within the hierarchies of the Church, as a boy-king with Deryni blood and Deryni friends assumes his murdered father's throne. The Histories of King Kelson—*The Bishop's Heir*, *The King's Justice*, and *The Quest for Saint Camber*—pick up after the Chronicles, as King Kelson comes into his young manhood. The short stories set out in *The Deryni Archives* are interspersed across the entire time line, the earliest falling in 888 and the latest in 1118, and mostly expand on minor incidents or characters first encountered in the novels. In preparation is the Childe Morgan Trilogy, falling chronologically just before the Chronicles, as well as a single novel concerning the bride King Kelson finally gets to keep.

Given this milieu of Deryni magic, now let's look at its different facets in detail.

# CHAPTER TWO

# Religious Framework I: Structure of the Church, Religious Orders, and the Sacraments of Baptism and Matrimony

In general, the official or institutional Church in Gwynedd is very close in structure to the medieval church of our own tenth-, eleventh-, and twelfth-century England, Wales, Scotland, and Ireland. The single greatest difference is the Church's acknowledgment of the existence of magic—leaving aside, for the moment, any moral judgment of whether that magic is good or ill, for at different times, Gwynedd's Church has at least tolerated careful, circumspect use of the magical arts, and sometimes even condoned it.

The second notable difference is in the hierarchical structure of the Church, owing more to the collegiate structure of our Church of England, with its two primate-archbishops as first among equals, than to Roman influence. In the Deryni universe, we may postulate a gradual shift from Roman to Byzantine influence in the cognate area of the Mediterranean around the fourth to fifth centuries—a shift that very nearly occurred in our own world. The subsequent failure of the Bishop of Rome to achieve recognition as Supreme Pontiff would have diminished Roman influence even further, to the extent that the Council of

11

Whitby (664), if it still occurred, probably would have been dominated by the native Celtic Christian church established by Joseph of Arimathea rather than the Roman version imposed by Saint Patrick.

In Gwynedd and its environs, this comparatively early shift away from Rome meant that the Church retained many of its Celtic roots and hierarchical forms, though the association endured long enough for Latin to become established as the official liturgical language and for many elements of Roman liturgy to become part of the accepted canon. Structurally, collegiality continued to develop, with a handful of powerful regional bishops gradually wielding influence over a larger number of lesser ones, but remaining only primates, first among equals, rather than any single one seizing preeminence. One might think of Valoret and Rhemuth as the rough equivalents of York and Canterbury, co-primates heading a college of titular bishops, based in key cathedral cities and towns; and a varying number of itinerant bishops with no fixed sees, who act somewhat as assistants to the titled bishops (who are largely administrators) and carry out primarily pastoral duties.

Thus, we hear no mention of a Pope or College of Cardinals in Gwynedd—though some similar institutions may exist beyond the desert regions far east of Djellarda, in the area analogous to Byzantium. Even as close as Torenth, just to the east, we know that a more eastern orthodox form of Christianity flourishes, for Kelson is informed that the Torenthi Patriarch of Beldour himself has blessed the gift sent by Duke Mahael of Arjenol, on the occasion of Kelson's knighting.

That the gift is delivered by a Moorish emissary of a Moorish Duke of Torenth underlines the existence of an Islamic parallel as well, somewhere to the east—the most specific reference yet encountered that Moors are a force to be reckoned with, as one goes farther east, though Christians and Moors seem to coexist peacefully enough at this time. (This was not always the case, of course, for King Bearand Haldane was canonized for his part in driving presumably more aggressive Moors out of Gwynedd's sea-lanes in 752.)

Indeed, Moorish influence presumably has permeated the (heavily Deryni) Forcinn Buffer States quite extensively by the time of Kelson's reign, for both Richenda and Rothana are the products of mixed Christian-Moorish marriages and received at least some of their training from Rothana's uncle, the Moorish adept Azim—for whom even the usually cocky Tiercel de Claron seems to have a healthy respect.

> "He's—ah—an acquaintance," Tiercel hedged. "Not an enemy, I assure you, but I can't explain further. Let's just say that he's an old friend and teacher of Richenda's and leave it at that, shall we?" (*The King's Justice* 165)

Azim's exact position in the hierarchy of Deryni adepti has yet to be clarified, but as brother of the Emir Hakim Nur Hallaj and precentor of the Knights of the Anvil—descendants and successors of the Knights of Saint Michael who fled to Djellarda after the Haldane Restoration and the long regencies that followed Cinhil Haldane's death—it is obvious that he wields both political and esoteric influence. We might posit yet unspecified connections with the Camberian Council, perhaps through the equally enigmatic Sofiana, herself of oriental if not Moorish persuasions.

As for Richenda and Rothana themselves, both women ostensibly are Christian, but the practices observed in the courts of their childhoods may have necessitated some interesting compromises by conventional Gwynedd standards. Though at first glance Richenda may seem more westernized than her more exotic cousin—and her first marriage brought her into a quite conventional western family—it is also Richenda who is the better trained and whose magic appears to have more eastern touches. That this training is also of a very high caliber is underlined by the fact that even the very discriminating Arilan has no objection to following her lead for Calling the Quarters at the ritual for setting Nigel's potential—a variation he would never allow if he felt at all unsure of her competence. Undoubtedly we shall be seeing more aspects of this Moorish-blended, eastern brand of Christianity as the histories of Gwynedd continue to unfold.

Incidentally, a number of readers have queried the apparent absence of Jews from Gwynedd. While it is true that Jews have not been mentioned as individuals, one should never assume that absence of proof is proof of absence. Neither Christianity nor Islam could exist without Judaism, after all, and Arilan already has quoted Talmudic precedent as authority for regarding the Reserved Sacrament as a valid witness to Duncan's irregular but licit marriage with Maryse. Such knowledge will not have been handed down in a vacuum.

The Jews as a race perhaps fulfill a slightly different function in Gwynedd than they did in our own Middle Ages, however. Jews need not be the scapegoats for hostility from those threatened by differences and apparent superiority at various endeavors—not when the Deryni fulfill this function even more blatantly. Given a race of sorcerers like the Deryni, whose abilities and powers could confer almost unimaginable advantages, those disposed toward racism found them a far more apparent and justifiable target for persecution than Jews.

Astute Jews would have realized this early on and capitalized on it, keeping a lower profile than their Deryni neighbors—not difficult, especially during the Interregnum—paying lip service to the outward social forms of mainstream Christianity much as the Marranos (Christian Jews) did in medieval Spain, but safer than the Marranos because the majority of hostility was being directed increasingly toward Deryni. As we have seen in *The Harrowing of Gwynedd*, the inquisitors of the immediately post-Restoration regencies began to employ tactics very similar to those used by the Inquisition in our own world, and with similar tragic results for the objects of those inquisitions—and the Deryni themselves displayed some of the same stubborn tendency to ignore the handwriting on the wall until it was too late to save themselves. In a sense, we might say that the Deryni *are* the Jews of Gwynedd, in their targetability and response to persecution.

However, this is not to say that we will never encounter any "real" Jews. Quite probably there are not as many of them in Gwynedd as there were in our analogous Europe, because of differences in the history of the area around the Holy Land, but those who have come to Gwynedd are a quiet part of its culture. When the time comes to tell a story in which being Jewish makes a difference from being merely human or merely Deryni, we will see Jews, have no fear.

We may surmise the existence of several other faiths as well. Ferris' veneration of the All-Father, in "Trial" (*The Deryni*

*Archives* 207, 226), suggests a Norse parallel, and there are several references to native, pre-Christian religious practices among the common folk, coexisting alongside Christianity. Most obvious is Prince Javan's questioning of Tavis O'Neill about the remnants of a ritual bonfire he discovers on a hilltop shortly after the Autumn Equinox and asking whether the little folk danced around it (*Camber the Heretic* 284–285). And we can surmise pre-Christian roots for Kelson's ordeal in the underground chamber at Saint Kyriell's, with its vapor-induced vision quest while he slept at the feet of the god-figure (*The Quest for Saint Camber* 377 ff.). At least on the surface, however, the religion of Gwynedd is Christian, and only passing tolerant of magic.

What, then, precisely, is the structure of the religious hierarchy in Gwynedd? The basic hierarchy consists of the Archbishops of Valoret and Rhemuth (of whom Valoret is senior, and styled Primate of All Gwynedd and first among equals); from four to ten additional titled bishops, each of whom administers his assigned geographic area or diocese from a cathedral, assisted by the canon priests of that cathedral Chapter; and up to twelve itinerant bishops, roving prelates with no fixed sees, who peregrinate in smaller assigned areas and carry out mostly pastoral duties rather than administrative ones. Supervision of parish priests comes under the jurisdiction of the diocesan bishop responsible for that parish.

(For a general breakdown of the areas covered by various dioceses, at various times, see Appendix I. For specific listings of Councils of Bishops in Gwynedd at various times during the period 905 to 1125, see Appendix II.)

In addition, there are numerous religious orders whose members assist the episcopal clergy in various ways, some of them running schools, hospices, and seminaries, some contributing more prosaic services in scriptoria, chanceries, and monastic farms. A few of the religious orders cater to purely Deryni needs, such as the Order of Saint Gabriel, primarily geared toward the training of Healers, or the Order of Saint Michael, which produced military officers with the distinctive Deryni edge to their style—though some Michaelines were human and still benefitted greatly from the rigid Michaeline training and discipline.

Various all-human religious orders exist as well. The one

dealing most directly with Deryni matters is the double Order, founded to replace the Michaelines early in the reign of King Alroy, called the *Ordo Custodum Fidei* (Order of the Guardians of the Faith), with its military arm, the *Equites Custodum Fidei*—the Knights of the Most Holy Guardianship. The Custodes became official Inquisitors for the new regime, and developed many and devious ways of dealing with their Deryni adversaries. (For a listing of all the religious orders mentioned to date, see Appendix III.)

Deryni magic is interwoven with all of this. Within the Eleven Kingdoms, it enjoyed a coexistence with institutional religion ranging from faint uneasiness to outright hostility. The Deryni themselves see no contradiction between practicing Christianity and continuing to use their magical powers, so long as those powers are used in an ethical manner. Indeed, within the context of esoteric Christianity, largely hidden from the average person whose religion consists of fulfilling periodic obligations of attendance at public worship, there exist diverse practices and meditation techniques suitable for enhancing an individual's relationship with the Creative Force. Deryni variations, some of them employable by humans as well, seem to enable some devotees to establish a closer link with and awareness of Deity, sometimes to the point that the meditator experiences what has been described by mystics throughout the ages as divine ecstasy.

This closer union with Deity—or the "supposed" closer union—can become an object of jealousy among merely human clergy, who sometimes come to resent the fact that Deryni appear to have a more direct line to God. In fact, the line is probably no more direct, only more obvious, on a conscious level, to someone linked in this way. Less enlightened persons, whatever their race, may tend to overlook the likelihood that those truly establishing close communion with the Deity, whether human or Deryni, probably are highly evolved souls to begin with and are not likely to boast of it.

But the fact remains that many humans feel disenfranchised because they cannot (or think they cannot) function in this mode, and thus cannot make the sacred connection. From there, it is only a short step of illogic to conclude that the Deryni themselves, and not any human failing, are responsible for denying humans this glimpse of Divinity.

Deryni Healers are probably the one group of Deryni per se who are not greatly resented by the bulk of humanity, for humans, like Deryni, regard healing as a God-given gift and the Healer's vocation every bit as sacred a calling as that to the priesthood. Indeed, Healers are governed by a code of ethics and conduct far more demanding than that required of ordinary physicians, and no less stringent than the moral code applied to priests. Unfortunately, Healers are rare, even among Deryni, so little tolerance spills over to Deryni in general.

Adding to the confusion is the fact that many of the "miracles" reported in sacred scripture can be duplicated by Deryni, especially those having to do with healing. Indeed, the method whereby Deryni Healers lay hands on their patients to effect healing is indistinguishable from biblical accounts—at least superficially. (As we shall see, when we examine the healing gifts more closely, a bit more is involved than simply laying hands on a patient; but neither are we ever given any insight into the actual mechanism of biblical healing.) By that reasoning, if healing comes of God, then Healers, at least, cannot possibly partake of the evil carried by the rest of their race. Yet, if this is accepted as a given, then it follows that other Deryni may not be evil either—which opens a floodgate of dangerous speculation.

The Deryni ability to project an aura of light about the head is also a talent of biblical significance—for is an aureole of light about the head not the sign of a saint or angel? And what of the Deryni ability to conjure fire (as in pillars of, and burning bushes), or to cause rain or lightning, or even to take on another's shape for disguise? Angelic attributes, one might say. And yet, is Satan himself not a fallen angel, with the same abilities as his heavenly counterparts, and a master of deception? What if the Deryni serve *him*?

Rational men are able to keep these kinds of doubts and worries under control when society is in balance and when those who can wield such powers restrain themselves, disdaining to use their powers to the disadvantage of mere mortals. But when power runs rampant, and those gifted with greater powers and abilities misuse those powers, resentment, anger, and impotence in the face of unarguable greater strength soon give way to fear, irrational generalization about *everyone* having such abilities (whether or not they use them unjustly), and justification for a backlash of reverse persecution, as soon as resistance becomes possible.

We see tragic illustration of this sad commentary on human shortsightedness in the months immediately surrounding the death of King Cinhil, as those long oppressed under the former Deryni dictators regain their freedom and force the pendulum back in the opposite direction, doing to Deryni the very things that Deryni were doing to humans. And because religious zeal is one of the more powerful tools available to society, the institutional Church becomes one of the prime arbiters of the new morality, "restoring" the balance to the long-oppressed human population and meting out "justice" to those who caused their discontent.

Keeping Deryni out of the hierarchy of that Church is one of the most effective ways of eliminating this aspect of Deryni influence, and keeping them out of the priesthood is the only way to ensure that. By the decree of the Council of Ramos in 918, they are forbidden to seek ordination, on pain of excommunication and death, for Deryni are judged to be "spawn of Satan" and less savory terms. Under the guidance of men like Archbishop Hubert and Paulin of Ramos, the Church is quick to develop clandestine and uniquely Deryni-specific ways of enforcing these restrictions—ways that will remain a secret from Deryni for nearly two hundred years, until the young Denis Arilan dares to defy the bishops' ban and discovers how it has been perpetuated (*The Deryni Archives* 100–157). One would rather not imagine all the good and pious Deryni, desiring only to serve God as His priests, who must have perished terribly in the intervening years, convinced that God had abandoned them to be struck down for their presumption, yet who really were sacrificed unwittingly on the altar of human fear and vindictiveness.

But the history of Deryni within the context of Christianity has not been all negative. At the height of Deryni supremacy in Gwynedd, before and during the Interregnum, regardless of what was happening on a secular level, Deryni functioning within the institutional Church added to the faith far more than they detracted. The magic of the all-Deryni and mostly Deryni orders such as the Gabrilites and Michaelines brought a richness to

Christian expression that is far too seldom glimpsed in our own world—not a substitute for traditional religious belief but an overlap, parallel, and augmentation of the "merely human" elements. In fact, there is no such thing as "merely human" religious expression, for religion, by definition, is magical, dealing with That Which lies beyond human comprehension. When the magic goes wrong, purely human motives of avarice, jealousy, or blind superiority generally lie at the root of the failure, as we may see as we examine a few examples of how Deryni magic touches a cross section of Christian sacraments illustrated thus far, for good or ill. Of the traditional seven sacraments, all but confirmation have been seen in a Deryni context.

*Baptism* is the first sacrament experienced by any Christian. In the baptism of Cinhil's firstborn son, Prince Aidan, we see Deryni magic gone tragically wrong. The ceremony seems to proceed without incident until Archbishop Anscom offers the former priest, King Cinhil, the opportunity to baptize his own son, "for even a layman may baptize in necessity, Cinhil, and I believe you more than qualify" (*Camber of Culdi* 273). But Deryni power turned to evil is already at work, for a Michaeline priest, himself Deryni, has been forcibly subverted by the perfidious King Imre and has added poison to the salt placed on the infant's tongue earlier during the ceremony. The infant Aidan is already dying by the time his father pours the water over his head. The only thing positive to come of this day's work is that Cinhil's outrage at this sacrilegious murder of his son catalyzes his own ability to use the magical powers awakened in him by his Deryni allies—an event long awaited by those trying to restore him to his throne, though the price is not one that any of them would have chosen.

The imagery of baptism is also the springboard for a more benign if decidedly unorthodox use of the outward form of the sacrament in Revan's Baptizer cult. The morality of such use gives qualms even to those who conceive the plan, but they eventually justify their action on the grounds that its intent is not sacramental but purificatory (and obfuscatory). Many faiths have used a form of baptism as a rite of purification and/or initiation. The outward form of Revan's rite of baptism utilizes the symbolism of dying to sin and a rebirth in new life, as a vehicle for utilizing Tavis' and Sylvan's ability to block the powers of certain Deryni so that they may elude the authorities and escape to build new lives. The ramifications of this concept are too numerous to recount here, but are examined in some detail in *The Harrowing of Gwynedd* and will be explored in even greater depth in *King Javan's Year*.

The sacrament of *matrimony* appears to be touched far more by human than by specifically Deryni concerns. We have not yet seen a wedding of two Deryni, though we have caught glimpses of a Deryni marriage in Rhys and Evaine, and Morgan and Richenda. The wedding of the browbeaten Cinhil Haldane with the young Megan Cameron is painfully human, with both of the pair agonizing over their decisions to carry through with what has been set in motion by forces bigger than either of them. Yet there is a very human magic in Megan's trust and determination that she *will* be a good wife to her future king, who so needs her gentleness and support, and for whom she is willing to sacrifice her own possible happiness with someone nearer her own age and interests, if only he will allow himself to feel at least some faint affection for her. And there is undeniable magic in that moment when Cinhil actually must face his bride and make his marriage vows, setting aside his priestly vocation for a king's duty, and the trembling wonder, verging on terror, as he looses her hair to place a consort's coronet on her head. Later, in the bridal chamber, the magic continues, bringing even the repressed and fearful Cinhil to at least a temporary glimpse of the wonder of the marriage sacrament, as they consummate their union.

The next royal wedding we are allowed to witness ends in tragedy, but even in the painful and duty-bound courtship and marriage of Kelson and Sidana, we see a magic at work. Here, again, the alliance begins out of duty—and hostility, on Sidana's part, exacerbated by her brother's spite and venom—but Kelson, his own moral scruples strained by the pressure of dynastic urgency, manages to persuade Sidana of the necessity of the match without, in the end, compromising himself, his kingdom's interests, or his intended bride.

Her consent once secured, it is unclear whether Kelson might, indeed, have resorted to force, whether physical or psychic, if he had not been able to convince her by reason. Burgeoning sexual chemistry has its own imperatives that, for good or ill, only reinforce the dynastic considerations. Given that the immediate purpose of the marriage is to get an heir as soon as possible, Kelson's growing physical desire for Sidana is neither unreasonable nor unwelcome. Still, it is to Kelson's credit that by the time he escorts his bride to the cathedral, he has also managed to convince himself that the practicalities of duty *can* eventually lead to mutual respect and hopefully eventual affection. So he prays, as he watches his bride come down the aisle.

Lord, forgive me if I approach Thy altar with reservations in my heart. . . . Let me love the woman I am about to marry—and let her love me. And help me to be a wise and compassionate husband to her. . . . O God, she wears peace like a mantle! . . . Please, Lord, let it be peace between the two of us, as well as our lands. I don't want to have to kill her people. I don't want to have to kill anyone else. I want to create life, not death. Please, Lord. . . . (The Bishop's Heir 335–336)

We sense that Sidana, too, may have managed to shed most of the negative influence of her brother and at least embraced the possibility that she could learn to love this handsome and puissant young king. But alas, even Deryni magic is not enough to save Sidana from her brother's final act of blind devotion to his own political cause—or perhaps he senses a little of the sexual tension and cannot cope with that. Morgan and Duncan, though they carry the Healer's gifts, have not the skill to apply those gifts quickly enough to save the ill-fated Sidana. And Kelson, constrained by his own scruples not to use his powers to learn his bride's true feelings for him, is doomed never to know.

The next Haldane marriage we see is less fraught with immediate tragedy, but no less a disaster for the principals. Rothana is a far more willing bride than Sidana, but only in the sense that her training and greater maturity allow her to recognize and accept the inescapable logic of Conall's proposal. If Kelson really is dead—and at this point, no one has any reason to suspect that he is not—then all of the reasoning Conall uses to persuade her to accept him is sound. Rothana's upbringing will not allow her the luxury of paralytic grief when a way still exists to accomplish so much for the good of her race. In that respect, Conall is entirely correct when he tells her that only the name of the king has changed.

And so the marriage of true minds, which might have been her lot in a marriage with Kelson, becomes a pale parody of what might have been—for Conall, despite many apparent similarities, is not Kelson. One might argue that Rothana should have been able to see behind Conall's façade—she is supposed to be well trained, after all, and certainly was more than Kelson's match when she forced him to experience Princess Janniver's rape memory. But we must remember that she has been bred to duty, to her gifts as well as her race. Deryni etiquette does not permit the forcing of another's mind without good cause, and Rothana has no cause to suspect Conall's motives. His shields might have given pause to a more world-wise Deryni than Rothana, but Conall *is* a royal Haldane, after all; who knows what they can and cannot do? Even the more experienced Deryni around Conall—Morgan, Duncan, Richenda, and *Arilan*—are deceived, for a time.

And would Rothana really expect Conall to initiate psychic intimacies that properly should not come until after marriage anyway? If he even knows of such things, Conall surely has enough on his mind, during the unexpected transition from prince to regent to king in all but name. He says he loves her—as, indeed, he does, in his own, possessive way—and he urges her to be the Deryni queen that Gwynedd needs, as Kelson himself urged her to do. He tells her no lies; he simply chooses which aspects of truth he will reveal to her. Truth-Reading will not detect the rot at this root.

So Rothana, numbed by the suddenness of falling in love, leaving the religious life, losing her intended bridegroom, and then being offered a chance to still have at least part of her dream, reacts with far more maturity than we might expect of most eighteen-year-olds. She makes the choice that still may make a difference for her people.

It remains to be seen how Rothana and Kelson will go on to deal with their situation, now that Conall is dead. One may surmise that Rothana, at least, will be far less circumspect about using her powers to confirm what she seems to perceive through merely human senses. And if Rothana and Kelson ever *should* get together, we may expect Deryni magic of a rare and magnificent sort.

Indeed, we know of at least two other marriages that certainly must have involved Deryni interaction of a very high level. We are shown no details of the wedding of Evaine and Rhys, reported to have taken place in the octagonal chapel of the Michaeline haven during that winter of hiding before Cinhil was restored to the throne, but it is evident from their relationship thereafter that this was, indeed, a marriage of true minds. "Rhys and I are mated in our souls, as well as hearts and bodies," Evaine tells Revan (*Camber the Heretic* 157). "We could not ask for closer union in this life." The ceremony itself would have been a modest affair, witnessed only by the handful of family and exiled Michaelines in residence there, but Joram might well have incorporated Deryni elements into the ritual.

The wedding of Morgan and Richenda provides scope for even more speculation, knowing what we do of their sometimes stormy relationship. Though the rank of both principals ordinarily would have justified a state wedding of no small scale, Richenda's fairly recent widowhood and Morgan's own notoriety as Deryni must have reduced the event to a somewhat more modest affair. In fact, it took place quietly in Marley, on the first of May, 1122, with Duncan as celebrant and Richenda's young son, Brendan, as one of the witnesses. And because neither Richenda nor Duncan was yet known to be Deryni outside a very small circle of intimates, we may be certain that outwardly, at least, there was no hint of Deryni augmentation of the usual, most basic marriage ceremony.

Deryni or not, however, Morgan's ducal status and his close friendship with the king probably would have justified a fairly sumptuous wedding feast, probably with Kelson himself as host. With both the principals and the celebrant being Deryni, it is not unlikely that some sort of private ceremony might have preceded or followed the more formal one in church, incorporating Deryni elements. One day, that story will be told.

# CHAPTER THREE

# Religious Framework II: Holy Orders, Confession, Extreme Unction, and Eucharist

The basic concept behind the Christian sacrament of *Holy Orders* is not unique to Christianity. Indeed, nearly all organized religions have some kind of setting aside of individuals who are to function in a special relationship to Deity, ranging from mere acknowledgment of those who function in a teaching capacity all the way through priestly ordination. In the sacramental sense, and in its optimum exercise, ordination to the Christian priesthood constitutes an esoteric initiation, opening the perceptions of the priestly initiate to a higher level of awareness, the better to perceive and serve God.

We have seen two ordinations of Deryni (Camber and Arilan) and heard mention of a third: Duncan's. We do not see Duncan's ordination, but there must have been Deryni elements aplenty, at least on the inner levels, because some years later, within an hour of going to his episcopal consecration (a higher degree of initiation, if you will), he elicits Morgan's troubled concern when he considers keeping his Deryni shields in place during the rite, to avoid dealing with the strong and possibly painful emotions associated with the martyred Bishop Istelyn's ring.

"Is that really the way you want to experience your consecration as a bishop?" Morgan asked quietly. "You remember your ordination to the priesthood—God knows, *I'll* never forget it. Do you really want to shut yourself away from that kind of magic, Duncan?" (*The Bishop's Heir* 231)

Until this episode of Duncan's life is explored in further detail (in the course of the Childe Morgan Trilogy), we can only guess at the particular kind of magic Duncan must have experienced then, but overall, it must have been profoundly moving—and intense, to have spilled over to Morgan as well (though not to anyone else present, or Duncan would have been revealed as a Deryni). Perhaps Duncan's experience was akin to Camber's at the hands of Anscom of Trevas. Though necessity dictates that Camber's ordination must be clandestine and outwardly modest, with only Joram, Evaine, and Rhys to witness, the Deryni Anscom is able to unleash for Camber the full potential of the priestly initiation, in all the added dimensions perceivable to an adept of Camber's caliber.

The rite that Anscom uses is an older, alternate ordination ritual, which, in fact, contains no historical elements later than twelfth century usage of our own universe. Other than the obviously Deryni warding of the area—and the visual keys of the quarter candles placed at the cardinal points in the little octagonal chapel—little in the ritual's outward form would give pause to even the most conservative modern-day bishop. What goes on inside the ordinand is far more subjective and ultimately can be known only by the ordinand himself. For Deryni, the process at least *seems* to be far more profound than it is for human ordinands, enhanced as it is by that altered state in which Deryni approach most important tasks.

Camber's ordination is a strong case in point. For him, both the warding and the framework of the Mass in which the ordination is embedded serve to help him enter that state of altered consciousness in which he can open his mind most fully to the descent of Deity. The mantralike repetition of the litany during the prostration serves to take him deeper still, so that by the time he kneels before Anscom to receive the laying on of hands, he is ready to experience what is intended.

Camber drew a deep breath and let it out slowly as Anscom's hands were raised above his head. This was the heart of the ordination: the mystical laying on of hands. Resolutely he let his defenses slip away, opening every channel of awareness that he could, that he might feel the Forces of Creation flowing through Anscom and Joram.

"O Lord of Hosts, Who hast made me, Thy servant Anscom, an instrument of Thy will and a channel of Thy power: now, according to the apostolic succession passed in unbroken line by the laying on of hands, I present to Thee this, Thy servant, Camber Kyriell, that he may become Thy priest."

The consecrated hands descended gently on Camber's head, and Camber felt a faint tingling sensation, the building of a pure flow of energy against the outer edges of his mind. His immediate instinct was to withdraw, to shut down, to raise every defense and ward against the awesome Power whose potential he could already sense. But he dared not hold back—not if tonight was to have any meaning.

He felt another hand join Anscom's, gently touching the side of his head, and knew Joram's cool and gentle probe on his mind. Forcing himself to relax and remain open, and reassured by Joram's presence, he closed his eyes and let out another deep breath, surrendering to whatever might come. He sensed his control slipping as Anscom continued speaking.

"*Accipite Spiritum: quorum remiseritis . . .*" Receive the Holy Spirit. Whose sins thou shalt forgive. . . .

There was more, but Camber swiftly lost the meaning of mere words as he concentrated instead upon the sensations he was beginning to experience at Anscom's and Joram's hands. A subtle pressure grew inside his mind, a gradual filling and expanding with Something which was so powerful, so awesome, that no corner of his being escaped Its insistent touch.

His hearing went first, and he knew that his vision also was gone—though he could not, to save his mortal life, have opened his eyes to test that knowledge.

Then all awareness of having a body at all began to recede. He was pure consciousness and more, centered in a bright, shining point, bathed and immersed in a golden brilliance, cool and fascinating, which was unlike anything he had ever experienced or imagined experiencing.

He was no longer frightened; he was engulfed in an emotion of peace and joy and total oneness with all that was and would be and once had been. He stretched and soared on rainbow wings, exulting in the certainty that there was far more to being than a mere mortal body and lifetime—that even when this human body died, whatever guise it wore, he—the essence of him—would continue, would grow, would move on to the fullness of eternity.

In a sparkling instant, he saw his past, and other pasts, in shimmering, quicksilver glimpses, immediately lost to memory; and then his present experience, as though observing his own body from above, quicksilver head bowed unflinching beneath consecrated hands whose touch was both delicate and relentless.

The thought whisked across his consciousness that perhaps he was fantasizing all of this; and a rational part of himself agreed. But another part of him banished that notion almost before it could take definite form.

What did it matter, at this point, whether he was experiencing true reality or one created, born of his own emotional need and reaching? No mere mortal could hope to experience the Godhead in *all* Its many facets. Man the finite could but glimpse the filmy shadow-trails of the Infinite, and that only if he were very fortunate.

But in his present mode, given all the weaknesses and strengths both of human and Deryni resources, was this not as close as he had ever brushed the Power which governed the wheeling of the Universe? (*Saint Camber* 264–266)

All of Camber's experience takes place within his mind, of course, within a real elapsed time of merely a few seconds. To any human observer witnessing the rite, only the physical act of laying on hands would have been apparent, though a particularly perceptive and spiritual human priest might have inferred some kind of inner process taking place, based on his own experience of ordination, and might even have perceived some change in Camber's psychic aura. Even without the agency of a Deryni bishop consciously channeling such a flow of power, we have reports of similar experiences of spiritual ecstasy in our own world. When the connection with Deity is made—when the receiver is open to transmission, the antenna focused to the right wavelength—the Power descends, whether or not the antenna is aware of it. (It is recognition of this principle that lies behind the Church's assertion, since the early fourth century, that the efficacy of a sacrament does not depend on the worthiness or spiritual state of the priest administering the sacrament.)

We may surmise that something of this sort was at work during Duncan's ordination, with the Divine power funneling down through his human bishop to be perceived primarily on the deeper levels of which a Deryni is capable. Remember that priestly ordination *is* a form of initiation, after all, and any outward form of initiation is at best a pale reflection of changes brought about in the initiate at inner levels, experienced by him or her in ways unique to the individual.

Returning to Camber's ordination, however. After his experience of the laying on of hands, the ceremony proceeds according to reasonably orthodox pattern, with peculiarly Deryni references coming in only toward the end, when Anscom addresses his newest priest.

"The rubric indicates that here I am to warn you of the potential danger of that upon which you are about to embark. However, I think you know that, and that you will exercise prudence. You will find, if you have not already guessed, that the rituals authorized by the conferring of the priesthood are no whit less powerful than any of our strictly secular Deryni operations, 'secular,' in the Deryni sense, being a somewhat nebulous term. Perhaps that is why, even in our 'secular' affairs, we are careful to perform our works according to specified and formal procedures. We know, or at least suspect, the length and breadth and height and depth of the Forces we draw upon. . . .

"And so, my dearly beloved son, I will not admonish you as I would any common priest—for you are one of the most uncommon men I know. I will simply wish you all fulfillment in the new responsibilities which you have undertaken here tonight, and will ask you to bear with me as we complete the last portion of your priestly investiture before allowing you to celebrate your first Mass.'' (*Saint Camber* 269)

The peculiarly Deryni responsibilities that Camber has taken on as a priest fall into two general categories. First, as a Deryni, inherently capable of exercising greater conscious control over energies unseen and largely unperceived by mere humans, he will be expected to perform a more efficient and consciously responsible mediation of the power raised by celebration of the Eucharist—itself one of the most powerful magical rituals ever devised by humankind, even in our own world, a continuous celebration of praise and sacrifice performed thousands of times each day, always in progress somewhere in the world. Even the energy focused by an indifferent celebrant ought not to be taken lightly; in the hands of a celebrant who is well aware of what is being done, the potential is staggering. All of the seven Christian sacraments can be enhanced by a priest who is spiritually aware, but the Eucharistic sacrifice remains the single most powerful expression of the Deryni priesthood.

The second uniquely Deryni factor bound into the exercise of the priesthood involves the sacrament of *penance* or *confession*. Because a Deryni priest can actually read the mind of a penitent, he is apt to be more effective as a pastoral counselor; after all, he has access to more information than a human priest. However—and this is the sticking point for many humans—he also will have access to confidences and information that might not ordinarily be divulged, even to a priest. Because of this easier access to confidences, a Deryni priest will be expected to guard the secrets of the confessional with even greater zeal than any mere human.

The inviolability of a penitent's sacramental confession to a priest is one of the most basic assumptions of Christian faith. Historically, priests beyond numbering have suffered torture and even death rather than betray a confidence so obtained. In a Deryni context, the entire concept of confession takes on additional dimensions, for it is uniquely open to abuse in the hands of a race that can read minds—though the Deryni have strict prohibitions against such misuse of their powers. The danger of this particular temptation must have been recognized very early on by humans living among Deryni, and probably contributed

to the general mind-set behind the clampdown on Deryni clergy
after the Haldane Restoration.

In fact, we see little evidence that Deryni priests were, indeed,
guilty of this abuse—though the occasional human priest seems
to have fallen prey to the temptation. But whether a human or
Deryni is the agent, betrayal of the confidences of the confessional
is viewed as one of the more abhorrent of crimes, carrying a
profound emotional impact. It accounts for Morgan's repugnance
at being forced to recite a litany of sins he did not commit, to
gain himself time while being held prisoner by Warin de Grey
and the fanatic Monsignor Gorony. It explains his suspicion of
Arilan, when he again is offered a chance to confess what he has
done, even though Arilan assures him that this need not be a
formal confession. It also figures in Prince Javan's awareness that
he dares not confess everything to Father Stephen or to Archbishop Hubert, for fear of recriminations. And the young Gilrae
d'Eirial certainly experienced the full sense of betrayal when he
confessed his oak leaf and acorn cap Masses to old Father Erdic
and the priest then violated the seal of the confessional to tell
Gilrae's father (*The Deryni Archives* 51).

Unfortunately, all these examples serve to show confession in
a negative and punitive sense, rather than the rite of reconciliation and healing that it is meant to be. Thus far we have seen
only two positive examples of confession being used in the sense
for which it was intended, both of them in the context of a final
confession connected with Extreme Unction. Evaine seeks out
the Deryni Bishop Niallan before going to perform the ritual
that ultimately will cost her her life.

"I have lied to Joram and Queron, Father," she whispered,
focusing on one end of the purple stole set around his shoulders. "I have told them there is but little danger in a mission
I must perform. But if I told them the truth, they would not
let me go—and I must."

Niallan nodded slowly, his steel-grey eyes shuttered and
unreadable. They were sitting in Niallan's cell, on the edge
of his cot, with Wards set round the little room for privacy.

"This danger," Niallan ventured, sounding her out with
consummate skill. "Is it to you alone, or does it involve them
as well?"

"There is some small danger to them as well, but they know the risk and are willing to accept it. My risk is far greater."

"And *you* are prepared to accept *that* risk?"

"I am, Father." She looked up at him with bright blue eyes. "I must. And if a sacrifice is required, then I must make that, too. Is it wrong to insist that I be free to make this choice?"

Niallan was looking at her strangely, a taut foreboding playing about the lines around his mouth, and for an instant Evaine was not sure of him.

"You obviously have thought long and carefully about this," he said, after a troubled pause.

"Yes, Father. And I have begged that this cup not be placed before me. But if it is presented, then I must drink it to the dregs."

"And must your children drink it, too, if you should perish in this venture?"

"That is the hardest part of all," she whispered, looking away. "To know that my children may become orphans because of my actions. And yet, I still must take that risk. I've—made arrangements, if I should not return." She handed him a sealed parchment packet. "Fiona will see to my little ones and be a better mother to them than I could be, if I decided not to dare what my heart tells me I must. But only I can do this other thing. Do you understand, Niallan?"

After a moment, he closed his eyes and nodded, laying his hand over her folded ones, his bishop's ring burning like a beacon between them. "Not entirely, child, but it's clear that you have powerful reasons for what you are doing. I—will not question you further, for I sense a power at work here which far transcends anything I might call into play." He glanced up at her with a sad wistfulness. "Will you at least allow me to pray for you?"

"Aye, of course," she said with a faint, tremulous smile. "And there is one other favor you can do for me as well."

"Anything that is within my power, dear child."

"You can give me the Last Anointing and Viaticum, in case my journey takes me—beyond where either of us would have me go. It would give me great comfort."

Niallan winced as if she had struck him a physical blow, but after a few heartbeats he gave a stiff nod.

"If you truly desire it, of course I will do it. You should be aware, however, that Joram and Queron may sense it. The mark of such sacraments is often discernable to priests of their caliber."

"They have their own concerns this morning, Father," she whispered, thinking of the preparations already in progress. "By the time it might become apparent to them, it will be too late to stop me from what I must do."

"Very well, then. If you'll wait here, I'll fetch the oils and a pyx from the chapel."

She slipped to her knees when he had gone out, bowing her head over folded hands to pray. (*The Harrowing of Gwynedd* 394–395)

Apart from the fact that we, the readers, know the specifics behind what Evaine reveals, her dialogue with Niallan is not so very different from any human confession, despite the fact that both principals are Deryni. Neither uses Deryni abilities to enhance the exchange. It is the mortal Evaine interacting with Niallan, not the Deryni sorceress. The only Deryni element at all is Niallan's warning that Joram and Queron may become aware of the imprint of the Last Rites she has requested—though there is no indication that this sacrament will be any more specifically Deryni than her confession was.

Both confession and the Last Rites certainly *can* take on dimensions beyond the usual, however. Camber, as Alister Cullen, confers both sacraments on the dying Davin MacRorie at a distance, joined to him only by the bond of their Deryni link but imparting the unction and his blessing just as surely as if the two had been physically in the same place.

In a breath, though there was no outward sign, Davin opened all his soul to the bishop, sensing the answering absolution and blessing like a whisper of a caress flowing across the link which bound them. Almost he could feel the touch of the anointing oil as the last sacrament was projected through the link as real as if the bishop had knelt by his side and physically touched him with the holy balm. (*Camber the Heretic* 294)

Clearly, this application is beyond the capability of mere humans, as is Camber's final farewell to the grandson he cannot help to live but can only help to die. It is not clear whether the dying Davin actually realizes that it is, indeed, his grandfather embracing him psychically, but one would like to think that Davin did know, at the very end.

> As he closed his eyes and sagged more heavily against Jason's supporting knee, he reached out a final time to the one who anguished in the Council chamber and tried to force his own strength across the fading link.
> He had time only to sense that last futile caress, and to wonder again at how Bishop Alister reminded him of his grandfather Camber; and then, for just an instant, the old Cumber presence that he remembered from childhood flooded through him and enveloped him in love.
> His last image, as the final darkness descended, was of the face of his grandfather, weeping, and of the strong hands reaching out to buoy him up—and then a nothingness that was pervaded by a blinding, incredibly beautiful light of all the colors of time. (*Camber the Heretic* 296)

Unlike Davin, the dying Cinhil receives both the physical and the spiritual imprints of Extreme Unction from Camber-Alister's hands. Examination of Cinhil's actual transition rightly belongs in another section, so we shall not dwell on it here, but Cinhil's passing does illustrate an important point about the sacrament of the *Eucharist*.

Of all the Christian sacraments, the Eucharistic sacrifice is the single most important one, lying at the very heart of the Christian faith. To a believer like Camber, capable of perceiving multiple dimensions of the descent of Divinity within the mystery of the Mass, the power inherent in that sacrament and its products is actually perceivable on certain levels. In a sacramental sense, the Eucharistic elements of bread and wine *become* the Body and Blood of Christ at the moment of consecration.

After the dome of the circle has been shattered from Cinhil's passing, Camber finds himself speculating on the nature of consecrated Hosts, for he suspects that he may have survived the event only by the protection of the Reserved Sacrament in the ciborium close beside him. Basic tenets of his faith have always assured him that right reception of this sacrament is a means to spiritual salvation, but now he considers whether it may have been his *literal* salvation as well—for the unexpected shattering of the circle's dome unleashed enormous power, unendurable but for *some* kind of supernatural intervention.

He sank back to his knees at that, carefully lifting the golden cover and setting it aside. In the glittering bowl of the chalice lay perhaps half a dozen of the precious, consecrated Hosts, exactly like the one he had given to Cinhil so short a time ago. Respectfully, he reached in with thumb and forefinger and extracted one at random, gazing at it attentively.

Unleavened bread, the uninitiated would call it. Flour and water. And yet, in this morsel of the plainest of foods resided the greatest Mystery of his faith, something which he could not begin to explain or understand with his mind, but which was nonetheless true for heart and soul.

And had that Mystery protected him tonight? Perhaps it had. Cinhil had shown him a half-forbidden thing, not realizing, even in his heightened awareness and grace, how broad was the sweep of the wings of the Angel of Death.

Or was it simply not yet Camber's time? Did the Lord— that same Lord present, or so he believed, in the consecrated Host between his fingers—did the Lord have other plans for him, other work for him to do?

He doubted he would get any further answer tonight. With a short but fervent prayer for continued mercy, and a little shiver as if physically to shake off this line of speculation, Camber deposited the Host with its brothers and replaced the cover. . . . (*Camber the Heretic* 99–100)

Camber does not attempt to analyze the power inherent in the Host he handles. To do so, after what he has just experienced, would be to place his entire faith under examination—and that is hardly necessary in light of what has happened. He has been a priest long enough, and a Deryni one, to know what happens in the course of the Mass. Unlike a human priest, who usually must accept on faith that there is an efficacy to what he does at the altar, a Deryni priest like Camber can be well aware of the connection he makes with Deity when he taps into the Divine as he says the words of consecration. (Some humans can perceive this power, too; often they are called saints.)

Cinhil is hardly a saint, and unlikely to become one, as he himself observes, but even before the empowering of his Haldane potential, with its access to Deryni-like powers, he, too, seems to have tapped into some of the extra energy of the Mass. At the last Mass he is permitted to celebrate, before being acknowledged as Prince of Gwynedd and compelled to set aside his priesthood, his emotion spills over to the watching Rhys.

"I think he sensed that this might be the last time," Rhys tells Camber, afterwards. "His distress was so poignant that I could sense it in the air, like a grey pall surrounding the altar. Didn't you feel it, too?" (*Camber of Culdi* 217)

Of course, this ability to transmit the emotion-charged atmosphere of the Mass is not exclusively a Deryni ability; it is only that they may be better at it. The flow of power does not seem to be dependent on Deryni abilities, though perception of that flow may be, at least in degree. As yet, we have seen no examples of the effect of the Mass on a purely human observer (though ample evidence exists in our own world to attest to its efficacy), but it is clear that Deryni observers are quite able to focus in on the energies being channeled by merely human priests, to good effect. Whatever the source and however it is perceived, the beneficial effect of the sacrament is apparent, in the world of the Deryni as well as our own, as a potential source of strength, healing, and reconciliation for the communicant. That the humans of Gwynedd are not able to acknowledge this is the source of much of the reactionary behavior of the hierarchy of Gwynedd's Church.

# CHAPTER FOUR

# Telepathic Functions I: General Definitions, Ethics, Shields, Mind-Speech, Energy Augmentation

Perhaps one of the most widely known—and feared—of all Deryni powers, real or imagined, is their ability to read minds. For a human, the thought of having one's mind invaded against one's will—or, even worse, without one's knowledge—represents the ultimate violation of person and privacy, the supreme self-betrayal, made all the more treacherous because it is totally beyond the individual's control. At the hands of a Deryni, who knows what secrets or confessions one might be compelled to yield up, at the cost of one's livelihood, one's life, or even one's immortal soul?

Of course the ultimate truth of the matter is that most people's thoughts are of concern only to themselves and, perhaps, to their immediate intimates. After all, what earthshaking secrets does the ordinary person carry around in his or her head, the revelation of which would have any impact beyond his or her immediate circle? Most folk are reasonably law-abiding individuals, with little to hide that is of genuine import to anyone but themselves. Petty peccadilloes and personal failings are not the stuff of which great intrigues are made.

But because of the paranoia surrounding the true extent of Deryni abilities, and the very human tendency to regard oneself as truly unique and important in the grand scheme of things (even if one is only a small cog in the machine), the typical human in a position likely to come into contact with Deryni is convinced that he or she is different—that of course a Deryni would be intrigued to learn what he or she is thinking, or what he or she knows that no one else knows, and is only waiting for the chance to rip into the innocent human's mind and extract that information by force!

The truth is something rather different, of course. Given the appropriate conditions and opportunity, a Deryni *can* read the mind of just about any human he wants, when and wherever he wants, whether his subject is cooperative or not. Realistically, though, the typical Deryni (if there is such a thing) is not likely to bother wasting time and energy reading a stranger's mind for trivial reasons, even if there were not conventions of etiquette governing ethical mind-to-mind contact. Kelson summarizes the general attitude quite succinctly in *The Bishop's Heir* when Dhugal, after dancing around the question for some time, finally summons the courage to ask him about it directly.

"I—thought that Deryni could read minds," Dhugal whispered. . . .

"We can," Kelson murmured. "But we don't, among friends, unless we're invited. And the first time, even among Deryni, it almost requires some kind of physical contact." (*The Bishop's Heir* 28)

And this statement, indeed, points up one of the first limiting factors in many Deryni functions: the necessity for physical contact. Indeed, we might go so far as to say that physical contact is all but essential for an initial mind-to-mind encounter—and it is at least helpful in nearly every other kind of psychic operation of which Deryni are capable, whether involving deep mental rapport, control of various kinds, trance induction, or whatever. Without physical contact—unless a previous link has been established between Deryni and subject—a Deryni's ability to read another's mind is limited to a cursory scan of surface thoughts, especially if the reading is to go undetected.

Physical contact allows optimum conditions for mind-to-mind contact, then. Convenience and convention have established several ways of doing this. Almost always—and this applies both to Deryni-Deryni and Deryni-human encounters—the Deryni touches some part of his subject's head: the forehead, temples, bridge of the nose, the carotid area beneath the hinge of the jaw, the nape of the neck, or some combination thereof. Individual preferences vary. In practice, a hand or wrist or any other skin-to-skin contact can work just as well, but custom seems to have locked on the head area for primary focus, perhaps symbolically reinforcing the notion of information being drawn from the mind. By the time of *The King's Justice*, at least for military applications, humans were beginning to adjust to the notion of having intelligence reports read directly.

All the scouts knew that being read was a possibility, whenever they came to report to the king or his champion, if clarification was in order—and most had learned not to mind, and certainly not to fear. They had also accepted the growing convention, deliberately fostered by Kelson and Morgan, that Deryni always must touch their subjects on the head or neck in order to read their minds, preferably bare-handed. In fact, a hand or wrist or any other part of the body would do as well, and Deryni *could* read through gloves or other clothing if they must; but Kelson had felt that if humans at least *thought* the Deryni limited in this regard, it might ease some of the apprehension attached to actually dealing with them on a regular basis. (*The King's Justice* 169)

What should be noted here, beyond mere technique, is the potential ethical dilemma of this particular application of Deryni power. Militarily speaking, the procedure has much to recommend it, for it is fast, silent, and eliminates the possibility of important details being forgotten or observation being misinterpreted. On the other hand, what guarantee has the subject that the reader will confine himself to the intelligence report, rather than delving beyond to infringe on the subject's privacy? It might be argued that a vassal should have no secrets from his king, but where does one draw the line between what legitimately is the king's business and what ought to be reserved to the individual? In theory and in fact, a Deryni has access to information that a subject might not share even with his confessor.

In practice, however, most Deryni will not go beyond the scope agreed upon in advance or implied by the nature of the subject's service. For a scout, this normally would be limited to his reconnaissance report and attendant observations. Unless strong suspicion arises regarding a given subject's integrity, most Deryni will not waste time and effort on "fishing expeditions."

Which is not to say that this would never occur. Humans are all too aware that *some* Deryni—and kings among them—have been known to take advantage before. This long-standing human fear, only recently beginning to be assuaged by Kelson's uncompromising stance on justice, is always lurking in the background.

One way of alleviating this fear is by having the process last as short a time as possible. For a specific application such as scout reports, rather than the broader, more intensive reading that would be used in questioning a prisoner or some other hostile and/or resistant subject, the process can be as quick as the space between two breaths. In fact, the first breath itself becomes another convention that we will come to recognize as an almost universal corollary to most Deryni activity. When Kelson asks Kirkon to take a deep breath, he not only is engaging the scout's active cooperation but also is triggering a very common physical prelude to relaxation and centering and opening one's mind to an altered state of consciousness.

Kirkon appears to have no awareness of what transpires between his first breath and the next, as his king extracts the needed information. His next conscious sensation is a slight momentary vertigo, eased by Morgan's steadying hands, and a faint (and understandable) feeling of relief as he realizes it is over. Implied, of course, in the cooperation of Kirkon and others like him is trust in the king's reassurance that neither he nor Morgan will delve beyond the intelligence report being sought, or seek to influence the individual's free will; in short, that the privilege will not be abused, to the detriment of the individual being read. This trust is a key to Deryni-human interaction—one that, alas for Deryni-human relations over the centuries, can be earned only by experience.

Once earned, it may be that such trust is all too easy to take for granted. A case in point is Kelson's first mental contact with his new young squire, Ivo Hepburn. Presumably Kelson would have no reason to doubt young Ivo's loyalty or discretion, or the boy would not have been appointed a royal squire. Yet, as the twelve-year-old kneels to remove Kelson's spurs and boots, the king drops his hand to the boy's bent head and reaches out with his mind.

> "Relax, Ivo," he commanded, intensifying his mental touch as the young mind unexpectedly sensed the intrusion and the body started to tense. "No, close your eyes and don't fight me. I promise I won't hurt you—on the oaths we exchanged."
>
> Kelson sensed that the boy had been half-expecting something of this sort—one could hardly spend much time around court and not have heard at least rumors of what the king could do with his mysterious powers—but he was pleased when the resistance immediately ceased and the young mind tried to still, though he could feel a faint trembling beneath his hand.
>
> Continuing to croon words of encouragement and reassurance, the king drew the boy's dark head gently against his knee and deepened control, then sat forward slightly so he could ease both hands to either side, thumbs resting against the boy's temples and fingers sliding among the crisp curls for closer contact yet. Immediately the trembling stopped. He let his gaze shift to focus through the fire as he set his instructions. (*The Quest for Saint Camber* 87–88)

The instructions seem harmless enough. Ivo is told not to repeat anything he may overhear of the king's business—to "forget it unless I, personally, ask you to remember. This is something I require of all my squires and pages" (*The Quest for Saint Camber* 88). At first reading, this may seem like a not-unreasonable request by a king of his vassal. What shifts this encounter into a hazy area, ethically speaking, is that Kelson has *compelled* a loyalty that already was freely given "on the oaths we exchanged." He has assumed that Ivo, if left to his own devices, either does not have the self-control to keep his mouth shut or else would deliberately gossip about what he hears.

On a level Kelson probably has not even considered, this represents as profound a lack of trust as that which he deplores in humans—and with far less provocation from the innocent Ivo than humans often have had, dealing with Deryni of far fewer scruples than Kelson. Nothing in Kelson's makeup suggests that he would knowingly abuse his powers to the detriment of others, but an inner rot can begin insidiously. One hopes Kelson will reexamine his policies and revise his practices before unconscious suspicion and lack of trust become a habit. He will find himself far better served by vassals who *choose* to be loyal and discreet than by those whose loyalty and discretion come by way of compulsion.

That said, we should reexamine what Kelson actually did, for it was not so much a reading of his subject's mind as the setting up of a receptive state wherein the subject will accept suggestions given by the operator. We might view the mechanism as a kind of *para*-hypnosis, an imposed or even forced hypnotic state in which suggestions implanted by the operator cannot be resisted by the subject. We will find that most direct control of a subject's mind by a Deryni will involve some degree of para-hypnosis—which, used positively, can be of immense value, such as enabling deep rapport for various more complicated procedures, or in forcing sleep on a patient so that healing may be facilitated, or imposing unconsciousness on an enemy as an alternative to killing.

The scope for abuse—the Deryni edge, as it were—is that suggestions made with the force of Deryni will behind them can overcome *any* resistance a human subject might ordinarily have to accepting *any* suggestions. Ivo's conditioning, ultra-light and essentially benign, is *nothing* compared to what Wencit did to Derry, for example. Under the compulsion of a para-hypnotic command, a subject can be made to betray anyone or anything and even to take his or her own life. Such a command precludes even token resistance from the guard Michael DeForest as Ian very clinically stabs him to the heart. It also induces Morgan's vassal, Edgar of Mathelwaite, to turn a dagger on himself rather than submit to close questioning by his liege lord.

Nor are humans the only victims of this kind of forcible conditioning. Humphrey of Gallareaux, the Michaeline priest captured by King Imre's men in *Camber of Culdi*, has his will utterly shattered at the hands of Imre and his cohorts, then is reprogrammed as Imre's agent and reinserted into the rebel community, with tragic consequences. Unable to break the conditioning, the unfortunate priest poisons the very salt used at the baptism of Cinhil's firstborn son, then turns on Cinhil himself when the prince realizes what has been done. The incident has its redeeming aspect, for it finally shocks Cinhil into conscious use of the powers that Camber and his kin tried to awaken in him; but the hapless Humphrey dies a traitor's death in a Duel Arcane that he had no chance of surviving, driven to self-destruction by Imre's compulsions.

Of course, we would like to think that Kelson and the other positive characters of our acquaintance are governed by scruples not present in the individuals just cited. Camber displays repeated concern about the charade he is forced to play—though he can see no way to avoid it. Joram worries about the morality of placing the identity of the young guard Eidiard of Clure on Davin MacRorie—not out of particular concern for Davin, for Davin is willing, despite the inherent danger to himself, and the reason for the substitution is compelling. No, Joram frets for Eidiard, who must have his identity and any chance of a normal life taken from him, without any say in the matter.

Joram worries about Cinhil being forced to forsake his priesthood and take up his crown, too, even though he can see no way to avoid it, for the sake of the kingdom; and he worries about whether he and Evaine have the right to try to bring Camber back. Time after time, we see Deryni being forced to make these decisions for others, usually for humans who have not the power to resist such manipulations—though in truth, such manipulations are and always have been present in our own world, if not on the scale of which Deryni are capable.

Still, Bishop Arilan has very definite ideas about the propriety of Morgan even Truth-Reading the Mearan priest-prince, Father Judhael, without sufficient probable cause. Kelson certainly recognizes self-imposed limits on how far he would assert his own power, though he feels certain usages are justified as king. He *says* he would never use his powers to make Sidana agree to the marriage he proposes—and worries when he finds himself seriously considering just that. But we never actually see him succumb to this level of temptation. ''This is the most I'll ever do to you without your consent, unless it's a life and death situation," he assures young Ivo, before releasing him to his duties. *(The Quest for Saint Camber 88)*

In other words, Kelson will make no trivial use of his powers, to read Ivo's mind or control him only for his own curiosity or personal gain. That resolve is underlined the next morning, when he and Dhugal banter briefly about possibly Truth-Reading Conall's squire to find out more about Conall's mysterious leman—though one is left with the distinct impression that the young men would never actually *do* it. Unlike other Deryni who have abused their powers, Kelson realizes that obedience given without free will lasts only as long as the compulsion that commands it and that long-term rule must be based on mutual trust. As a king, Kelson's actions may sometimes reflect expediency more than the ideal, but the ideal remains, nonetheless, as an ultimate goal.

One might argue that this sort of reasoning smacks of situation ethics, pure and simple—and indeed, it does. But the realities of life dictate that ethical considerations sometimes *must* be subject to situational evaluation, especially when one must make one's decisions based not only on one's own best interests but the best interests of others entrusted to one's care. Time and again we will see Deryni apply this balance to decisions they must make, weighing the good of the many against the possible detriment of an individual. Kings must make these kinds of decisions all the time; Deryni kings are no different, except that wider options may be available to them to accomplish what they must do.

When Camber and his kin control Prince Cinhil to spirit him out of his monastery and, later, awaken his Haldane potential, they are acting in what they believe to be the best interests of their country. Likewise, when Camber assumes the identity of the slain Alister Cullen—and all his actions that follow as a direct necessity of his decision to maintain that façade—he is using his powers for what he regards a greater good than that of himself as an individual. Time after time, we see Deryni controlling the actions and even the thoughts of others for what they perceive to be a greater good. So long as their motives remain pure, we may perhaps regard this as a positive thing, in the long term; certainly, overall, Camber and his kin cannot be said to have acted out of any hope of personal gain. Nor can it be said that Kelson has abused his power, or Morgan or Duncan or any of the several other Deryni serving the cause of Order in the latter ages in Gwynedd.

But Deryni have not always been innocent of such abuse, and it is this that humans remember. If absolute power can be said to corrupt absolutely, it perhaps follows that nearly absolute power can lead to a great deal of corruption as well. When Deryni act in honor, in the cause of justice and the furtherance of the race of mankind, they can be powerful forces indeed. When they use their powers to further their own interests at the expense of others, their destructive power can be appalling.

This certainly was the case during the Festillic Interregnum, with Imre and Ariella representing perhaps the epitome of Deryni power abuse for selfish interests. Unfortunately, it is the history of such abuses that has colored human memory for nearly two centuries. The wary and guarded tolerance of Deryni beginning to emerge during Kelson's reign is a relatively late development in the human-Deryni saga. Up until Kelson's accession, even in the years before the Restoration when Deryni operated openly in Gwynedd, people perceived few if any limitations to their power. Indeed, the overlords of the Interregnum undoubtedly encouraged the perception that they were omnipotent and could be omniscient if they chose, simply by looking at a human subject with intent.

Fear of a Deryni's mere glance has been mostly dispelled by Kelson's time—though Truth-Reading requires no physical contact and constitutes mind-reading of a sort—but wariness of a Deryni's touch persists, and with good reason. As Arilan reminds Duncan on that fateful Ash Wednesday morning of 1125:

> "You're just damned lucky no one bolted this morning, when you were distributing ashes. I hope you realize that. You and I both know that if you'd wanted to, even that brief contact—long enough to trace a cross on a man's brow—would have been long enough to take over just about any mind that approached that altar rail. Fortunately, they don't know that." (*The Quest for Saint Camber* 103)

Arilan perhaps overstates the point just a little—encountering any resistance at all, a Deryni would need *some* time to establish control over a determined human—but the fear is a very real one, and humans do not know of the limitations. Deryni are well aware that their magic cannot just be called into force instantaneously, that it takes time to put themselves into the proper mind-set to engage the powers at their disposal, and that an arrow can end a Deryni magician's life from a distance while he is still gathering his powers to launch an attack—or defense.

While we're considering defense, this might be the opportune time to mention a Deryni's very first line of defense: shields.

## Shields

All Deryni have shields, to some degree—or at least the potential ability to generate shields. Shields are a Deryni's natural psychic protection against intrusion by other minds. Unless threatened, the shields of a trained Deryni generally will remain largely quiescent, permitting casual input of Deryni-enhanced perceptions. The visualization of the shields may range from glass domes to shimmering curtains to steel shutters, depending on individual taste and possibly the person's training.

A Deryni who refuses to lower his or her shields is practically invulnerable to influence by another Deryni—depending on the strength of the shields, of course. Pitted against a Deryni subject with shields intact, even a skilled Deryni is very limited in what he can do. He cannot use Truth-Say to force his shielded subject to speak the truth or impose controls of any kind. He cannot put his shielded subject to sleep or force unconsciousness or read his mind. If he is a Healer, he can work around his subject's shields for the purposes of healing, but his work is far easier if his patient cooperates.

Deryni fortunate enough to receive formal training learn very early how to control their shields. Being able to raise them and maintain them under assault is necessary for the sake of defense; but being able to lower them and keep them down is just as important. The snap of suddenly returning shields apparently constitutes at least a sufficiently unpleasant prospect that Rhys voices his concern about it before demonstrating his newfound blocking ability to Queron.

"I'd like to be assured that you won't panic and snap your shields shut on me," he tells the Healer-priest—who assures

Rhys that he has better control than that (*Camber the Heretic* 179)! But indeed, when Rhys restores his subject to full power, Queron's shields do rebound into place "with an almost audible snap, nearly brushing them all with the force of the return" (*Camber the Heretic* 181).

This "snap" seems to be a characteristic description of shields going into place, and it appears to be largely a reflex reaction. If it happens unexpectedly, the person working behind those shields may get caught in the backlash. The most usual preventive measure against accidental snaps is for the subject to give over control of the shields to the operator; but this requires a bond of trust that may not always be present.

Being able to lower shields *is* important, however, for shields can make a prison as well as a fortress, closing one in as well as keeping others out. In order to experience the full benefit of the Deryni pantheon of talents, shields must be lowered. Indeed, very little psychic interaction is possible between two Deryni with shields between them. We have seen Dhugal's initial inability to lower his shields as a graphic example of the difficulties that can arise.

Shields *can* be forced down, of course. The balance and concentration involved in maintaining really powerful shields against a determined assault is actually fairly precarious and can be disrupted by several different Deryni-specific drugs, in slightly varying ways. Other substances actually erode the shields for the duration of their physiological effect on the body, allowing a skilled operator virtually unlimited access to the subject's mind.

In addition, shields can be rent by the brute force of a more powerful mind—a process tied in with mind-ripping, which will be discussed below—though this process is liable to do devastating if not permanent damage.

Finally, only Deryni and those with assumed Deryni-like powers have shields. Humans do not. Upon closer examination, supposed humans discovered to have shields usually can be found to be descendants of Deryni, even if at some great remove. It is likely that most of these individuals are descendants of Deryni who were forced to go underground during the great persecutions, whose true inheritance was first suppressed as dangerous knowledge and eventually lost in the transmittal to children for whom the knowledge would have been mortally dangerous. Nonuse of one's Deryni powers can cause the genetic material to lie dormant, sometimes for generations, often reactivating only at a time of great stress, when the individual's need triggers the potential anew. Dhugal's gradual awakening of his Deryni inheritance is a mild example of this kind of rediscovery.

We will deal more with these aspects of shielding and buried Deryni inheritance. But for now, let us begin examining specific aspects of Deryni use of the telepathic functions of mind-magic.

## Mind-Speech

Mind-speech describes a telepathic communication between two individuals, at least one of them Deryni. The information is verbalized, just as if the participants were speaking aloud—except that the verbalization takes shape only in the minds of sender and receiver. Mental pictures may accompany the verbal message, but the essence of mind-speech is essentially a silent conversation. Especially at a distance, it generally presupposes previous telepathic interaction by the participants, thereby precluding the need for physical contact. However, it is possible that a "wild card" psychic cry for help might be high-powered enough to be picked up by someone not previously known to the sender.

Indeed, if a potential receiver is predisposed to pick up telepathic communication, if he or she is "open" to such a contact, it is quite possible to "overhear" mind-speech intended for another. Because transmission across a distance requires a stronger and broader "band" of energy, spillage can occur, to be picked up by anyone in range and "listening" for it. Several characters display concern about psychic eavesdropping and often use physical contact to close the "leak" and prevent it. Morgan and Duncan are sitting close beside one another when they use mind-speech to communicate after being interrogated by Arilan and Cardiel at Dhassa, even though they do not yet even suspect that Arilan is Deryni. And Camber-Alister, to prevent being overheard by the assembled bishops, utilizes blatant formal contact with Joram, hands to temples, outwardly pretending a judicial probe of Joram's mind but at the same time communicating on hidden telepathic levels as well as open verbal ones, all the while

cobbling together a forthcoming explanation for his audience
that will extricate Joram from perjury yet still retain Camber's
identity as Alister. It succeeds in that, though not precisely as
Camber had planned. As so often happens, Camber has not
foreseen *all* the ramifications. Still, it is a masterly piece of work
and a good example of what can be done with mind-speech.

But mind-speech, though it may be facilitated by physical
contact, generally takes place across a spatial distance, usually
when other forms of communication are not possible. The energy input required to make a contact by mind-speech seems to
be directly proportional to the physical distance separating
sender and receiver. Under optimum conditions, an individual
Deryni's range may extend to the distance of several days' ride,
but the practical limit for an unassisted contact is considerably
less. However, when large distances are involved, it is possible
for participants to augment their own energy resources by drawing upon the energy of others, ideally with their consent and
cooperation. Hence, Kelson draws energy from Caulay and
Dhugal when attempting to bring in the probe he senses emanating from Morgan (*The Bishop's Heir* 79–82); Morgan, when
seeking out reports from Duncan in the field, allows Kelson to
augment his power, to spare him ongoing and repeated depletion
(*The King's Justice* 97); and Dhugal draws on the energy of
Ciard and his other henchmen to warn Kelson of Duncan's
capture (*The King's Justice* 217–220).

Incidentally, Deryni power itself cannot be increased by augmentation—power is not cumulative—but an individual's potential for energy capacity can be ''topped up,'' as it were. Also,
augmentation can be useful for many other kinds of operations
besides enhancement of communication. When setting up a field
Portal at Llyndruth Meadows, Arilan augments his energy from
active links with Kelson, Morgan, and Duncan, also pulling
passive energy from Nigel, Cardiel, and Warin (*High Deryni*
293–294). And Tavis O'Neill, before attempting a healing on
his mangled wrist, asks to pull energy from Prince Javan—also
providing us with a description of what it feels like to have
energy drawn voluntarily.

''You may feel a faint sensation of pressure inside your
head, as if something were being pulled slowly through your

body and out through your head, but it's nothing to be afraid of, and I won't even start until you're nearly asleep. That's right. Let go and let me guide us both. Sleep now. You're safe.''

And as Tavis' voice died away, Javan felt the familiar lethargy of the Healer's touch steal across his limbs; he sensed himself slipping into that twilight state he had felt so many times before, and he dreamed. He felt the warm, satisfying shift of energy stirring within him, prickling at the base of his skull, not at all unpleasant. . . . (*Camber the Heretic* 227–228)

Kelson gives Dhugal a much sketchier description, warning him to expect "a slight sort of a tickling sensation in your head" if he has to draw energy (*The Bishop's Heir* 81), but it is clear from Dhugal's reaction that resistance, even if unwitting, produces a very different sensation. The pain caused by resistance may warn of a very real danger, as illustrated by two negative examples of energy augmentation.

Twice Lord Ian Howell uses unwilling but unresistant accomplices to channel his communications with Charissa, setting up an almost mediumistic link whereby Charissa actually takes over the subject's voice to speak to Ian. The ease with which he sets this procedure into motion suggests that it is neither difficult nor dangerous for the operator (for Ian himself is not Deryni by birth, only holding Deryni-like powers by Charissa's grace and gift); but Charissa's warning not to drain his subject beyond recovery (*Deryni Rising* 116) suggests that a danger does exist for the subject. The prospect does not worry Ian in the first instance, since he plans to kill DeForest anyway, but he deliberately chooses a stronger specimen in John of Elsworth—and again is warned by Charissa not to tire his subject beyond recall, because an untimely death could arouse suspicions (*Deryni Rising* 201).

These warnings suggest very strongly, then, that it must be possible to drain a subject's energy reserves to a dangerous if not fatal low, perhaps without the operator even being aware of the subject's distress until too late. To guard against this possibility, most ethical practitioners will try to monitor their subjects quite closely during any operation requiring large energy outlays, as Arilan undoubtedly had Kelson, Morgan, and Duncan do when setting up the field Portal at Llyndruth Meadows (*High Deryni* 292–295). Indeed, we shall see how active monitoring of breathing and heart rate is taken almost for granted among high adepts in workings involving very deep trance, for a practitioner fully engrossed in Inner Work may well become too distracted to attend to such mundane matters. The classic example is Rhys monitoring Camber during the assimilation of Alister's memories (*Saint Camber* 172–187). Monitoring of energy outflow is slightly different from monitoring for vital functions, but Healers and most other high adepts who work in disciplines requiring frequent augmentation generally learn to do the former almost instinctively, as Tavis surely must have done when he drew from Javan.

Still, the logical extension of being *able* to pull energy without limitations means that an operator without scruples could deliberately strip a subject's energy reserves to the point of collapse or even death, either to gain the maximum amount of energy or to put an end to a subject who has become inconvenient. There are users and vampires in all worlds and universes.

The brighter side of the coin is that an operator whose scruples go beyond mere self-interest could willingly choose to deplete him or herself beyond safe survival levels, if that was necessary to ensure the success of an important magical working. Indeed, we have seen at least two outstanding examples of this kind of self-sacrifice: when Dom Emrys pours his life-energy into the destruction of the Portal at Saint Neot's, and when Evaine channels hers so that Camber may make that vast quantum leap into his next phase of existence.

Finally, returning briefly to the general topic of mind-speech, we should consider a very specialized application that is used primarily by members of the Camberian Council, functioning on much the same principle as the Saint Camber medallion Derry uses to communicate with Morgan. The Council's focus is a silvery crystal sphere suspended above the table in their chamber, charged with the energy of the group mind. Using this energy, which is bound and transmitted at each new member's oath-taking and reinforced every time the Council meets, the convener or, indeed, any member of the Council can send forth a tightly focused psychic call to members only, summoning them to attend. We see Arilan use the sphere as a visual focus as well, as he composes himself before calling his colleagues to explain their support of a Duel Arcane (*High Deryni* 296).

In addition, the crystal can be used to facilitate what we might call telemonitoring, as the Council did for Davin while he was working incognito in the royal household. At first, when Davin's Deryni powers were blocked, the monitoring would have been a fairly active proposition, with someone always on duty in the Council chamber, assessing intelligence information gleaned from Davin's ordinary perceptions and from Jaffray's periodic interaction with him, and keeping watch for dangers that their temporarily powerless agent might not have perceived. Later on, however, after Davin's powers had been restored, direct contact probably would have been limited to specified times, for fear of being detected, with someone always lightly but passively linked into the "listening circuit," free to pursue other activities such as reading or study, but instantly accessible if Davin should Call.

And when Davin *does* Call, mortally wounded in the course of protecting the princes, the link of full rapport locks in, so that Camber, as Alister Cullen, may comfort the dying Davin and ease his passage into the Nether World. We see a similar arrangement when the Council are awaiting word from Queron in January of 918—not actively scanning in any focused manner, but alert for the "psychic flare" that will be triggered when Queron, standing on the new Portal at Saint Mary's Abbey, reads the message psychically set for him in Rhys' Healer's seal. In all these examples, information gained through such a link tends to be the specific, mental vocalization of mind-speech rather than the wordless surge of information that is associated with true rapport—the subject of our next chapter.

# CHAPTER FIVE

# Telepathic Functions II: Rapport

Rapport is the term used to describe a mutual melding of thought between two Deryni, going beyond mere verbalized communication to include other sensory involvement. Its depth may range from fairly focused and superficial, for the exchange of specific information, to a deeply intimate exchange and disclosure at multiple levels, edging into a sexual intimacy, with all possible variations in between. One of the more common uses is for an enhancement of memory, as when Camber, as Alister, briefs young Jesse MacGregor regarding the band of Deryni bravos who accosted him and Joram on the road near Dolban. This example also illustrates a fairly typical first contact between two very competent Deryni.

"Well, Jesse, do you have any particular approach you prefer to use for establishing rapport with someone new? I don't believe we've worked together before, have we?"

"No, sir, to both questions," Jesse murmured, looking across at Camber trustingly. "My father trained me, though, if that's any help. I know you're used to working with him."

Camber smiled and stood slowly, signing for the boy to remain seated. "Well, this should be easy, then," he said, resting one hand on Jesse's near shoulder and moving quietly around to stand behind him. "It's been a long day, and I'm tired, so let's just make this a nice, easy, passive link, and I'll feed you the information as soon as you're ready." He slid his hands to rest on both the boy's shoulders, kneading the tight neck muscles briefly with his thumbs.

"Center down and relax," he breathed, feeling the boy draw breath deeply and let it out in response, already accommodating to his instruction and first tenuous contact. "Excellent. This is going to be a pleasure, I can tell. Breathe again now, and let it out. . . ."

With that, he dropped down two levels at once and found the boy's consciousness sinking in perfect unison with his, approaching a linkage and touching and merging as smoothly as he could have wished for. He closed his eyes in response to the growing rapport, knowing that Jesse no longer saw through sight either, then simply let his hands rest easily on the boy's shoulders, the need for physical contact no longer necessary except that it would have been more bother to move than simply to remain standing where he was.

Jesse's shields receded with a practiced ease which Camber should have expected, knowing Gregory, and the link was forged and the memory of the encounter near Dolban exchanged with no more effort than the wink of an eye. A moment he lingered in quiet balance and communion, then withdrew easily before the returning shields and opened his eyes to see Jesse turning his head to look at him. The boy wore a pleased and fascinated smile, as if he, too, had been surprised at the ease with which they had adjusted to one another. (*Camber the Heretic* 130)

When Jesse has gone, Camber comments to Joram that "either I'm getting better in my old age, or else the younger generation is better trained. That Jesse is as smooth as silk, even better than Gregory. I shiver to think what he might be like with some Michaeline or Gabrilite training."

So rapport can be a instrument of memory sharing—and Camber's rapport with young Jesse represents an optimum example of it. Rapport can also be a tool of healing (of which more later, when we discuss healing in particular), a preparation for more involved working (of which examples abound), or even an end in itself, to allow two individuals to interact on levels not possible to ordinary consciousness alone. Almost inevitably, the latter are the most dramatic, especially when they illustrate the first full rapport between two individuals.

One of the most poignant of these examples is that between Duncan and Dhugal, just after Duncan has discovered Dhugal's true identity and has revealed himself as his father. It is an encounter filled with joy, but it also holds its share of tension, for up until now Dhugal has not been able to lower his now-explained shields to permit close psychic contact.

"I'll do most of what needs to be done," Duncan tells his son, bidding him clasp a *shiral* crystal in his fist and close his eyes while he tries to remember his mother. "Close your eyes and try to see her. . . ."

As he spoke, gently insinuating thoughts along with words, he could begin to read the image forming in Dhugal's mind as well as his own, just on the surface at first, then gradually eroding the pulsing, troublesome shields.

"She had a laugh like silver bells . . . a serenity as still and deep as the lake at Shannis Meer. . . ."

Even as Duncan's voice trailed off and he tried a stronger probe, he was past Dhugal's shields and in his mind, driving the memories across the unconscious links and into Dhugal's consciousness, holding the channel open relentlessly when Dhugal sensed what was happening and would have drawn back in momentary panic. He felt Dhugal gasp as something psychic snapped, but he damped the sharp wrench of pain which followed even as he pulled Dhugal closer and gave him physical comfort.

All in an instant, all the barriers were down and Dhugal was with him, reliving those halcyon days with Maryse. . . .

The sheer force of emotion which surged with Duncan's remembrance flooded through Dhugal's mind with such a pressure that no resistance was possible; nor, once the pathways were in use, did Dhugal feel any further fear or apprehension. Duncan sensed almost the exact instant when Dhugal made that conscious choice to let the mind-link fill him—and the surge, as Dhugal opened to his father's mental touch, gave new impetus to the sharing Duncan now pursued even more.

Sparing only the areas of confidence which might not be shared with anyone—his priestly secrets and duties, the confidences of others—Duncan poured forth all the memories of the years he and Dhugal had lost, intertwining them with Dhugal's own—sparser, for sheer number, but no less potent and treasured, for his part. And Dhugal, once he sensed how it was done, entered joyously in the sharing. (*The Bishop's Heir* 321–322)

Another striking example of rapport as a healing device in the broad sense is the first psychic encounter between Camber-Alister and the rebellious young Healer, Tavis O'Neill, toward the end of *Camber the Heretic*. After several false starts, during which Tavis finally comes fully to terms with the loss of his hand, he finally allows a light rapport with Camber, their hands linked around a lighted candle.

[Camber] brushed the other's shields almost immediately; but to his relief, they began to subside, slowly, tentatively, at first, then with greater confidence, as superficial levels of Tavis' consciousness encountered and accepted Camber's gentle questing out. Camber went carefully, gathering all of his Camber essence back beyond what he intended to share with Tavis and beginning to reveal the Alister aspects, intending to go slowly, gingerly, so as not to startle the Healer.

But then, to his surprise, Tavis lowered every vestige of shielding and subterfuge, in one dizzying surge of blind, submissive trust. On instinct, Camber swept in behind the disintegrating shields, ready to pull out quickly if Tavis started to panic, but then letting himself merge with Tavis' thoughts in a breathless mingling of memories and perceptions.

It was the most nearly perfect rapport Camber could have dreamed of, under the circumstances, approaching that long-ago first contact with Jebediah for sheer ecstasy of psychic communion outside the bonds of blood kin—excellent by the most exacting of standards. He was dazzled, by turns awed and appalled, but all of it was Tavis, and real. (*Camber the Heretic* 431–432)

Camber's rapport with Jebediah, toward the end of *Saint Camber*, is an even more positive case in point, for ultimately, unlike his bond with Tavis, it involves a total sharing, holding back nothing. Camber has tried to avoid this contact for months, for the Michaeline Grand Master was closer to Alister Cullen than any living soul and does not know that Alister is dead, his identity taken on by Camber.

But now Jebediah has forced the issue, making it impossible for Camber to refuse the contact without seriously undermining his credibility. So in this encounter, not only must Camber ease another man's façade into an intimate and long-established relationship strained by months apart and unexplained, but he must balance the integrity of his alter ego against what is really a first rapport, Camber with Jebediah, knowing all the while that his secret must take precedence even over Jebediah's life— that if he cannot win Jebediah to his support, the Grand Master must die. Camber begins with manipulation on a master's scale, at which he ably shows his adeptship, but he is able to transform it, in the end, to a full and joyful communion of equals, with results that neither he nor Jebediah could have predicted.

He dropped his hands to Jebediah's shoulders and pulled him back to lean against his knee, at the same time gathering his own essence deep within him, so that only the Alister part of him might show at first. As he raised his right hand, the one which wore the bishop's ring, he hesitated for just an instant to clench and unclench his fist as though warming his fingers—long enough for the purple gemstone to catch Jebediah's eye and remind him, if only on some deep, inner level, of the reason for this unequal sharing.

Then he brought that hand to the back of Jebediah's neck, to cup the already tilting head in the fan of his fingers. Jebediah responded immediately to the familiar touch, breathing out with a sigh and letting his head loll against Camber's hand, eyes fluttering dreamily as he began to open to the contact. Camber let a little more of Alister's personality seep through the bond being forged and felt Jebediah's consciousness stilling in further response, no hint of suspicion yet fogging the clarity of that well-ordered mind.

"*Let go now,*" Camber said softly, as much a thought as a whisper, as he stretched to the furthest limits of revealment which he dared, using only Alister's memories.

And to his amazement, Jebediah did let go, taking the

sparseness of the Alister contact for natural caution as his old friend explored the limits to which he might share and still retain the security of his office.

Camber marveled at the naive trust, at the same time hating himself for having to betray it. Gathering all his resources for one massive onslaught, quick and without warning, he poised and then swooped, seizing so many avenues simultaneously that Jebediah never had a chance to realize what was happening until it was too late to resist effectively.

Jebediah gasped and flinched under Camber's hands at the force of the contact, mind staggering with the shock of an alien consciousness overwhelming his own. He could not do more. Physically and psychically blind now, he struggled helplessly against the bonds already formed, shrinking from the constant new incursions, fruitlessly trying to prevent the imposition of knowledge which he had not expected, had not wanted, would not have considered, had he retained control of his own mind.

Only in sheer body reflex was he at all able to resist Camber's bidding, warrior's muscles responding to the threat even if the warrior's mind could not. Almost independent of his mind's frantic struggling, his right hand crawled to the dagger at his right side, closing half-paralyzed fingers around the ivory hilt, dragging the blade slowly from its sheath.

Camber saw the movement, and shifted quickly to block the rising hand. Relenting not one iota from his task of education, he twisted around to straddle the now-sprawling Michaeline and redouble his assault, left hand locked around Jebediah's powerful wrist in a separate war of strength as his will forced knowledge into Jebediah's mind, giving all the necessary details, from Alister's death to the present.

Jebediah shook his head in denial and cried out, a despairing animal moan of grief, as he stared up at Camber with blank, unseeing eyes. His left hand lashed out to twist itself in the neck of Camber's mantle, pulling Camber down closer as the dagger hand rose slowly against the grasp of Camber's, nearer and nearer to Camber's throat.

But Camber would not be distracted. Relentlessly he drove home the final realizations: the benefits already accrued to Cinhil; the smallness of their numbers who knew the truth of

Camber-Alister; the consequences if the play did not go on, in terms of anti-Deryni backlash already brewing in small ways among the restored human nobility; the trap of all of them who were now committed to play out the charade—and that Camber and his children were willing to make any necessary sacrifice for the sake of Gwynedd. Was Jebediah?

With that, Camber disengaged from all controls save one: a touch which would bring swift unconsciousness and, if necessary, death. At the same time, he bade his long-borrowed shape melt away from him, his own Camber face gazing down at Jebediah in hope and compassion. The dagger was resting against his throat now, near to drawing blood, but he ignored its deadly pressure, praying that Jebediah's good common sense would keep him from rejecting what had been revealed and forcing Camber to use his ultimate weapon.

And Jebediah, sensing his release but not yet the significance of what had happened, arched his body from under Camber's in that first instant of freedom and rolled him to the floor, to straddle his former captor and sit upon his chest, dagger pressed close against the quickened pulse, his other hand twisted in the mantle to choke out what life the dagger spared.

Camber went totally limp, quicksilver eyes beseeching as they stared calmly up into Jebediah's crazed ones, arms outflung to either side in an attitude of total physical surrender.

And finally Jebediah saw, and knew, and realized what he was about to do. With a strangled gasp, his eyes once more reflected reason and his hand opened in reflex horror at what it held. Camber could almost see the succession of memories which flashed through Jebediah's mind as he froze there, open-palmed hand still poised beside Camber's neck, though the dagger now lay on the floor beside the silver-gilt head.

Then the staring eyes closed, and the frantically working throat choked out a single sob, and Jebediah was collapsing to weep unashamedly in Camber's arms. (*Saint Camber* 403–405)

Jebediah eventually accepts what Camber has done, and the reasons for it, finally bringing himself to ask what Camber would have done if Jebediah had *not* accepted it.

. . . Camber pursed his lips and glanced down for an instant, then reached out to his final control and exerted the slightest amount of pressure as he looked up again.

"I'm afraid I was not as honest as you would like to believe," he whispered, as Jebediah felt the effect and reeled on the edge of unconsciousness. He released the pressure and the final control and grasped Jebediah's upper arm in a steadying hold. "As you can see, I held back one last, desperate weapon. If I'd really had to use it—I'm not sure what I would have done."

Jebediah winced, nodding slowly in acceptance of that revelation. "You would have killed me," he said, quite dispassionately. "And you would have been right. You couldn't let me leave here as anything less than an ally. The cause you've been working for is far too important to endanger by my angry betrayal."(*Saint Camber* 407)

Jebediah's new understanding and acceptance of the circumstances leads to yet another offer of help; and this time, Camber does not refuse.

For an instant, Camber searched the sorrowing eyes—bloodshot now, with their former weeping—reading the trust and loyalty which he had always known was there for Alister, and which he had sensed he might find for himself but had never dared to verify, for fear of losing all. As he stretched out his arm, to lay his right hand on Jebediah's open palm, he let first Alister and then Camber flow out and mingle with the timidly offered Jebediah, gasping with the sheer delight which the unexpected three-way interaction evoked.

He had not realized the fullness of the Alister part of him before this very instant, feeling it interact with the mind of the man who had known and loved Alister Cullen perhaps better than any other living person. Jebediah, too, was astonished at the contact, his own memories and experiences of Alister merging and fusing with the pseudo-Alister almost as if a physical presence held that essence and urged its participation in this strange sharing which neither Jebediah nor Camber had dreamed possible.

They sat there, wrists clasped across the space between

them, for nearly an hour, delighting in their mutual discoveries, sorrowing at their disappointments, even laughing aloud from time to time as some new facet of sharing fell beneath their scrutiny. Then finally they stirred, Camber to resume the shape of the man he now understood far, far better than he had ever dreamed possible, and Jebediah to watch in awed fascination as a new friend took back the form of an older one who was not totally lost after all. (*Saint Camber* 408)

This, then, is a taste of what rapport *can* be.

## Rapport with Animals

As a final commentary on rapport, we should mention the special affinity some Deryni have with animals. In fact, it is one of the first things we learned about Deryni magic. The very first time Morgan is mentioned, long before we actually see him, Brion has him able to "charm the deer right to the city gates if he chose. . . . He has a way with animals—and other things."(*Deryni Rising* 4).

Morgan himself, standing by the pool in his ducal gardens at Coroth the following year, observes that he could call the fish and they would come (*Deryni Checkmate* 36), just as his sister Bronwyn is able to call birds to her hands (*Deryni Checkmate* 145). And Dhugal, years later, employs the same talent to charm eyeless fish into his hands for food for himself and Kelson. Indeed, long before we know that Dhugal is Deryni, his "knack with animals" gives us some clue of his future—and his past. Our suspicions should be aroused when he influences the guards' horses at Ratharkin so easily; and by the time he uses a horse to augment the physical link he needs to gain rapport with Ciard, we know what he is. Hence, his affinity with the cheetah Kizah should not surprise us at all, though one might suspect from the reaction of Kizah's master that this goes a bit beyond what even Deryni might expect. Morgan's gentling of the injured horse in "The Knighting of Derry" and the young Rhys Thuryn's affinity with Evaine's cats are also examples of animal rapport.

# CHAPTER SIX

# Telepathic Functions III: Truth-Reading, Memory, Mind-Control, and Staring Patterns

Truth-Reading is a Deryni talent with extremely useful applications. In its purest form, it is a noninvasive tool that can be used whether the subject wishes it or not, for the subject's mind is not broached; the operator simply knows whether any given statement made by the subject is true. Its mechanism perhaps is tied in with reading physiological signs even more subtle than those measured by modern polygraph machines, or "lie detectors." It is a skill that Kelson had begun developing on his own, even before he became king, and seems to be one of the easier Deryni skills to master.

One has to ask the right questions, though—or have someone else ask the right questions, if a human and a Deryni are working as a team. And a subject aware of the limitations of the process often can get around it by the way he or she answers, or by not answering at all—for only actual lies are detectable. Camber-Alister's performance before the bishops, as he and Joram are being questioned about "Saint Camber's" appearance to Guaire of Arliss, is masterful in what he does *not* say, never quite lying, but telling only that part of the truth that will support their position or be construed as innocence.

Kelson also is well aware of the limitations of Truth-Reading.

61

"I'm not omnipotent," he tells Dhugal shortly after their re-union. "I can tell whether a man is lying, with very little effort—it's called Truth-Reading—but to actually learn the truth, I need to ask the right questions" (*The Bishop's Heir* 28).

But what if the subject refuses to answer, or is caught in lies but refuses to tell the truth? To deal with this contingency, a Deryni can *compel* his subject to answer truthfully. The process, sometimes called Truth-Saying, is used somewhat more spar-ingly than simple Truth-Reading, since it involves overshad-owing the subject's free will—a violation of individual choice that most ethical Deryni will avoid, given a viable alternative. For extracting information from a prisoner or suspected male-factor, it is far preferable to torture or other strong-arm tactics, and infinitely more reliable. Still, because the process *is* so re-liable and relatively easy to use, the temptation to use it for lesser applications can be nearly irresistible.

Sheer expediency is a common and commonly invoked jus-tification, as when Morgan and Duncan are en route to Dhassa, searching for a shortcut, and Morgan compels the clerk, Thierry, and several others to tell all (*High Deryni* 89–91). Given a choice between physical intimidation and a simple compulsion to lend cooperation that will not harm or even greatly inconvenience the subject, the latter obviously is the choice of preference, even if the subject's free will *is* slightly violated, but it does edge into an ethical grey area.

The ordinary human has little defense against this kind of questioning, unless previously protected by a Deryni more skilled and powerful than the questioner. The captured rebel bishop, Nevan d'Estrelldas, has no such protection and con-fesses all when Morgan puts him to the question, his few at-tempts at resistance easily overcome by Morgan's compulsions. Derry, who does have some protection, makes a heroic attempt to resist the questioning of Wencit of Torenth, but he is no match for the Deryni sorcerer when deprived of his Saint Camber medal and plied with appropriate drugs. In the end, Derry is broken, his body in thrall to Wencit's will, and his mind intact enough to know exactly what has happened. He is all too aware that he has betrayed Morgan and his king, that he will continue to betray them if Wencit commands it, and that even the volition of taking or preserving his own life is totally at Wencit's whim.

A Deryni subject may be able to resist Truth-Saying to a degree commensurate with his or her general skill level, but as both Queron and Rhys point out, at different times, anyone eventually can be broken, given the time and drug support. Ultimately, the only sure defense against being subjected to the compulsion of Truth-Saying is that a would-be subject, whether human or Deryni, can be given the dubious protection of a suicide command, either self- or other-imposed, to come into play before his or her integrity can be breached. We have mentioned Edgar of Mathelwaite already, as a human victim, compelled to turn a dagger against himself rather than submit to reading by Morgan. Deryni victims include Dafydd Leslie, who panicked under interrogation by Tavis O'Neill and died in convulsions rather than betray his friends, and Denzil Carmichael, whose suicide block likewise was triggered by the Healer Oriel's attempt to read him.

The compulsion of Truth-Saying differs only in degree from an actual forced rapport, whereby an operator goes forcibly into a subject's mind to extract information. If the subject is able to sustain any resistance, the process may cause pain or even injury to him or her.

We have already seen how certain perfectly legitimate procedures can cause varying degrees of discomfort to the subject. In nearly all cases, resistance is the cause. Until Dhugal consciously learns how to lower his shields, he experiences excruciating pain whenever anyone besides Duncan attempts to ease past those shields—and this with the best of intentions on the part of all concerned. Even *wanting* rapport with Duncan, once he learns that they are father and son, Dhugal's first time is far from pleasant, in the beginning, for Duncan must force his way past the instinctive and unconscious initial resistance and then hold the link, despite Dhugal's discomfort, until the flow of shared rapport can stabilize on unconscious as well as conscious levels and the resistance ceases.

If the subject truly resists, however, and if the operator proceeds without regard to the damage that may result—which may be necessary in some circumstances—the consequences may be grave, indeed. The forcible extraction of information is sometimes known as *mind-ripping*, a procedure whose very name suggests violence and destruction. We may perhaps consider it the brute-force version of what can be done less traumatically with skill, time, and drug support to break down a subject's resistance. Joram first alludes to it in the context of Archbishop Jaffray's suggestion that Joram should submit to a deep probe regarding Camber's final resting place—a probe Joram is bound to resist with all his might, because of compulsions set in his mind by Camber.

> Jaffray pursed his lips suspiciously. "Such lapses of memory can be overcome, Father." The words were neutral enough, but they carried an edge of threat, nonetheless.
> "To do so, in this case, could shatter my mind. Please do not force me, Your Grace," Joram pleaded. (*Saint Camber* 380).

Dom Queron already has made voluntary submission to a deep probe by Jaffray—called Truth-Reading, in this context, for general convenience, but actually a one-sided rapport for examination of a specific subject. Were such a procedure to be forced upon Joram against his wishes, however, his mind might, indeed, be shattered—depending on how far Jaffray was willing to go to get at what he believed Joram was hiding. After Jaffray has agreed, in principle, that "Bishop Cullen" may have a go at getting past Joram's "compulsions," Joram mentions mind-ripping more specifically—no longer because of any immediate fear that it may yet be done, but as a means of reiterating the ostensible reason he cannot submit to anyone except, perhaps, Camber-Alister.

> "Well, Father MacRorie, how say you?" Jaffray asked sternly. "Will these 'compulsions' permit you to yield to Bishop Cullen's reading?"
> "I—don't know, Your Grace," Joram whispered, feigning uncertainty. "I think so. I feel—some resistance, even to that, but I would trust Bishop Cullen above all other men to try to read beyond it. Believe me, Your Grace, I have no desire to disobey you, but I am even less inclined to have my mind ripped from me by force." (*Saint Camber* 383)

We are left with the distinct impression that mind-ripping is an extreme measure, not often used by ethical Deryni, but a very real threat under certain circumstances and greatly to be feared by potential victims. Certainly, when the drug-fogged and groggy Rhys invokes the specter of mind-ripping, it is done for its deliberate shock value, gambling his very sanity in the hope that Tavis will recognize the taunt as a desperate earnest of his honesty—for no one seriously would suggest that a Healer use so devastating a tool as mind-ripping, least of all another Healer.

> "Well, why not just rip it from my mind?" Rhys lashed out, anger at their procrastination taking the better part of prudence. "Fill me full of some more of the drugs that you swore to use only for Healing, and then wade right in! You'll probably find out what you want to know!"
>
> . . . He consoled himself with the thought that at least if Tavis took him at his word and ripped his mind, he would probably never know what hit him—he had probably goaded the other Healer beyond all possibility of reasoned response—but Tavis surprised him. He could only guess that Tavis had been reading him all the while, and knew it was truth behind the words he spoke. (*Camber the Heretic* 394)

Mind-ripping may be seen as a basic abuse of Deryni power, then, *perhaps* marginally justifiable as a tool for professional inquisitors who have no other practical options—for ripping a subject's mind by force must do near irreparable damage, leaving the victim a psychic cripple even if the physical body survives the experience. It remains to be seen whether knowledge of the procedure persists into Kelson's time, when so much of the lore of the Deryni has been lost or hidden. One is moved to hope that it does not, for there can be little information whose acquisition justifies such wanton destruction of a mind.

## Memory

Deryni have a particular affinity with memory functions. We have not seen enough examples to know whether Deryni, as a group, have superior memory capacity per se, but specific mention is made of Duncan's "precise" Deryni memory (*Deryni*

*Checkmate* 203); and Dom Emrys' "perfect" memory (*Saint Camber* 193) probably is what we would call eidetic or "photographic." The latter, in particular, would only be enhanced by Deryni skills, as when Evaine assists Joram to recall a map their father showed him years before, so he can draw a duplicate copy.

"Close your eyes now and let me direct you," she whispered, drawing him back to lean against her, cool fingertips slipping up to rest against his temples. "Go deeper now, and deeper still. Suspend all conscious thought and let yourself drift back to that day at Grecotha, when Father showed you the plans he'd discovered. See him spread the plans before you now. Remember your fascination as his finger traces what he's discovered. Study what he shows you. Recall every detail with such clarity that you can read each word and line."

Drifting at her command, Joram let the image form—smiled lazily as the requested details came bobbing from memory to focus in his mind's eye.

"Good," came her encouragement, just at the edge of his awareness. "Now fix the image in your consciousness and, when you're ready, open your eyes and see the lines superimposed on the blank parchment in front of you. When you open your eyes, you'll remain in trance and the image will persist, as real as actual lines, so that all you have to do is trace over the lines on the parchment. Begin when you're ready."

Slowly he opened his eyes to the now familiar plans, dreamily reaching across to pick up the quill and dip its point precisely in the inkwell Evaine steadied. His hand seemed to take on a life of its own as he bent to his task. The pen glided along the ghostly lines with uncanny sureness. . . . A detached part of his consciousness laughed with her at the sheer joy of being able to tap such resources of the mind. (*The Harrowing of Gwynedd* 226–227)

This example also illustrates aspects of classic "automatic writing," in that a direct circuit is set up between the unconscious and the subject's hand, with the conscious standing aside as a passive observer. Something similar occurs when Camber sketches out troop deployments after scrying with the Haldane necklace (*Saint Camber* 52–53), tapping back into the memory of what he saw through Ariella's eyes and relaying it directly through his hand without the intermediary of conscious control.

By extension, what Morgan does when he reads the young page's memory of Duke Jared's capture (*High Deryni* 218–220) is simply a more dramatic approach to what essentially is the same process, using voice as the medium rather than the pen. We have no indication that memory retrieval of this sort represents any particular danger to the operator, despite the fact that Morgan twice mentions that the procedure is not without its dangers to him personally (but not to his subject or his audience). We must take his statements partly as a reflection of his own inexperience in the use of his powers, which is a very real factor, but partly also as his flair for the theatrical—for the incident provides an unprecedented opportunity to demonstrate his powers in a setting of supposed vulnerability, willing to put himself at considerable risk in the service of his king.

Finally, taking the idea of memory enhancement to its ultimate expression, we have Dom Queron's very graphic demonstration with Guaire of Arliss of "a process taught by our Gabrilite Order which enables an adept to reach into another's memory and project a visual image of that other's recollection which anyone may see" (*Saint Camber* 369). In what essentially is a holographic playback of what Guaire saw, Queron is able to re-create the incident for Guaire to reenact, Queron's own voice channeling the memory of Camber's words. (One can see how this variety of role playing could very easily have applications in treating "certain sicknesses of the mind," as Queron notes.) The procedure must not be commonplace, for neither Camber nor Joram has seen it done before (though they have heard of it, and Camber notes that Rhys probably is familiar with the technique), so perhaps it belongs to that twilight area of esoteric practices taught by the Gabrilite Inner Order, surfacing only on a need basis. What results is not just an example of mass-induced para-hypnosis, because Camber and Joram and the other Deryni in the chamber see and hear it, too, and presumably they could detect any manipulation of their perceptions.

But the above is an extremely specialized and dramatic aspect of memory recall. More unusual applications tend to be of a

more immediately practical nature. We have already seen how
direct reading of memory sometimes is used for military intelligence, to save time and avoid errors of interpretation; a Deryni
often will allow another Deryni to read a memory direct, for
the same reasons. The other major application of memory function is to alter a subject's memory or even implant new memories. Rhys' alteration of Tavis O'Neill's memory of the night of
King Cinhil's death is a particularly good example of the usefulness of memory manipulation, and blurring or erasing a painful
or inconvenient memory also has its uses. All of these applications
utilize some aspect of the para-hypnotic functions mentioned earlier, and all except the direct reading of memory are accessible,
at least to some degree, by real-world hypnotic techniques.

## Death-Readings

What the Deryni also can do regarding memory, which has no
analog in our own universe, is to "read" the memories of a
recently dead person. Most often, this is done in order to find
out more about the circumstances surrounding an individual's
death (as would have been done for Tiercel, had his death been
discovered earlier), or to retrieve important information that
might have been at the individual's disposal—as, indeed, Conall
did for Tiercel.

The major factor in success or failure of a death-reading is
the elapsed time since death, though the mental state of the
reader also can be a factor. Morgan gains little information from
a death-reading on the boy who attempted to assassinate Duncan
(*The Bishop's Heir* 38–39), perhaps because of his own emotional reaction to the deed (and a physiological reaction to the
*merasha* in Duncan's wound). Kelson does slightly better on a
Mearan prisoner (*The King's Justice* 94–95) but gains little useful information beyond the identity of the man's liege lord. Anscom is able to read enough from the slain Father Humphrey
(*Camber of Culdi* 277) to exonerate him of any conscious or
willful betrayal of the king, but Anscom has the advantage of
formal training in the technique and immediate access to the
body. After nearly two centuries of decline in the transmission
of Deryni training, we cannot expect that Arilan will have had
skills comparable to Anscom's, but the question is rendered ac-

ademic since Tiercel has been dead for nearly a fortnight before Arilan can attempt a reading on him (*The Quest for Saint Camber* 166), with predictably negative results.

Nor can much be said about the death-readings we know were done on Rhys and Jebediah. Almost certainly it was Camber who performed that last service for Rhys, surely very soon after death, but we will never know what he might have learned. Joram probably was designated to Read Jebediah, since they both were Michaelines, but enough hours had passed that little would have remained; attempts to Read Camber were unsuccessful for altogether different reasons.

While Reading a subject's immediate predeath memories and other superficial information may have its practical applications, however, a vastly more far-reaching potential is the retrieval of knowledge and personality attributes that otherwise would be lost when a person dies. Some Deryni have the ability actually to assume another person's memories and assimilate them, so that those memories become integrated with the operator's own personality.

## Memory Assumption and Integration

The major factor limiting the actual assumption, aside from the skill of the operator, seems to be one of time. Memory integrity tends to deteriorate rapidly after death, perhaps linked with the relationship we know exists between oxygen deprivation and irreversible brain damage. We might posit a distinction between brain function and mind function as a mechanism to suggest how the process works for the Deryni.

As a physical function, memory appears to be stored in the brain, much as a battery might store an electrical charge. The energy of the living body keeps the circuits unbroken, enabling the brain to operate more or less as it should. But the *will* to drive the brain mechanism for retrieval of memory information from the brain is a *mind* function, closely linked with that ineffable life force that we call the soul. Once the soul spark leaves the body at death (or once the silver cord is severed, to use biblical and Deryni imagery), access to the brain must be bridged by another mind before the physical storage capacity of the brain begins to ground out in a manner similar to an electrical charge seeping into earth.

This random earthing of the charges that compose the brain aspect of memory would account for the patchy nature of memories being assimilated that is always observed when making a death-reading. It also suggests the means by which skilled Deryni such as Dom Emrys or the dying Davin MacRorie could purge their own memories as they died, earthing that mind energy in a supreme act of will, so that nothing remains to be read that might betray their people.

Thus far, we have seen two major excursions into memory reading on a large scale: Camber's assumption and assimilation of the memories of the dead Alister Cullen, and Conall's assumption of Tiercel de Claron's memories—though the latter's assimilation of the memories gained was never formally accomplished, and may partially account for personality aberrations later on. Unlike the relatively untrained Conall, Camber knows precisely what he is doing and takes on the dead Alister's memories in full awareness of what must follow.

[He] laid both his hands on the forehead. He closed his eyes and let his awareness center and then extend, reaching out for what was left of Alister Cullen.

The remaining memory fragments were chaotic, jumbled and rent already with death-wrought gaps which he could never hope to fill; but he had expected that. Without pausing to read those memories, he let them siphon off into a closely guarded vault of his own being, slowing the flow only to sift it from the shadows of death—not to impart any kind of order or understanding. Later, he would—he must—integrate the alien memories with his own, but for now such as remained of Alister Cullen must be merely locked away, partitioned off beyond kenning. There was no time for more.

He knew the price he would pay for that haste. To take another's memories whole, without assimilation at the time of taking, was to court the throbbing, pulsing pain of all the other's dying once he did find the time to do things right. And he dared not delay to find that time, not beyond a week or two, at best—for pressure built with passing time, like a wound festering with infection, and had been known to drive men truly mad, when at last they did dare to let the pressure out. (*Saint Camber* 115–116)

A week later, Camber does integrate those memories, with astonishing results. His method is couched in quasi-ritual to establish the appropriate mind-set, but it basically involves a profound turning inward to own and experience for himself these fragments that were part of the essence of the man whose identity he has assumed. From then on, he is able to access those memories as if they were his own, giving him the flexibility to continue playing his role to perfection. Indeed, so thorough is his integration of the Alister memories that, at times, it is almost as if the Alister part continues as a distinct entity—a circumstance that must have given an unexpected degree of comfort to the faithful Jebediah when he experienced rapport with Camber for the first time.

Conall achieves no such success, perhaps because he is not aware of the need for memory integration, perhaps because he has no intention of *becoming* Tiercel de Claron but only drawing upon Tiercel's memories of "forbidden knowledge." Some form of ordering and integration apparently takes place during the ritual intended to set his Haldane powers in place, but we are left with the impression that this is an unintended and incomplete by-product. Conall's guilt will not allow him to own the personal memories he has taken on; he is interested only in the forbidden knowledge he has gained. The headaches that increasingly characterize Conall, and his susceptibility to the lure of using his powers to have his own way, particularly in his courtship of Rothana, are all symptoms of a memory integration never really resolved—perhaps verging on the very madness that Camber feared. Jealousy of Kelson has been a major facet of Conall's personality almost from the start—he is a selfish, self-indulgent young man, all too conscious of his rank and privileges—but one would like to think that some outside force was the final factor to push him over the edge into treason and betrayal. We can only mourn as we see this flawed Haldane gradually reduced to a scheming, petty boy and hope that the headsman's sword has brought him some level of expiation and peace at last.

## Mind-Control

Mind-control of one kind or another governs all of the functions we have discussed so far, whether it is control and discipline of the operator's own mind or actual control and direction of another's, for virtually all Deryni functions require an altered state of consciousness—some level of trance, if you will. The parahypnosis we have already discussed is a most powerful tool in this regard, whether to give the edge to one's own, internal processes or to direct another's trance. Shields are a Deryni's natural defense against mind-control; humans may have a certain amount of resistance, but they do not have shields.

A Deryni's shields can be a liability as well as an asset, however, as we saw in the case of Dhugal. It is doubtful whether his shields were set in place deliberately, for his mother, though of the border folk who possess Second Sight, was not aware of the probable source of that border trait, and in any case lived only a few days after the birth of her son. More likely Dhugal's shields simply arose spontaneously at puberty, as often happens if a child does not have the benefit of training. In the days when Deryni were in ascendancy, parents usually set controls in their children in infancy, to enable them to bypass the child's shields when they eventually developed. (We have already seen the controls Rhys and Evaine set in their children for that purpose and the reason such controls might be needed, especially in the case of Tieg.) These controls normally would be relinquished when the child reached the age of majority, but meanwhile they allowed parents and designated surrogates such as teachers to bypass the shields that might have prevented responsible guidance. Part of the educational process for young Deryni was to learn to lower their shields, once they had learned to raise them, for one cannot relinquish control of one's mind behind closed shields; certain processes cannot even be contemplated without giving control over to another.

Such control usually was accompanied and enhanced by trance, for which the Deryni had a number of preferred induction techniques. Many of them will be familiar to those acquainted with modern hypnotic practice. More often than not, physical contact was involved, preferably on the forehead.

A favorite technique for engaging the attention of a human

subject was to direct the subject's attention to the operator's fingertip, held slightly above eye level—which the operator then brought slowly to touch the subject between the eyes. Tracking the fingertip (or indeed, any object) as it approaches in this manner puts a slight physical strain on the subject's eyes, encouraging the tendency for the eyes to roll up in their sockets and close—a physical sensation of weariness to reinforce the simultaneous suggestions of the operator to relax, to sleep, to let go. . . . When enhanced by a Deryni's para-hypnotic power, the suggestion is near irresistible.

Other standard induction techniques are common among the Deryni as well. Some involve breathing exercises, motor cues, visual keys, or any combination thereof. A trained adept can go into trance at the blink of an eye, shifting mental gears with little if any outward preparation, but physical cues almost always enhance the establishment of the mind-set necessary to enter an altered state.

The Thuryn technique, the only one we know by a specific name, involves both visual fixation and a breath trigger. In fact, it does not differ markedly from most other concentration aids we have encountered, but the fact that Morgan and some of his contemporaries refer to it by this name may indicate descent through an authentic Camberian connection—an imperfect descent, perhaps, for much knowledge has been lost or altered over decades of persecution, but Rhys Thuryn may well have taught such a technique, which was passed on by his descendants. Indeed, both Morgan and Duncan can claim direct descent from Rhys and Evaine—though the exact relationship will unfold only in later books.

Visual fixation is an important key for going into trance, then: a deep breath in and out to collect oneself, to release tension, paired with focus on a physical point of concentration—a ring, a candle, a fingertip, a point of reflected light. Morgan fixes on his gryphon signet; Tiercel has Conall gaze into a candle flame. Wencit dangles a *shiral* pendant from a chain to fascinate Bran Coris and ease him into trance. Tiercel uses Conall's Saint Camber medal as a pendulum to guide him in use of another Deryni aid to trance induction: a staring pattern.

## Staring Patterns

The intricate spiraling motifs called staring patterns have been known for millennia in our own Earth history. They are a sub-class of labyrinths and sacred mazes, except that the Deryni user traces not only a physical labyrinth but an explicitly psychic one. The purpose, in either case, is the same, however: to draw the user toward the center, or toward a centered state—toward a trance state, or a pretrance state, if you will, or certainly a state of altered consciousness. From this state, the adept should be able to tap powers and/or insights not usually accessible to nor-mal waking consciousness. For this reason, the Deryni desig-nate certain patterns to trigger certain responses (or mind-sets, or spells), as shorthand methods for reestablishing certain psy-chic connections.

Permanent staring patterns tend to be carved in stone or wood, or cast in metal, like the staring patterns on the bronze door to the *keeill*, underneath the Camberian Council chamber. Often these must be activated or charged before use, as Ansel charges the *keeill* pattern with handfire before instructing Queron to use it.

"I'll release your controls now," Ansel murmured, shift-ing his grasp to Queron's left elbow, "but don't raise your shields." His free hand seemed to press the handfire into the carvings of the top spiral so that it glowed like molten silver. "Work the first staring pattern. It's a spell for centering. I'll follow it with you."

Nodding, Queron drew a deep breath and complied. He knew the pattern well—probably far better than the younger, less experienced Ansel, but that might not be a safe assump-tion, based on the last quarter hour. So he made himself trace it slowly—no short cuts—savoring the gradual stilling and centering as his eyes tracked every curve of the mystical maze. At the centerpoint, the spell in place, he closed his eyes for just a moment and took another deep breath, letting it out slowly as he opened his eyes again to await further instruc-tion. The glow of the staring pattern was fading as Ansel pushed the door open with the flat of his hand and ushered Queron in. (*The Harrowing of Gwynedd* 70–71)

More transient staring patterns might be drawn with pen and ink, but more commonly are traced in sand or earth, such as the one with which the Marluk attempts to ensorcel Brion, sketched in the dirt with the tip of his sword (*Deryni Archives* 169). Such staring patterns may even have New Testament antecedents. Perhaps Jesus was utilizing a staring pattern in the story of the woman taken in adultery, when he "stooped down, and with his finger wrote on the ground, as though he heard them not" (John 8:6).

Certainly it was a staring pattern traced in the sand by the grey-cowled man to guide Kelson and Dhugal to a vision of Saint Camber's final resting place—a scrying aid, in this instance, to allow images to appear on the stretch of smooth, wave-washed sand (*The Quest for Saint Camber* 434). Nor are staring patterns confined to use only with Deryni. Raif, in a move both blatant and clandestine, uses a staring pattern to induce a deeper trance in the already susceptible Hoag.

"You know, today's strategies were really quite brilliant," he murmured, beginning to sketch a pattern which, to the uninitiated, would appear to be a battle diagram. "Do you realize what the king did, when he ordered the charge from the east?"

Hoag's eyes had followed Raif's every move, and now they tracked the pattern he traced, with increasing attention, slipping unerringly into the deeper trance state that Raif demanded.

"But, perhaps that's too complicated, after a long day's fighting," he murmured, touching Hoag's hand with the end of the twig.

Instantly, Hoag's eyelids fluttered and closed, his breathing deepening to that of sleep, though he leaned on his elbow still.

"Ah, yes," Raif whispered, never taking his eyes from Hoag's as he tossed his twig into the fire, "you look very tired, Hoag."

Hoag's only sound was a tiny, relieved sigh as he collapsed back against the saddle. (*The King's Justice* 269–270)

Raif goes on to use the entranced Hoag as a communication link to report to Sofiana. The point is that the staring pattern is used to induce a trance or altered state, either with or sometimes without the cooperation of the subject.

# CHAPTER SEVEN

# Clairsentient Functions

Clairsentience involves those functions that permit the acquisition of information from outside the bounds of normal sensory input, by means other than direct telepathy. One of the broadest Deryni applications of this function is *casting* or scanning or probing for danger—a nonspecific, nonfocused general sweep of an area or object with one's powers, through partially opened shields. Without specific preparations, the range for such a sweep may extend as far as 8 to 10 yards in any direction, or about the maximum size of a magical circle in which one might work. Casting beyond that distance, and especially beyond line-of-sight, requires a more focused target and intent. Within these limitations, however, the process can be quite useful. One means of moving beyond these limitations is called scrying.

*Scrying*, often associated with crystal-gazing in our own world, is an ancient method of seeking out otherwise hidden information. To scry means to fix one's gaze upon a suitable focus and enter an altered state of consciousness—we might call it a form of self-hypnotic trance—allowing previously unconscious knowledge to surface, usually as images. Typical points of focus have been crystal balls, mirrors both bright and dark, still or rushing water, shiny gems, flames—whatever will arrest the attention, preferably in a monotonous manner, freeing the mind to elaborate according to the guidance of the unconscious.

The Deryni have been known to use a variety of foci for scrying operations. Duncan stares into a large, amber *shiral* crystal in Morgan's study and lets his mind drift (*Deryni Check-mate* 47), recoiling when his troubled unconscious conjures up images of Archbishop Loris' menace. Camber scries in a silver bowl of ink-blackened water (*Saint Camber* 40–52), seeking a link to Ariella via a necklace she has worn. This inclusion of and focus on an article associated with the target subject is a Deryni variation on normal scrying procedure, drawing on the principles of psychometry: that an object worn or used regularly by an individual tends to absorb some of the essence of that individual, retaining a distinctive "signature" that is identifiable by an operator trained in such disciplines. Depending on the duration of former proximity and, to a certain extent, the material of which the object is made, a link of varying strength persists between object and subject. It is this link that is intended to serve as a guideline, when an operator scries for particular information. Morgan has Kelson use a backdrop of flames as a visual focus when seeking information on the missing Dhugal, attempting to link with his essence through a black silk ribbon Dhugal has worn to tie back his border braid.

Here a slight digression is in order, to mention that silk, of all textile materials, is most closely associated with holding a psychic "charge." Ideally, magical implements are wrapped in silk for storage, both to insulate them from outside energies and to help contain the energies built up in them from use. Even in our own world, one will find few teachers of the Tarot who do not recommend that a Tarot deck be kept wrapped in silk, if at all possible, and many suggest that a silk cloth should be spread on the table where the cards are to be laid out. Tabernacles set aside for housing the Reserved Sacrament traditionally are lined with silk (or possibly with pure linen), and the ciboria stored in those tabernacles almost invariably are veiled with silk. Just about any object used habitually in a ritual manner will benefit from being wrapped in silk when not in use.

Silk also is the preferred material for ecclesiastical vestments and other magical robes, though natural fibers such as fine wool, linen, and cotton also are effective. At least one Christian theoretician postulates that the very cut of the traditional chasuble, with its decorative cruciform bands of gold-embroidered silk, helps in channeling the energy raised by the priest during celebration of the Mass. We may recall that Jodotha's robe, very possibly a ceremonial garment, was of purple silk.

Dhugal's silk ribbon is an excellent focus, then, when Kelson tries to scry for information about his whereabouts. Note that additionally, in this case, Morgan gives Kelson the option of augmenting his power, since they expect the distance to be great between themselves and wherever Dhugal is.

> "Let's use the flames as your first focus," Morgan said softly, himself locking on the king's eyes. "Let yourself slip into trance and stare into the fire. I'll not share your vision, but feel free to pull energy from me as you begin to build an image of Dhugal in the shifting patterns of light and dark. Draw on his essence that remains in the ribbon and start to reach out across the miles and See him. Let your eyes unfocus. That's right. Use the flames as a background for your Vision, but know that the flames themselves are not your goal. See Dhugal as you last saw him, and now bring that image forward in time. Let yourself flow with it. Good . . ." (*The Bishop's Heir* 143–144)

The key in all these examples is that the visual focus serves as a backdrop for the images that the mind conjures, once a suitably receptive mental state has been achieved and the will has been directed via some link with the sought-after subject. A physical link with a desired "target" is often useful, but scrying can be done just as effectively without a specific focus.

Using a link with a target can be useful in casting or scanning as well. Duncan, when searching for some clue to Morgan's fate in the chapel at Saint Torin's, uses Morgan's fallen cap as a focus to scan for him specifically (*Deryni Checkmate* 202–205). And Morgan focuses on the ring alleged to have been braided of Duncan's and Maryse's hair (*The Bishop's Heir* 317) to confirm that part of it did, indeed, come from Duncan's body.

A slight variation on the above techniques has the subject use a scrying surface as a focus for memory amplification. The young Charissa scries in a goblet of dark-red wine, projecting her memories of her father's last battle onto the surface for her audience also to see (*The Deryni Archives* 165–171). Tiercel has Conall focus on his cup of wine while he reads Conall's memory of the sacked convent and meeting Rothana. (*The King's Justice* 128). And in yet another variation, Charissa "sees" in a crystal that is linked magically/psychically to a similar stone in the pendant of the chain of office that Morgan wears to Kelson's coronation (*Deryni Rising* 228–229).

*Dowsing* is another "oddball" psychic skill that has its counterpart in the Eleven Kingdoms—a method for locating underground water and sometimes applied for locating other things, such as buried pipes and power lines, in our own time. We have seen only one example of its use so far, when Morgan and Duncan dowse to trace the route of the underground river where Kelson and Dhugal were lost, but we can assume that it is a fairly common if little talked about practice in the borders and highlands, for it is Ciard O'Ruane, Dhugal's faithful old retainer, who suggests its use. Ciard attributes it to the pantheon of knacks and ways that borderers call the Second Sight—which may, in turn, be the surface manifestations of Deryni inheritance buried under generations of repression. Ciard expresses doubt that *he* can focus the dowsing process finely enough to distinguish underground water from surface water but opines that a Deryni might be able to do it.

[Morgan and Duncan] watched with honest curiosity as Ciard picked through the piles of driftwood at the edge of the pool until, after inspecting and rejecting nearly a dozen, he found a forked branch that suited him. Quickly he trimmed it to the shape of a short-tailed Y and peeled it, pausing often to pare away a knot or test the proportions of the arms. When he had sheathed his dirk, he held out his work for their inspection.

"Now, why did you pick this particular bit of wood, Ciard?" Morgan asked.

"Why, because it spoke t'me, sair. Some o' them hae th' yen tae bend tae water, an' others dinnae. Feel th' life in this one—not th' life o' the tree it came from, exactly, but a—a vitality, if ye will."

As the two Deryni ran their fingers along the smooth, pale wood, Duncan nodded, opening his perceptions to Morgan as well.

"I think I see what you mean," he said. "Now, how do you use it?"

A little tentative now, Ciard took the two arms of the forked branch lightly in his fingers and turned so that the tail of the Y pointed toward the water. After a few seconds, the tail dipped a little between his hands.

"Are you doing that?" Morgan asked.

Duncan shook his head at the same time Ciard shook his.

"No, sair," the gillie murmured, his seamed face very still, eyes a little unfocused on the end of the stick. "I—cannae exactly explain what I'm doin', but . . ."

As his voice trailed off and the tail of the Y jerked more strongly between his hands, Duncan moved enough closer to touch his forearm gently.

"Try not to pay any attention to me, Ciard," Duncan said, pushing a tentative probe toward the gillie's mind. "You've worked with Dhugal, so you know a mind touch won't hurt. I just want to see if I can figure out how you're doing that."

He closed his eyes then, reading all the nuances of energy flow that went into what Ciard was doing.

"We'll have to make our own dowsing sticks," he said, when he looked up at last and let his hand fall away. "Each one has to be chosen by and for the user. But I think I've got the general idea." (*The Quest for Saint Camber* 319–320)

Further examples of clairsentient acquisition of knowledge might include the feedback a Deryni gets when probing inside an object, such as the ability to suss out the inside of a lock (the *knowledge* part, as opposed to the *action* part of moving tumblers and levers); the general procedure whereby a Healer may probe the condition of hidden body parts; the somewhat more specialized talent for detecting the sex of a child *in utero*, and even the general ability to sense the presence of other living things at a distance (presence of bodies rather than identification of specific individuals).

# CHAPTER EIGHT

# Telefunctions I:
# Telekinesis

Telefunctions include those applications of Deryni power that result in physical movement of something or someone across a distance by a nonusual means. We may divide these into two general categories: telekinetic functions, in which the operator causes movement of an object without physically touching it, and teleportal functions, in which the operator causes himself (and possibly another) to move instantaneously across a given space. We will consider telekinetic functions in this chapter.

## Opening Locks

Manipulating the innards of locks without benefit of key is a particularly handy Deryni application of telekinetic ability. To accomplish this, the operator projects a tendril of mental energy into the lock to quest out the mechanism and shift the appropriate levers and tumblers. It is a specialized application of the casting/scanning function mentioned previously. Joram uses this skill when he and Rhys sneak into Saint Foillan's to kidnap Cinhil, unlocking a gate in the rood screen with his mind (*Camber of Culdi* 183)—but he bests an earlier lock, on the outer door at the porch, with the more time-honored expedient of slipping the narrow blade of his dagger between the latch and the door jamb (*Camber of Culdi* 181), much as we might employ a plastic credit card today. (This is a good example of *not* using magic when an easier nonmagical method may be employed. We may also assume that this lock was of a simpler variety, that could be sprung with a dagger blade rather than actually having to be picked—perhaps even a simple latch to be lifted.)

Morgan also has mastered this particular skill—obviously very useful to one in his position—and uses his powers to open a more complicated lock guarding the gate to the crypt under Saint George's Cathedral in Rhemuth, when he takes Kelson there the night before the young king's coronation (*Deryni Rising* 145–146). Duncan reluctantly does the same for a door under the shrine of Saint Torin (*Deryni Checkmate* 222–223)—reluctantly, because he must do it in front of Warin de Grey and Lawrence Gorony, thereby revealing that he is Deryni.

Camber uses his powers to gain access to Archbishop Jaffray's apartments and the Transfer Portal therein.

> [He] bent to the door latch and reached out with his mind, found the pins, nudged them with that peculiarly Deryni skill which not all of his race could wield with this degree of accuracy. He kept a little tension on the latch while he worked, finally feeling the handle drop beneath his hand (*Camber the Heretic* 118).

We also know that Duncan unlocked the tabernacle containing the Sacrament, in his father's chapel, on the night he and Maryse exchanged wedding vows (*The Quest for Saint Camber* 16). And Dhugal uses the same talent to loose his father's shackles (*The King's Justice* 245).

Locks are not always secured with mere metal, either. Cinhil observes a "strangely glowing doorlatch" (*Camber of Culdi* 262) as he is being led into the Michaeline chapel for his ritual of power assumption—a latch that Alister Cullen touches to open, obviously involving something besides merely physical manipulation of a lock mechanism. Evaine, retrieving scrolls hidden by her father before he went off to the battle of Iomaire, mentally articulates "a series of syllables highly unlikely to be combined at random" while she presses a protuberance of rock—and the compartment opens (*Saint Camber* 152).

Some locks are "keyed" by application of a suitably charged ring or seal or the like, as when Duncan uses Morgan's signet ring to open a secret compartment in the altar at Saint Hilary's, or when Morgan uses the same ring to open the box that Duncan has retrieved (*Deryni Rising* 88–89). Later on, Kelson's Ring of Fire, suitably charged, is used to open the box that contains the Crimson Lion brooch (*Deryni Rising* 159). All three examples involve the same kind of psychic energy as that used to open locks directly, except that the energy already has gone into the lock, preset to be discharged against the appropriate mechanism by the designated trigger item—a kind of psychic storage battery, if you will. And of course, locks can be *locked* with Deryni powers as well as unlocked.

## Deflecting Arrows

Another very practical application of telekinetic ability—a "Deryni advantage," as Kelson terms it—enables arrows to be deflected or even guided in flight. Kelson and then Morgan demonstrate this quite graphically to the newly aware Dhugal on the archery range, though Kelson concedes that it would be an unfair advantage in a competition (*The King's Justice* 10–12). There on the practice range, shooting at a straw target in a non-stress setting, it is a lighthearted display, intended only to open Dhugal's mind to possible further applications of his inherent Deryni ability. But the exercise takes on deadly urgency later on, when Duncan is the target of enemy arrows, and Kelson and Morgan must try to deflect those arrows while at the same time keeping themselves alive as they battle toward him through the rebel forces (*The King's Justice* 239–242). Again, a major Deryni limitation is illustrated: that magic does one no good unless there is time for the concentration to use it.

## Other Telekinetic Functions

Deryni power can be used for more frivolous things, too. Several times, we see accomplished Deryni "float" objects for one reason or another. Arilan calls a cup to himself (*The Quest for Saint Camber* 29). Charissa makes a gauntlet return to her hand (*Deryni Rising* 255). And the young Rhys and Joram move pieces on a game board with their minds (*The Deryni Archives* 11–12).

Morgan's thought makes a bully's whip tangle around his feet and trip him (*Deryni Rising* 29). Conall ties a knot in a blade of grass by staring at it and employing his powers (*The King's Justice* 168). On a more serious note, Charissa is able to make Morgan's chain of office choke him briefly, throwing him off balance for Ian's flung dagger (*Deryni Rising* 245). And Dhugal is able to shift bars securing doors from the other side, when he and Kelson are trying to find their way out of the serial burial chamber in *The Quest for Saint Camber* (325–326), and to untie knots binding his wrists (*The Quest for Saint Camber* 338).

Such power gone awry also can cause destruction, as when the delirious Gregory launches crockery and weapons around his sickroom (*Camber the Heretic* 6, 8–9). We may imagine a similar scene of chaos when the Healer's novice Ulric went berserk and "tried to bring down the entire abbey" after killing the Novice Master in a forbidden Duel Arcane; and it is virtually certain that Dom Emrys' means of stopping Ulric's killing rampage involved using his powers to guide his arrow to Ulric's heart (*Camber the Heretic* 235).

The ability to cause physical movement at a distance also can be employed directly as an instrument of death, as in the heart-stopping spell that Charissa uses to kill first Brion and then Ian (*Deryni Rising* 20, 246), and that Kelson finally must also use, to give Wencit and his three henchmen the *coup de grace* (*High Deryni* 343–345). Indeed, how to stop a heart is something that even King Cinhil learns early on, instinctively using it to cut short the curses of the wounded Deryni dissident who has just tried to kill him (*Saint Camber* 14). In essence, the spell is one of sympathetic magic, reaching out with the psychic echo of the physical hand to symbolically squeeze the heart until it stops. The effect on the victim must be very like a heart attack.

Fortunately, one of the most common uses of telekinetic powers is more constructive. Part of a Healer's function, beyond the actual focusing of healing energy (which will be discussed in a later chapter), is the actual physical manipulation of cleaning a wound and then pulling and holding severed body parts back together. "Healing's much easier if you can get the injured bits back in the general area where they belong, before you start. Hard to heal across a handspan of empty space when you're trying to reattach two cut ends," as Dom Sereld, the king's Healer, observes in "Catalyst" (*The Deryni Archives* 25), having engaged Camber's assistance in repositioning the boy Rhys' severed Achilles tendon.

Camber is not a Healer, of course, but years later he again must try to save the gravely injured Rhys, this time by lifting the depressed skull fracture whose pressure is slowly snuffing out Rhys' life (*Camber the Heretic* 410). Unfortunately, the physical manipulation alone is not sufficient, but nearly two hundred years later, Dhugal tries a similar maneuver with far greater success.

> It was not a healing function, in the Deryni sense. It certainly did not sound like what his father and Morgan had described about the healing process—visualizing the damaged area as it ought to be and having the healing take place under one's hands. But was there not a physical side to surgery, as well as a biological one? Provided that no irreversible damage had been done to the tissue beneath the skull, relief of Kelson's condition might come simply by restoring the bit of bone to its proper place and letting natural healing take its course. . . .
>
> Not daring to think too much about it, Dhugal extended his Deryni senses into the body beneath his hands, centering on the circle of bone that lay beneath his fingertips. All at once he could see it in his mind, as if it were exposed by a surgeon's knife—a rounded triangle of bone, one edge still neatly in place and the opposite angle depressed almost to the depth of the tip of a man's little finger.
>
> Gently, gingerly, he eased his powers around it and lifted. It moved more easily than he had expected, smoothly pivoting on the edge still in place until all three sides were flush again. (*The Quest for Saint Camber* 211–213)

But more of healing applications when we discuss the healing function in detail. For now, let us shift to the other side of telefunction—the use of what Deryni refer to as Transfer Portals.

# CHAPTER NINE

# Telefunctions II:
# Transfer Portals

Transfer Portals are the means by which Deryni exercise what we would call *teleportation*, or the ability to move a person or object across a distance, more or less instantaneously. As Tiercel de Claron says (*The Quest for Saint Camber* 122), "It's a Deryni way of getting somewhere in a hurry." Portals should not be viewed as *dei* in the Deryni *machina*, however, because Portal use does have important limitations.

## General Limitations

*Primus:* Portal travel is possible only between pairs of previously established Portals. Deryni cannot just pop out of existence in one place and pop in at another. Properly activated Portals must exist both at departure and arrival points.

*Secundus:* A Deryni cannot transfer directly to a Portal to which he or she has never been. The operator must know the "coordinates" of the destination Portal, either from direct experience or from mind link with someone who does know the destination in question. (The sole exception noted to date is the Portal outside what became the Camberian Council chamber, the location of which was deduced from "a chance reference in one of the ancient manuscripts which still occupied most of Evaine's leisure time" [*Camber the Heretic* 243]. Many months passed before anyone was confident enough of their visualization of the desired destination to risk an actual Transfer—

presumably by Evaine herself or by Camber, as the most adept among them.)

*Tertius:* Actual use of a Portal must be controlled by a single individual. If the operator wishes to take another person through the Portal, the extra traveler must allow the operator to assume complete control, lest discordant psychic activity upset the delicate balance necessary to shift the energies.

For Deryni, even if the extra Deryni knows the coordinates of their destination, this involves lowering primary shields and shifting to a passive, receptive mode, permitting the operator to assume full initiative. Human companions can learn to mimic this passivity sufficiently that they will not interfere with Portal operation, but most operators prefer to induce temporary unconsciousness in their human companions, either through physical or psychic means, to minimize potential psychic interference. Tavis O'Neill uses carotid pressure to induce unconsciousness in Javan, the first time he takes the prince through a Portal (*Camber the Heretic* 421–422). Arilan, on the other hand, is sufficiently confident/competent to take the human Cardiel through merely by distracting him (*High Deryni* 119).

*Quartus:* Portal transfer requires an energy outlay on the part of the operator. This outlay is nominal in the case of single short jumps by an operator whose handling of the energies is efficient, but the drain on the operator can be cumulative if efficiency is less than optimal or the operator must execute a series of jumps in a relatively short period of time. In addition, very long distance jumps take considerably more energy than shorter ones, perhaps in a geometric rather than arithmetic ratio. When Tiercel first begins teaching Conall about the use of Portals, he warns the prince against overextending (*The Quest for Saint Camber* 122–135).

This would seem to indicate that a certain energy expenditure is required simply to activate the Portal, each time the Portal is used—to which is added an additional expenditure that is directly related to the distance to be traveled. The individual operator's efficiency/ability level also would be a factor, as would the residual energy level of the Portal itself.

## Specific Limitations

Very shortly after they discovered how to construct and use Portals, Deryni adepts would have become aware of the need to regulate the use of particular ones, to prevent indiscriminate access by persons who learned the location of private Portals but were not necessarily welcome at all times. One way of doing this was to set a Portal to resonate only to certain individuals. Before Evaine and her children fled Sheele, for example, the Sheele Portal was locked and sealed to all but those of blood relation (*Camber the Heretic* 441). Perhaps Camber-Alister's Portal atop Queen Sinead's Walk was a variant of this, operable and even findable only by Camber himself.

An even more sophisticated method of guarding Portals from unauthorized use is the use of Trap Portals. Camber and Evaine encounter one of the more benign forms when they go to the Michaeline Commanderie at Cheltham.

"Where are we?" Evaine whispered, as her eyes adjusted to the near-darkness and she pressed a little closer to her father's side.

Wainscotted walls and ceiling surrounded them at arm's reach all around, covering solid rock such as lay beneath their feet. The walls glowed faintly—arcane wards to keep one's power in, not out. Camber reached out tentatively to explore the fastness of the warding spell, then sighed and withdrew, pressing his daughter's shoulder with his encircling arm. . . .

Evaine scanned the walls around them—it was getting more difficult to breathe—and acknowledged that this was one of the most secure confinements that she had ever experienced. Even without the wards, this chamber would have been impervious to invasion, for no Deryni could reach through so much solid rock and loose the bolts which held the rock door closed. If no one chose to give admittance, a would-be intruder had but two choices: to stay and slowly suffocate, for there was no ventilation, or to quit the place entirely and go back the way he had come.

That could be a problem, if one had been forced to destroy the Portal used to get here, she realized, as her eyes continued to sweep the panelled walls. If one had no place to go back to, and knew no other portal place, he could die here. (*Camber of Culdi* 158–159)

More treacherous varieties are possible, too. Tavis O'Neill describes a few of them to Prince Javan after the events of Christmas 917, in a curious mixture of theory and myth.

> "What do you mean, 'traps' and 'can't get back'?" Javan asked in amazement.
>
> Tavis sighed. "Well, you can Transfer into them, but then you can't leave, even to go back where you came from, unless someone at that end releases you. I've also heard stories of other things that can be done to Portals so that you—never come back anywhere. No one knows where those unlucky souls go." (*Camber the Heretic* 418)

The implications are most disquieting, but Tavis doubts that the fugitive Archbishop Alister and his colleagues have resorted to such drastic measures at Dhassa—though he does feel that a Trap of some sort probably has been set. "If that is a Trap Portal at Dhassa, we could wait a long time, and it might be very unpleasant in the waiting," he warns the persistent Javan. "Do you remember how you felt the night I made you sick? The mental part of it, not the physical illness, though it could also have physical manifestations. . . . Well, it could be worse than that, depending upon what they've done." (*Camber the Heretic* 419)

In fact, the physical manifestations of this particular Trap Portal seem to be confined to a shimmer of purple light restraining the newcomers from leaving the immediate area of the Portal square—the sort of measure we might expect of Camber and his allies, aware that friends as well as foes might be seeking the sanctuary of neutral Dhassa—but we can surmise that some discomfort or at least uneasiness is involved, for Tavis gives an audible sigh of relief as the light dies around him and Javan (*Camber the Heretic* 423). In fact, this may be a variant of the Trap put on the Portal at Cheltham, with a different effect because of being out in the open.

In fact, lesser Trap functions in the form of lock-outs probably are placed on private Portals fairly routinely. The Portal that serves the Camberian Council chambers very likely is locked against entry by anyone but sworn members of the Council, unless brought through by a member. Tiercel de Claron hints at this when he tells Conall about Portal accessibility.

"I'm aware of a few dozen [Portals], but they're not all accessible to me. For security reasons, some are attuned to the use of selected individuals, or they have special warding at the other end to keep a user from leaving the immediate vicinity of the Portal until the owner authorizes it. And then there are Trap Portals that will prevent an intruder from jumping back out of an unauthorized Portal until the owner releases him. That may not sound particularly dangerous, but suppose the one in this room were trapped, and we'd come into it while Duncan was on campaign last summer? A person could starve."

"Good Lord, can you tell, before you jump, whether a Portal is trapped?" Conall asked, aghast.

"Sometimes. Sometimes not. It depends on the skill of the trapper and the trappee—which I hope will give you pause before trying any of this on your own, if you should find any Portals on your journey. As I said earlier, I don't recommend Transfer Portals for recreational purposes." (*The Quest for Saint Camber* 129–130)

## Using Portals

Perception of a Portal location requires close proximity to or contact with the Portal square—the term most often used to describe the boundary of the Portal location, despite the fact that an octagon is used in construction. The energy pattern of a "live" or operational Portal usually is perceived as a tingling or a pulsing sensation, though this clearly is a psychic rather than a physical phenomenon, since humans do not feel it. A Deryni accustomed to Portal use can lock onto a familiar Portal merely by stepping onto the square; a neophyte may need to make contact with a bare hand before the distinctive energy pattern can be felt.

The interweaving of energies that causes the tingling or pulsing sensation sometimes is called the Portal matrix. It is this matrix that holds the coordinates of a particular Portal and that must be learned before an operator may use it. An adept *can* learn the coordinates of a new Portal merely by standing on the Portal square, but individuals memorizing Portal coordinates for first-time use generally will place one hand flat on the floor or ground, in order to complete a physical circuit and allow the psychic information to percolate to appropriate levels of consciousness. Physical contact, especially with a hand, also is helpful in attempting to locate an unknown Portal or one grown weak through disuse, as when Duncan searches for a long-destroyed Portal site in the ruins of Saint Neot's (*Deryni Checkmate* 235–239).

Actually using the Portal involves setting in mind the two Portal loci, departure and destination points, balancing the energies thereof, and then "shifting the balances" or "warping the energies." This may be conceptualized as a literal act or tied up with a mnemonic/spell of some sort. Arilan lets "the Words begin to take shape inside his head" (*High Deryni* 119) and wrenches the spell into being. Morgan merely visualizes his destination and opens his mind to the energies binding the two locations, reaching out to shift their balance (*The Bishop's Heir* 244). Camber gathers the energies close about himself and Joram, visualizes their destination, makes the proper mental shift, and warps the energies just—so (*Camber the Heretic* 164).

The actual process is instantaneous, or nearly so, and is accompanied by a brief sense of vertigo, of greater or lesser severity in different individuals. Duncan, being taken through a Portal under Arilan's control, feels "the vague, stomach-wrenching shift of the jump, subtly blunted by Arilan's silken control, and an instant of suspended *not-ness* into which not even the grief penetrated, almost as if Duncan had managed to leave it behind in Rhemuth" (*The Quest for Saint Camber* 219). The untrained but partially Deryni Kelson experiences his first Portal travel as "a sickening wrench in the pit of his stomach, a fleeting impression of falling, a slight dizzy sensation" (*Deryni Rising* 144). The human Guaire, already faint from loss of blood, experiences it as "a sickening, swooping sensation, as if he were falling, and a blast of pure, brilliant energy which nearly held back the darkness" (*Camber of Culdi* 177).

The flashes of light reported in the above scene, when Camber and his kin are evacuating Caerrorie via the Portal in Camber's study, are not normally associated with Portal usage. Most likely, the effect was added as a visible sign of magic being worked, to intimidate the humans among the soldiers waiting to arrest the MacRorie family. A flash of light is also associated with Rhydon's arrival on Thorne Hagen's Portal, but this latter case is probably indicative of an alarm system of some sort, designed to alert Thorne of the arrival of authorized visitors.

Duncan, using the Portal at Valoret Cathedral for the first time, learns its coordinates and uses it almost immediately, with the typical aplomb of an experienced Deryni.

> Closing his eyes, he reached his mind into the tangle of power he could already feel throbbing under his feet. The Portal was a potent one and required far less effort than he had anticipated to lock into its pattern. As he reached for the link in the study Portal, he wondered briefly whether active use reinforced Portals.
>
> Then he drew the link closed with his mind and felt the pit of his stomach give a little wrench, and he was in close darkness, in the familiar confines of the Portal in his study. (*The Quest for Saint Camber* 165)

The *mechanism* of Portal operation—how it actually works—no doubt is largely a mystery even to the Deryni, but we may speculate. Given that a Portal always is constructed within protective Wards, let us postulate that some residual effect of warding remains with an active Portal, helping to contain and preserve the energy matrix established when it is erected. A useful analogy might be that of a horseshoe magnet with a bar across the poles to keep the alignment of energy. Imagine such magnets linking all possible pairs of Portals, tied in with earth energies. Placing a Deryni across the poles of the magnet, with an enabling boost of energy, shifts the balance between those poles, realigns the earth energy, and takes the Deryni to the other pole. Any excess of energy would tend to reinforce the Portal matrix—which explains, at least in part, why Portals in regular use often are more stable and require less energy to activate. Similarly, a Portal out of use for a long time may "fade," even to the point that it is unsafe or nonfunctional.

## Portal Construction

The setting up or "construction" of a Portal is a multi-Deryni operation, requiring both time and energy. Optimally, one would want at least two Deryni who know what they are doing and an additional two to four persons from which to draw additional energy. (In theory, it *may* be possible for a single Deryni to construct a Portal. Richenda, when asked about Morag's ability in this regard, replies, "Nay, few could," implying that some few *can*.) Some or all of the additional two to four persons could be human, but the efficiency of the operation is directly proportional to the ratio of Deryni to humans. For an excellent example of less than optimum conditions for Portal construction, see *High Deryni* 289–295, with Arilan as principal operator, Morgan assisting him with Kelson and Duncan (all three of whom know nothing about the procedure but are Deryni), and Nigel, Cardiel, and Warin providing human reserve energy.

Physical preparation of a Portal apparently requires a base of natural earth or rock. When Arilan prepares to construct a Portal in Kelson's tent in *High Deryni*, he makes a point of turning back the carpet to expose the turf beneath, carefully raking it free of stones and even small twigs; Joram and Ansel are noted to have spent several days tearing up the flagstones of the north transept at Saint Mary's to expose the living rock.

Once the surface is prepared, an octagon seems to be the required shape for defining the Portal bounds. (The octagon figure is echoed in the great ivory table that dominates the Camberian Council chamber, suggesting that the symbolism of eights may be a key facet of Deryni magic.) Arilan uses Nigel's dagger to cut a six-foot octagon into the turf, and Joram chalks one on the rock.

At this point, the area to be activated as a Portal must be warded. The exact form may vary according to the tastes of the principal operator. Arilan has Morgan set Wards Major with a set of Ward Cubes, but augments this warding with an unspecified procedure involving white candles set at the points of the octagon cut into the earth. We are not told how Joram warded for the Saint Mary's Portal, but we may postulate that perhaps he brought his father's Ward Cubes with him from Dhassa for that purpose.

The Portal atop Queen Sinead's Walk, at the bishop's residence in Grecotha, may represent a different sort of Portal altogether.

"This is something I've already gleaned from my archival reading: how to construct a new kind of Transfer Portal—or perhaps I should say that it's an old kind that had been forgotten. The location changes from corner to corner of this area, in a deosil rotation, so that the same spot is used only once in four times. Another feature is that it's attuned so that only I can sense its presence or use it." (*Saint Camber* 302–303)

Joram is amazed that he can't detect the Portal and remains mystified one book later, when he presumably has had access to the same archives from which his father learned the technique yet still doesn't really understand how Camber keeps track of the rotating Portal location. "Oh, I know the theory, but I can't help being suspicious of a Portal that moves—and that I can't feel" (*Camber the Heretic* 164).

We can only speculate as to how Camber actually constructed this unusual Portal. Presumably it involved different procedures from those required for more usual ones—though perhaps its attributes differed, too. It clearly is not the Portal in use at Grecotha, for Camber states (*Saint Camber* 313) that there are several other Portals available in the bishop's residence—which he apparently uses with sufficient regularity that the human Guaire takes it all in stride. (Since the building is a former Varnarite property, we may assume that the Portals are of Varnarite origin.) Also, the fact that Joram did not know about the odd Portal until it was an accomplished fact suggests that Camber had no Deryni assistance, for it is unlikely that he could have dared to work with others who were unaware of his true identity a mere four months after assuming his Alister façade, even if other Deryni had been numerous in that part of the kingdom. (And Alister Cullen, most conservative of Deryni, had never been given to public displays of his abilities.)

Of course, it is possible, in theory, that Camber recruited human assistance to augment the sheer energy drain necessary for creation of a Portal matrix—young Guaire is an obvious candidate, though the procedure would seem to require more than one human—but using humans in this way and then erasing their memories (as would be necessary, after an operation so flagrantly magical) is not consistent with the characters of either Camber or Alister Cullen. So we are left with the conclusion that the Portal atop Queen Sinead's Walk is a different sort from the others we encounter routinely throughout the Eleven Kingdoms.

## Portal Locations

Given the technical skill and energy output required to construct a Transfer Portal, we can surmise that Portals probably were never really numerous, even at the height of Deryni ascendancy. We do know that an ecclesiastical Portal network existed, at least among the religious houses with Deryni members, but we have no indication of the size of this network. In any case, it seems to have been in decline even by the time of Camber.

We know, however, that at least two cathedrals, Rhemuth and Valoret, are mentioned specifically as having Portals in their sacristies, so we may assume that some or even most other cathedrals in existence at the time of the Festillic Interregnum might have had Portals as well. Certainly those cathedrals with Deryni bishops, or those that had Deryni bishops in the past, might be expected to have at least one Portal tucked away somewhere. We know that Rhemuth, in addition to its sacristy Portal, had a second ecclesiastical Portal in the priest's study adjacent to the basilica, built during the Interregnum for the convenience of Deryni confessors to Deryni kings. And since a similar Portal existed in a side oratory off the bishop's chapel at Dhassa, within the bishop's residence, we may speculate that probably there was a second Portal in Dhassa's cathedral sacristy, in keeping with Rhemuth and Valoret.

Various other religious establishments, institutions, and private individuals had Portals as well. For a comprehensive listing of identified and presumed Portal locations, see Appendix IV.

## Destruction of Portals

Judging by the examples we have seen, destroying a Portal is fairly hazardous work. Of the three Deryni who attempt it— Dom Emrys, Bishop Kai Descantor, and Bishop Denis Arilan— all succeed, but two of the three perish in the process. We do not know enough of Kai's background to judge whether lack of training or some other failing was at fault in his case, but surely, if anyone should have been expected to know how to perform the operation successfully, Dom Emrys should have known; yet Emrys dies, while Arilan survives.

Obviously, more factors are at work here than first meet the eye. The primary priority, of course, is the matter of the procedure itself, which involves handling enormous levels of energy—an operation for which the sheer volume and intensity of energy to be channeled and earthed must be balanced against the capacity of the operator to handle it. Thus it comes as no great surprise that Arilan, very well trained for his generation (though hardly in the same league with Dom Emrys), can deal with a Portal like the one in Kelson's tent at Llyndruth Meadows—essentially jury-rigged to serve an immediate but temporary purpose—with little aftereffect beyond the extreme fatigue one might expect.

Kai Descantor, on the other hand, gives no impression of particular adepthood or specialized training, yet he is faced with neutralizing one of the principal links in the ecclesiastical Portals in Gwynedd. If, as we have postulated, Portals intensify and stabilize with use, then Kai's challenge, to defuse the Valoret Portal, would have been far greater than Arilan's—and Kai had far less potential for dealing with it.

Yet the Portal had to be closed. Kai would have realized the necessity, even if Camber and Joram were too devastated by Rhys' mortal injury to think about it. Left open, it might have become a weapon to be used against other Deryni, for the regents could have forced collaborators to utilize the Portals for ultrafast communication. The previous night the Regent Rhun and his troops already had been foiled in their attempt to capture the main Saint Neot's Portal intact—and Dom Emrys had set the example.

So without adequate preparation, either by training or by actual time available to establish a realistic mental set for what he must attempt, Kai made the decision so often made by men of valor. To safeguard his colleagues' escape and ensure that the Portal would not fall into hostile hands, he would stay behind and do his best to destroy it, setting aside the realization that he almost certainly would die in the process.

And he would let that happen—or at least would take no extraordinary measures to ensure that it did not, for escape would be impossible if he succeeded in destroying the Portal. Far better to perish in selfless sacrifice than to fall into the hands of the regents, who would show him no mercy.

This is all conjecture, of course, but it is in character for what little we know of the man. We are not privy to Kai's reasoning process or his work—only the result.

> They found Kai Descantor sprawled in the center of the sacristy floor without a mark upon him. Oriel told them later that a Portal had previously been sited there beneath the carpet, and judged that Kai had died destroying it, after the escape of his colleagues. (*Camber the Heretic* 412)

Similar circumstances surround the more detailed account of Dom Emrys' destruction of the main Gabrilite Portal at Saint Neot's, reverberations of which are detected nearly two centuries later by Morgan and Duncan. Under attack by soldiers of the Regent Rhun, Dom Emrys and an experienced Healer named Kenric use illusion to hold back the attackers for as long as they can, enabling many of their brethren to escape. But when the Portal is about to be overrun, Emrys sends Kenric on through, then kneels beside the Portal and slips his hands beneath the carpet to touch the stone, "questing forth with his mind to rip the Portal's existence from the universe" (*Camber the Heretic* 370). At the same time that he turns the energy of the Portal back on itself to destroy it, he sets in place a psychic warning for those to come—and is dead before the weapons of the intruders can touch him.

Emrys' death appears to be instantaneous, then. We do not know about Kai. On reflection, however, one realizes that Emrys, unlike Kai, must have had time to prepare for just such a contingency—not that night, but at some time previous. The mere destruction of the Portal would have presented no difficulty for an adept of Emrys' known ability, but the message he leaves seems rather too calculated to have been composed completely on the spur of the moment, while he and Kenric were busy maintaining the illusions that helped hold off their attackers.

Kenric himself surely must know what "final task" Emrys intends to perform, yet he obeys unhesitatingly. It is as if Emrys knew that Saint Neot's eventually would be destroyed and had already determined to make of it a symbol for Deryni to come— and was willing to pay whatever price was necessary.

But was death the necessary price? Granted, Emrys' target was the principal Gabrilite Portal, surely carrying an energy potential at least as potent as any other Portal in the ecclesiastical network, but we also have the impression that Emrys was one of the foremost, if not *the* foremost, adept of his time. Earthing the Portal's energy should have been child's play. Nor should the setting of the warning have presented any particular challenge, even combined with the earthing—a mere extension of the ability to embed a psychic message in a seal or the like.

What *would* have concerned Emrys were the reprisals he could expect if captured alive—for the regents would not be lenient on a man who had helped so many potential victims to escape, and highly trained victims, at that. As a Healer and a teacher of Healers, the old abbot would have known all too well how his art could be perverted—that *anyone* could be broken, himself included, given enough time, skilled interrogators, and the right combination of medications. It was not without reason that Rhys taunted Tavis about misusing the skills and drugs he had sworn to use only for healing; some Healers *were* misusing them thus.

What probably happened, then, was this. Emrys knew he *had* to succeed. He also knew that he dared not be around to deal with the consequences afterward—and to escape physically, via the Portal, was out of the question, if he was to destroy it. Nor must the vast knowledge at his disposal fall into the hands of the enemy. Triggers must be set to earth everything, just as the dying Davin MacRorie did, to keep from being read by Tavis.

In addition, turning the energies of a Portal inward to self-destruct takes power in and of itself, as does the setting of a psychic warning, even one largely prepared in advance. Under the circumstances, then, while we may assume that Emrys did not actively *will* his own death—suicidal tendencies were not a part of the man's character—neither must we assume that he would have been inclined to divert any scrap of his own energy to self-preservation, if that at all decreased his chances of success.

What would have happened, then, though all at once, and very quickly, is that Emrys would have triggered everything simultaneously—and taken no steps to compensate for the massive power drain on himself as well as on the Portal. Channeling the vast energy of such destruction surely would have caused destruction in the channel in addition, but Emrys would have done nothing to balance it out or repair the damage it might cost—which, as a Healer, he might have done.

As a conclusion to this chapter, this might be an apt time to comment on suicide. Some readers, noting that the Church forbids the taking of one's own life, have asked whether some of the deaths of otherwise blameless characters do not fall into this category.

Here we need to make some fine distinctions—situation ethics again, perhaps, but all determinations of this sort must be subjective, in the end. In the most technical sense, suicide is the taking of one's own life—which the Church forbids, since it reflects despair, an abandonment of hope in God's solicitude for His creatures. Ultimately, however, only God can know whether other or additional motives might conceivably justify death in such a manner. Active self-destruction with the primary intention of taking one's life is one thing; a self-destructive act that is a secondary result of some other intention may be something else again.

That there are degrees of accountability for death has long been recognized, by both secular and religious authorities. The taking of human life, while never viewed as a particularly desirable thing in and of itself, has always been accepted as sometimes necessary and unavoidable. Self-defense is a survival imperative, whether at the individual level or in times of war. Malicide, the slaying of evildoers, has been sanctioned by nearly every ethical system over the centuries of man's existence on this planet.

If we accept that warfare sometimes is a necessary evil, then it follows that men often will be horribly wounded in the course of its pursuit—and that sometimes nothing can be done to save them. From this grim reality came the practice of giving a mortally wounded warrior the *coup de grace*, literally, the stroke of mercy. Unless the method of dispatching the victim was brutal or inhumane (or became a matter of mere convenience, to avoid giving medical treatment to those who *could* have been saved), the *coup* was not considered to be murder, but a compassionate ending of another's suffering, and even if the victim requested it, the *coup* was not considered to be suicide.

Thus Davin's death is not suicide, even though he causes the guard's hand to move on the arrow in his back, hastening his death—nor is Ewan MacEwan's, begging the *coup* of Declan with a glance and offering his throat for Declan's mercy stroke.

Archbishop Hubert declares that Declan's own death will be judged a suicide, since Declan turned the dagger on his own wrists, but this is the sort of sophistry we might expect of Hubert. Murdoch's order to disembowel Declan constituted murder—or execution, at the very least. Further mitigating Declan's own action is the time-honored principle that soldiers often have been willing to die in the course of performing their duties, or to die rather than fall into enemy hands. The secret agent who bites a cyanide capsule to avoid giving up information that would endanger or betray his allies has much in common with Deryni like Daffydd Leslie and Denzil Carmichael, who set death-triggers for the same reason, or the assassin Andrew, who takes poison rather than be questioned by Morgan—or Declan, who hopes to keep his family from suffering just because *he* can no longer bear to collaborate. Alas, his action brings tragic consequences to his family as well as himself, but his judgment belongs to God alone.

In a final category, we must consider those who take measures that they know are almost certain to result in death. We have already mentioned Kai and Emrys and their reasons for doing what they did. In this category also fall Cinhil, who knows that potentializing his sons will hasten his own death; Sicard, refusing to surrender to Kelson, though he knows he will be killed; Evaine; and a host of others.

For these individuals and others like them, we must note that the motive of self-sacrifice for others, or for a greater good than the individual, is one of the noblest of human sentiments.

"Greater love hath no man than this: that he lay down his life for his friends." It is what makes soldiers march into battle against overwhelming odds, knowing that most of them will die; what makes a parent leap into the raging torrent to rescue a child, knowing that both of them may die in the process; what made Evaine willing to approach the very gates of death to accomplish a task that she believed far more important, in the greater reckoning, than her mere continuation in a physical body.

In all these examples, something besides death is the desired end result, but death is a possibility (and often a probability, perhaps even a certainty) that the individual is willing to accept as a consequence of his or her action, when weighed against the actual goal. It is not suicide; it is the selfless offering of one's very life as the possible price of a desired goal. A just and loving God will have no difficulty making the proper determination, at the day of judgment.

# CHAPTER TEN

# Operative Magic I: Utility Spells and the Duel Arcane

Operative magic describes spells or operations/procedures with both physical and mental/psychic components, whose combination causes a direct effect. Following certain procedures by rote, with appropriate concentration, will produce certain predictable results. Again, the repetition of ritual action assists in creating an appropriate mind-set, so that more or less standardized physical motions or gestures, coupled with particular intent and concentration (and sometimes key phrases), trigger certain releases of energy to produce certain results. We might call the first category of such spells utility spells or procedures.

## Conjuring Handfire

Conjuring handfire is one of the first such spells that most young Deryni learn in the course of their formal training. It is a very useful spell, especially for a child, since it produces a cold light that requires very little energy to maintain. Part of the mechanism for conjuring handfire involves clenching a fist and visualizing the light enclosed within. Opening the hand reveals a sphere of handfire in the cupped palm, ranging from walnut size to about the size of a baby's head. (Some practitioners prefer to visualize directly on the open palm. A few can conjure handfire without using the hand at all, merely concentrating on a point in space and bringing forth a sphere of light.) For all outward variations, the inner process is the same: establishing the proper mental set and then triggering a prelearned series of mental/psychic operations that will produce the required result.

Because light has no weight (or negligible weight, by the theories of modern physics), the operator requires little effort to set a sphere of handfire to floating. Such handfire can be directed to a maximum distance of about two to three times the practitioner's arm span. More than one sphere can be maintained at a time, though three or more might begin to tax the operator's concentration if anything else were required.

Handfire usually takes on a color peculiar to the particular practitioner, generally the same as the person's aura. The color can be altered at will, but Deryni tend to associate their magic with a particular color early in life and to stay with that color thereafter. Healers often develop green auras and handfire, though Gabrilite Healers seem to prefer white or silver.

Of the characteristic handfire colors we have seen so far, the following can be tabulated. Names in parentheses have been inferred from aura or shield color.

Red—Kelson, Conall, Jebediah
Green—Morgan, Rhys, (Barrett de Laney)
Silver—Duncan, Dhugal, Denis Arilan, Jamyl Arilan, Tiercel, Emrys
Blue—Charissa
Blue-violet—(Warin)
Violet—(Dame Elfrida)
Gold—(Dhugal), (Darrell)

Examples abound of the use of handfire. Joram conjures a tiny sphere of handfire when he and Rhys sneak into Saint Foillan's Abbey to kidnap the sleeping Cinhil Haldane. In the clearing at Iomaire, where Camber and his son find the blasted bodies of Alister Cullen and Ariella, Camber conjures handfire and later draws more handfire into being'' (*Saint Camber* 108, 110). And when Morgan conjures handfire in the underground passages beneath his capital of Coroth, we see it from a human's point of view.

\* \* \*

. . . Morgan was turning to face them, a sphere of softly glowing verdant light cupped in the hollow of his left hand.

"Relax, Bishop," Morgan murmured, gliding toward Cardiel with the light in his outstretched hand. "It's only light, neither good nor evil. Here, touch it. It's cool, perfectly harmless."

Cardiel stood his ground as Morgan approached, watching Morgan's face, not the light itself. When the young general at last came to a halt before Cardiel, only then did the bishop lower his eyes to look at the light again. It was cool and green, a softly shimmering glow like that which had surrounded Arilan's head the night he had revealed himself as Deryni.

Finally, Cardiel put out his hand. There was nothing there to touch per se, only the cool illusion of a breath of breeze as his hand passed through where the light should be and then touched Morgan's hand. At that touch, Cardiel let his eyes rise to meet Morgan's and forced himself to smile. (*High Deryni* 175)

Handfire is particularly useful and practical for exploring underground, for unlike torches or candles, it produces no smoke. In the ruined corridors beneath the bishop's palace at Grecotha, light flares in Camber's hand, "cool and silver-hued, to coalesce in a shining sphere a handspan above his palm. With a gesture he set it to hovering slightly above his right shoulder, then ignored it as he moved beside Joram" (*Saint Camber* 303). A little later, when a single sphere proves too dim on entry into a much larger chamber, Camber cups his hands and breathes life into another sphere, "seting that to hovering an armspan from the first one with a wave of one amethyst-ringed hand"—a slightly different technique from what we usually see for conjuring handfire (*Saint Camber* 305).

Needless to say, handfire is a distinct attribute of Deryni only—and a betrayal, if observed by someone previously unaware of the Deryni's identity. *"Are you going to keep that handfire lit while you work?* Kelson asked [Dhugal]. *If anyone looks in, it's a dead giveaway of what we are"* (*The Quest for Saint Camber* 342–343).

Handfire's corollary is the Deryni aura, which might be described as a visual display of a Deryni's psychic shields. (Deryni also can sense and sometimes See shields psychically, but that is another process.) The aura can be a particularly unnerving sight for humans, for not only does it mimic the classic depiction of haloes and aureoles, traditionally associated with saints and Divinity, but it was used by the Deryni overlords of the Interregnum as an outward reminder of their power over humans. We see Imre and Ariella project their Deryni auras for precisely that purpose when they make their first appearance, "light glowing around their heads in arcane splendor, as High Deryni were wont to appear on formal occasions" (*Camber of Culdi* 52–53).

A century and a half later, when the backlash of anti-Deryni persecutions had yet to begin ebbing, the sight of Barrett de Laney, enmantled in the emerald-green fire of his Deryni shields, could strike panic into the hearts of scores of ruthless soldiers about to execute Deryni children (*The Deryni Archives* 85). Nor was Bethane's husband Darrell unaware of the effect as he flared magnificent golden shields for protection while galloping in to attempt Barrett's rescue (*Deryni Archives* 88).

Even at the time of Kelson's accession, when the general attitude toward Deryni has shifted from grudging compliance through vengeful hatred to merely blind and superstitious fear, the appearance of a Deryni aura is almost sure to cause a fear reaction in humans who witness it unexpectedly. The imminently reasonable but unsuspecting Bishop Cardiel is shocked into a dead faint when he glimpses Arilan's silvery aura—following, one must admit, the already unsettling experience of an unanticipated and unexplained Portal jump (*High Deryni* 119). Those who witness Dhugal's knighting are better prepared for such a display, for there have been ample rumors about Duncan, and many of the court have seen Kelson's magic at work, but the light that plays down the sword in Duncan's hand and grows to surround him and his son can have had no interpretation save that of confirming what they are.

[The sword] held the magic of a long line of Haldanes—no doubt of that. With his Deryni senses, Duncan could feel it pulsing in his fist. Trembling, he steadied it with his other hand on the pommel so that he could bring it slowly to his lips to kiss the sacred relic encased in its hilt and, in doing so, loosed his own Deryni essence to show as silver light along the blade—a light that flowed bright as water down the steel and welled as quickly up his hands and arms to settle like a cloak of light around his head and shoulders, openly and unmistakably Deryni at last. The awed gasp of those watching was immediately caught in rapt silence as Duncan dipped the glowing blade, two-handed, toward Dhugal's right shoulder. . . . As the sword touched the crown of Dhugal's head, and Duncan sighted down the blade to his son's eyes, Dhugal's own Deryni aura flared like a halo around his coppery hair, sunburst golden. . . . (*The Quest for Saint Camber* 58–59)

Unexpected handfire can elicit much the same kind of reaction, though its remove from its creator, compared to an aura, serves to distance the Deryni from his or her magic just a little. Morgan, after healing the unconscious Dhugal (yet unknown by himself or Morgan to be Deryni, too), quenches his handfire so that Dhugal will not be frightened when he comes to (*The Bishop's Heir* 245). And a year later, when Dhugal himself casually conjures handfire, descending ahead of Kelson into the ruined and partially flooded MacRorie burial vaults at Caerrorie, it is sufficient to make their guide, Brother Arnold, cross himself in a warding-off gesture, even though he knows what Kelson and Dhugal are and has been invited to leave if Deryni "assistance" will offend him (*The Quest for Saint Camber* 174–175). These unmistakable signs of being Deryni are likely to elicit fear for some time to come, as humans only gradually learn that what they have been taught about Deryni for generations is mistaken.

## Conjuring Flame

Lighting and extinguishing fire is a side application of handfire conjuration. We see the two linked as Camber conjures handfire in the hidden Michaeline chapel after his ordination to the priesthood, just before magically extinguishing all the remaining candles in the chapel save the Presence light. (In this instance, Camber does it at considerably greater distance than is usually done.)

But conjuring flame is fairly common among Deryni—or was, when the Deryni were in their prime. In a ritual setting, we may perhaps view it as wielding control of Fire Elementals. The night of Camber's ordination, Joram lights a candle by passing his right hand over the wick—the candle that Evaine then uses to light the quarter candles (*Saint Camber* 260). And Evaine and Davin together conjure the cleansing fire for the funeral pyre that will consume the bodies of her firstborn son and others of their kin (*Camber the Heretic* 455).

Experienced Deryni often become quite casual about conjuring fire. Thorne Hagen lights candles in his bedchamber with a sweep of his hand and a phrase muttered under his breath (*High Deryni* 63). Arilan lights the torches in the Camberian Council chamber with a gesture as he enters (*High Deryni* 296). Tiercel lights a candle in Duncan's study, after Conall has controlled his first Portal jump with Tiercel in tow (*The Quest for Saint Camber* 129).

Even the ill-trained Morgan gestures absently with one hand to bring fire to life on the hearth in his study at Coroth (*High Deryni* 181), though he uses a more conventional taper to light the candles in the room. He also uses his powers to light a torch beside the wounded rebel Mal, though he *claims* to have used conventional flint and steel. "Do you think I'm Deryni, that I can call down fire from heaven simply to light a torch?" he blusters (*High Deryni* 8), knowing he has done precisely that. And by the time he conjures fire on the hearth in Duncan's study, before an amazed Dhugal, he is able to deliver quite a calm and reasoned discourse about the use of magic, like fire, being capable of both good and evil results. (*The Bishop's Heir* 274)

## Fatigue-Banishing

Fatigue-banishing is more in the nature of an actual spell than most of the procedures we have examined so far, though here we should take "spell" to mean a preset, shorthand trigger for a longer procedure—a posthypnotic suggestion, if you like—that can be activated at will to produce a given effect. Fatigue-banishing can be done actively and deliberately, of course, by relaxing and visualizing fatigue draining away, and of energy being taken into the body with each breath; but using the spell bypasses the need for such time-consuming procedures. Because it *is* a "spell," or a preset trigger, it either must be learned from someone who already knows how to do it or it must be assumed as part of a body of knowledge, such as occurs when a Haldane assumes the Haldane power.

However the ability is gained, triggering it generally follows a standard pattern. The subject draws one or more deep breaths, either passing a hand across the forehead or closed eyes or else palming both hands across the eyes—or sometimes pressing the bridge of the nose between thumb and forefingers—meanwhile triggering whatever mental key has been set for that individual. This may take the form of a key word or two, a "charm" (usually a phrase or short verse), or a key action. Different individuals approach the process differently, depending on their training.

Cathan, his face buried in his hands, inhales deeply, forcing himself to hold the breath for a moment and then exhale slowly, the while reciting the words of the Deryni charm that will mask his fatigue. Another deep breath, and he feels his pulse steadying, the flat taste in his mouth receding (*Camber of Culdi* 61).

Camber, though he does not specifically use a fatigue-banishing spell when preparing for the Alister memory integration, certainly uses the full arsenal of knowledge at his disposal, stretching out supine on the bed while he employs "diverse Deryni relaxation techniques to ensure that he would be fresh and alert when the time came for him to do what he must." Relaxation leads to several hours of profound sleep, followed by another hour in more active meditation,

> . . . making the mental and spiritual preparations he felt necessary for the task approaching. The steady rain outside was a constant reinforcement to his intent, helping to drive him to ever-deeper centering points of consciousness (*Saint Camber* 39)

Queron, though Gabrilite trained and inclined toward introspection, is far more direct about his fatigue-banishing than Camber. After projecting Guaire's recall of his Saint Camber visitation for the Synod of Bishops, Queron merely sinks back momentarily on his haunches and passes a slightly trembling hand across his forehead "in a gesture which Camber knew masked a fatigue-banishing spell" (*Saint Camber* 374). The significance of the action would have gone unnoticed by the human observers in the chamber and even some of the Deryni, perhaps, for Queron does not falter in the least. Drawing a deep breath to settle the spell, the Healer-priest gets to his feet no more slowly than might be expected of a man who has just performed a feat that even the most naive of the observers will realize took no little effort, and appears to be completely restored by the time he is fully standing. It is the first time we really see Queron work, and we may surmise by its ease and polish that Dom Queron Kinevan is an accomplished master, indeed—as certainly is borne out by further experience of the man.

Morgan and Duncan are not so polished, but they, too, seem simply to draw a single deep breath and "apply a fatigue-banishing spell" rather than pursue a particular procedure as such—though in their case, we should perhaps ascribe such brevity to rote training, neither of them truly understanding how the process works or how to alter its use for particular applications. (Both men tend to push themselves beyond the point that they should go, sometimes paying the price in sheer exhaustion that no longer can be eased by the spell. They "run" the spell, they reinforce it by repeating it, and they realize that they can do this only so long—but this does not change their behavior.) Dhugal, having learned his skill from Duncan and Morgan, does it the same way they do—as a rote process. Nor is Kelson any more adept, even if his knowledge comes partially from a different source, in his Haldane legacy.

Only from Arilan—who uses the spell almost offhandedly—do we really get a sense of what the spell actually *feels* like, as he lays his head back against the chair and closes his eyes, "wearily running a spell to banish fatigue. . . ." We still haven't a clue *how* he does it, but we do sense a little of what it feels like.

Sighing, Arilan pressed his palms across both eyes and took a last deep breath to set his spell, feeling the fatigue wash out of his brain like indigo running from fresh-dyed cloth in a mountain stream, finally clear (*The King's Justice* 261)

## Attuning an Object

We have seen a magical "charge" placed on a variety of different objects, for a variety of reasons—a process sometimes called "attuning" an object. The object so charged or attuned may function something like a psychic storage battery, holding energy in reserve to augment the owner's own power, or it may merely serve as an identity key. Using a charged object as a trigger for opening a lock or secret compartment is a fairly common application, as is embedding a psychic message in an object such as a wax seal or the signet that made it.

Sometimes the charged item is designated as a psychic link between two people, such as the Saint Camber medal that Morgan attunes to Derry—and which Kelson later augments in a storage capacity, for psychic protection, before sending Derry out to look for Bethane. Charissa gains access to the chain of office that Morgan is to wear to Kelson's coronation and keys its medallion to act as a psychic transmitter of everything around its wearer. Through that link, she is also able to animate the chain to choke Morgan and throw him off balance while the bested and wounded Ian throws a dagger.

We have seen, too, how objects formerly associated with particular individuals but not specifically attuned to them sometimes can become psychic links. The Haldana necklace formerly worn by Ariella, the silk ribbon from Dhugal's border braid, and the martyred Henry Istelyn's episcopal ring, apparently forged from a piece of altar plate somehow associated with Camber himself, come to mind immediately.

Rings, in fact, are one of the most common items to become attuned, often not even by design, partly because they become intimately linked to their wearers by proximity and partly because gold and silver tend to hold a psychic charge more easily than most materials. A ring deliberately charged by its owner can carry strong psychic connections, indeed. The Haldane Ring of Fire is one of the most notable examples, tuned to those of Haldane blood *by* Haldane blood and sometimes designated as a final trigger to loose the potential at a Haldane's accession or coronation. Morgan's Gryphon signet is a personal focal point of his concentration, as his Champion ring is a personal link

with Kelson. And the cold, silvery ring put on Derry's finger by
Wencit carries exceedingly strong compulsions to obey.

Other items also carry prodigious psychic charges. The Lion
brooch, with its three inches of gleaming gold that must be
plunged through the palm of a Haldane aspirant's hand, has built
its psychic load through the reigns of many kings. The Haldane
sword has been described as a magical blade—and *is*, in far
more pronounced terms than just any sword used for ritual purposes. The Eye of Rom, a great, dark cabochon-cut ruby the
size of a man's little fingernail, is said to have fallen from the
heavens the night Christ was born and to have been one of
the gifts of the Magi to the Child. Passed down in the MacRorie
family for twelve generations and endowed with certain catalyzing powers by Camber and his kin, it became the single most
powerful focus of Haldane sovereignty and has been used to
empower nearly every Haldane king since Cinhil. Also seen
from time to time, and endowed with unspecified arcane mystery, is a coat of gold-washed mail that has a cold, unearthly
glow about it.

Then there are the charges placed upon an object as individual
spells, such as the "charms" used by old Bethane.

> Charms for love and charms for hate. Charms for death and
> charms for life. Charms to make the crops grow tall. Charms
> to bring pestilence to the enemy's field. Simple charms to
> guard the health. Complex charms to guard the soul. Charms
> for the rich. Charms for the poor. Charms yet unborn, but
> waiting for the touch of the woman. (*Deryni Checkmate* 164–
> 165)

Such "charms" edge into the realm of folk magic, and some
may work as much from the recipient's expectation as from any
magical work done by the operator, but we have seen tragic
results of one gone awry. The charm requested by the lovesick
architect Rimmell to win Bronwyn's love is set in a *jerraman*
crystal, a large blue stone embedded with blood-colored flecks.
Afterward, Kelson remarks that *jerramani* can be used for many
purposes, some of them quite beneficial, though this one proved
not to be.

Certainly the charm was never intended to harm Bronwyn,

for Rimmell loved her, and only sought to make her love him in return. But when Bronwyn is snared in the beginning of the spell's enchantment, her cries of alarm bring interference that cause the energy patterns to shift and mutate, with tragic consequences. Kevin's intrusion upsets the fragile balance of the working—or perhaps it was ill-set from the start—and both he and Bronwyn die in the ensuing burst of uncontrolled energy.

## *Shiral* Crystals

In a magical category essentially by themselves are the smooth, honey-colored stones known as *shiral* crystals—which are not really crystals at all, but a Gwynedd-analog of amber, usually found rough-polished in streambeds and on the seashore. Like amber, which is fossilized resin, *shiral* can be worked and polished. And where amber holds a static electrical charge, *shiral* holds a psychic charge, perhaps better than any other substance. Its peculiar property, so far as Deryni are concerned, is that the stone glows when held by a Deryni working in a deep meditative or trance state. Because of this characteristic, it often is used as a focal fixation while working inner magic and it increasingly has been used to test for psychic potential.

*Shiral* seems to have been known for a very long time in Deryni history, for drilled nuggets of *shiral* were found knotted at the intersections of a silk stasis net protecting the body of the great Orin, who lived in the seventh century. Their apparent purpose was to help prolong a preservation spell woven into the net, like tiny psychic storage batteries.

Incidentally, stasis nets are an application of a specialized arcane discipline known as "cording lore," which usually is considered to be primarily a feminine magical discipline. Cording lore covers a variety of utility forms ranging from the stasis net already mentioned to similar nets observed in the serial burial chambers of the folk of Saint Kyriell's, to stitchery techniques such as Richenda employs on a tapestry, to the cords Evaine weaves together at the induction of individuals into the Camberian Council. Presumably, *shiral* could be incorporated in any or all of these examples.

Camber himself appears not to have learned about *shiral* crystals until fairly late in his life, for it is late in 903 when he tells

Evaine how, on his last trip to Culdi, he fished his first one out of a mountain stream in Kierney, only accidentally discovering its properties some time later, while meditating. "It—Well, watch," he tells her. "It's easiest to show you."

Holding the object lightly in the fingers of his two hands, Camber inhaled, exhaled, his eyes narrowing slightly as he passed into the earliest stages of a Deryni trance. His breathing slowed, the handsome face relaxed—and then the stone began to glow faintly. Camber brought his eyes back to focus and extended his hands toward Evaine, still in trance, the stone still glowing. . . . Taking the stone in one hand, Evaine passed her other hand over it and bowed her head, mentally reciting the words that would bring Rhys's trance. The stone did nothing for several seconds as she explored its several avenues of approach; then it began to glow. With a sigh, Evaine returned to the world, held the stone closer as the light was extinguished.

"Strange. It hardly takes any effort at all, once you know what you're doing. What is it for?"

Camber shrugged. "I don't know. I haven't been able to find a single use for it yet—other than to fascinate gullible daughters, that is. . . ." (*Camber of Culdi* 8)

Within six months, Evaine, at least, has found a use for *shiral*: a point of curiosity on the part of the oddly shielded and hitherto uncommunicative Prince Cinhil. When Cinhil observes her meditating and notices her handling the stone afterward, he asks to see it; when he returns it, somewhat gingerly, Evaine realizes that he has felt something from it, even if he is not consciously aware what it is.

"You must not fear it, Your Highness—no more than one should fear to approach the Sacraments when one is in a state of grace," she breathed, couching her words in terms she thought he might understand. "The crystal itself contains neither good nor evil, though it does have power. But one must approach it with respect and awareness of what one is doing. It can be a link—perhaps with the Deity?" (*Camber of Culdi* 252)

She goes on to explain to the increasingly intrigued Cinhil that *shiral* crystals can be an aid to concentration.

"Anything can be used as a focal point, but the *shiral* is better than most, because it shows you, by glowing, when you've reached the minimum level of concentration. Anything bright will do: a ring, a fleck of sunlight on glass. For that matter, you don't really need anything physical, though it does help, especially in the beginning." (*Camber of Culdi* 253–254)

His interest gives her the entree she needs to guide him into a profound hypnotic trance; from there, after a time, it is a relatively simply matter to extend that trance enough to seize control despite his shields, so that what will become known as the Haldane powers can be placed upon him.

Evaine gives that first *shiral* to Cinhil. Somewhat later, Rhys gives her a replacement, shaped and sized like a hen's egg, with tiny inclusions that catch the light. Other *shiral* crystals appear with increasing regularity as the years pass, most notably a clear, fist-size sphere in Morgan's study; a walnut-size one on a gold chain, used by Wencit to test Bran Coris' potential; a honey-colored one the size of an almond, strung on a leather thong, given to Duncan by Maryse on their wedding night; and a huge one, the size of a man's head, owned by someone in the Camberian Council around 1104, possibly Stefan Coram. In all cases, the crystals function as focal points, as testing devices, and as psychic amplifiers.

## Sympathetic Magic

Spells of sympathetic magic involve performing some smaller, symbolic action to induce a similar result on a larger scale, "as above, so below." Ariella's weather magic is one example, as she stares at a deployment map for the coming campaign and visualizes storms hampering her enemies, meanwhile sprinkling water over the corresponding areas on the map to reinforce her imagery. (*Saint Camber* 2, 5, 49). The physical gesture that goes with the spell to stop a heart also has an element of sympathetic magic, for the clenching fist echoes the psychic force that squeezes the victim's heart until it ceases beating.

What Rothana at first believes may be an example of sympathetic magic gone wrong is her venture with the dead Sidana's ring. Kelson had asked her not to wear it, because it was tainted with Sidana's blood. But Rothana, after letting herself imagine what it would be like to marry him—harmless enough, in and of itself—puts on the ring anyway, while imagining that it is Kelson who does it. This combines visualization with physical action in what could be construed as sympathetic magic—except that the desired outcome will not be achieved because the ring is tainted. When word comes of Kelson's accident, and Rothana believes him to have died, she convinces herself that her disobedience was contributory (*The Quest for Saint Camber* 247). It was not, of course, and Kelson is not dead, but her heartsick fear underlines the very real existence of sympathetic magic as an aspect of Deryni magic.

## Pure Conjury

Spells there are, of course, that fall into none of the categories we have mentioned thus far. They are spells whose workings even the most advanced Deryni do not understand—only that the spells work. Conjuring magical beasts comes under this heading—summoning stenrects, lyfangs, and caradots, none of which are found in the usual dimensions.

Deryni illusion is another odd category, some of which is achieved by means of para-hypnotic suggestion, but much of which simply occurs, according to the will of the operator(s). Rhys and Evaine dull their hair to nondescript dust tones before going to visit Revan among the Willimites (*Camber the Heretic* 272), and Dom Emrys and the Healer Kenric conjure cobwebs and mire to slow the attackers of Saint Neot's (*Camber the Heretic* 370). Derry, whom Morgan has taught to see through at least some illusion, tries to use pain to see the truth of what Warin is doing, but neither the rebel leader's misty blue-violet aura nor his healing turns out to be an illusion (*Deryni Checkmate* 135). And when Kelson calls up a line of fire to stop his men from charging Wencit's army, the illusion—if illusion it is—

is powerful enough that apparently no one even *thinks* of testing it (*High Deryni* 274–275).

Deryni sometimes work with the sheer expulsion of energy, too. The green fireball that Duncan launches at one of Morgan's attackers, when they return from Kelson's ritual of power assumption, stuns the man into unconsciousness. The blue sphere of fire conjured by Charissa becomes an armored blue knight to taunt and threaten Kelson. And of course, the very concept of the Duel Arcane involves the direct pitting of one participant's energy against the other's.

## The Duel Arcane

We have seen the Duel Arcane only seldom, but it must rank as one of the more awesome of Deryni activities, both to participants and to observers. Briefly defined, it is a ritualized testing of the power of one Deryni against another, often to the death. In practice, this means the contention of power levels almost inconceivable to most humans. By the time of Kelson, its conduct had been codified by a fairly rigid set of rules and procedures, under the supervision of the Camberian Council.

With few exceptions, a Duel Arcane takes place within a warded circle, to contain the emormous powers summoned by the combatants and prevent spillover to innocent observers. "It's partly for the safety of the onlookers," Morgan tells Nigel, as Kelson and Charissa square off. "Without the confining circle, the spells sometimes tend to get out of hand. They're going to be dealing with fantastic amounts of power today, from many sources" (*Deryni Rising* 257).

Usually the combatants themselves raise the wards, each providing half the retaining circle, which then is energized by mutual intent. The circle raised by Charissa and Kelson is a classic example.

Charissa smiled and stepped back a few paces, raised her arms in a low-murmured spell. Instantaneously, a semicircle of blue fire sprang up behind her, a graven line of sapphire ice which took in half the great circle of saints' signs.

She lowered her arms and stepped back several paces more, then gestured patronizingly to Kelson. . . .

Breathing a silent prayer to the renegade saint on whose seal he stood, Kelson raised his arms above his head—a single, fluid movement as he had seen Charissa do.

And unbidden, the words came to his lips—words he had never heard before, a low chant which made the air crackle with power around him in response, which seared a line of crimson fire behind him—a line which bent itself to the semicircle shape required and joined the two arcs together in a complete circle, half red, half blue. . . . Then he forced himself to concentrate on what must now follow as Charissa stretched out her arms and began another incantation. This one was in a tongue he understood, and he listened carefully, mentally pulling forth the response he would make when she finished.

Charissa's voice was low but clear in the stillness of the cathedral.

"By Earth and Water, Fire and Air,
I conjure powers to flee this Ring.
I clear it now. Let all beware.
Through here shall pass no living thing" . . .

Kelson's voice was low, steady, as he answered Charissa's spell.

"Inside, all space and Time suspend.
From here may nothing outward flee
Or inward come. The circle ends
When two are one and one is free."

As Kelson finished, violet light flared where the two arcs had been, the cold violet line now inscribing an unbroken forty-foot circle where the two must duel. (*Deryni Rising* 255–258)

The following year, Kelson faces another Duel Arcane, this one somewhat unusual even by Deryni standards, for it involves not a classic one-on-one confrontation but a "team" effort, four on a side—these eight within an inner circle and four members of the Camberian Council to arbitrate from a neutral zone between the inner circle and an outer one conjured by the Council four. The words are more ritual and pompous and perhaps less banal than those initiated by Charissa, but the end result is similar to other examples we have seen: a hemisphere of pale blue-violet surrounding the twelve, transparent but veiled, and an inner hemisphere of a deeper, purplish hue—the Outerness and the Innerness. "Mark well," blind Barrett de Laney warns them. "Until all men of one defense shall perish, the Innerness remains. Only victors leave this ring" (*High Deryni* 334).

This particular Duel Arcane is never really fought, of course, since one of Wencit's side turns out to be a double agent—for whom, we never learn, except that neither Wencit nor the four arbitrators apparently were prepared for anything like this. Kelson wins by default, since his opponents no longer are able to fight—and, in fact, are dying.

But the matter cannot simply end there. By specifying that this Duel Arcane would be to the death, Wencit ensured that all four losers must perish before any remaining winners can enjoy the spoils of their victory. That victory came by treachery is not an issue. The circle will stand until all four losers are dead—and Kelson must kill the remaining three outright or else condemn them to a painful and protracted dying.

But how? Kelson has never killed a man before, even with steel—though at least he knows *how* to do that. And giving someone the *coup de grace* is a far more deliberate act than simply slaying a man in the heat of battle. That Kelson's potential victims are also his enemies makes the matter no less complicated. It is one thing to give mercy to a friend or a companion in arms, as an ultimate gesture of compassion; it quite possibly is yet another matter to give it to an enemy, especially when one cannot be certain that vengeance has not become entangled in one's motives. Kelson learns a far more important lesson than simply how to stop a heart, when he finally does put an end to the three survivors.

Four years later, Kelson must face his own cousin in a Duel Arcane. The young king has learned both sophistication and a degree of informality in the intervening years—and a self-confidence that must have been unnerving in the extreme for his slightly younger opponent, even though Conall gained his knowledge from a member of the Camberian Council itself.

"This is pointless," Kelson murmured. "Cast the circle."
"Me?" Conall squeaked.

"Yes, you. You started all of this. You can start this final folly, too. Or don't you know how?"

The gibe had its desired effect. Drawing himself up in wounded pride, Conall backed off three stiff paces and, without further preliminary, raised his arms above his head and then to the sides, murmuring a setting spell under his breath. A semicircle of crimson fire sprang up on the floor behind him and around him, sending courtiers scurrying farther back to flatten themselves along the south wall of the hall, those on Kelson's side also retreating into the window embrasures on the north side.

Kelson tested at the barrier Conall had raised, satisfying himself that it would not require a death to release it, once he completed his part of the spell, then swept his own arms up and outward in a graceful arc, holding as he uttered the words that would produce the counter. More crimson fire sprang up behind him, matching Conall's, enclosing them both now in a circle of red.

"Your turn again," Kelson said, lowering his arms.

The lightness of the king's tone, suggesting the triviality of whatever Conall might attempt, angered the wayward prince, but Conall only raised his arms to shoulder level again, his palms turned inward toward the center of the circle.

"If you're expecting some trite piece of poetry, don't," Conall said. "My teacher didn't believe in such things. I affirm that the circle shall contain all power that we shall raise within it, so that none outside may be harmed, and that it shall not be broken until one of us has achieved a clear victory over the other. Is that your understanding?"

"It is," Kelson agreed, also raising his arms again. And at Conall's nod, Kelson began to pour energy into the binding of the circle as Conall did likewise, only barely aware, in his concentration, that the fire of the two arcs they had cast was rising to define a dome above their heads. When they were done, it was as if they stood beneath a dome of pinkish, faintly opalescent glass. (*The Quest for Saint Camber* 423–424)

The outward manifestation of the protective circle may vary, then, but the protection itself is an essential component. The one time we see a Duel Arcane begin *without* a protective circle being cast, as the enraged Cinhil prepares to face down Humphrey of Gallareaux, the suborned Michaeline priest who has just poisoned Cinhil's firstborn in the course of baptism, Camber and his kin scramble frantically to erect protective shields—which are not as efficient as a warding circle, but better than nothing in an emergency.

It was just in time, for Cinhil's next words shook the very air, the ancient, awesome phrases echoing from arch and joist and mosaicked panels.

Cinhil's words brought crimson fire to encircle him—a dancing, living flame which was not so much seen as felt and experienced, by those on the outside. It was a fire which was sensed, if at all, out of the corner of the eye—which disappeared when sought head-on, but which was no less deadly should it come within reach of the unprotected. . . . The Michaeline moved toward him in a haze of gold, until only a few meters of sparkling air separated them.

The air glittered with power, visible lightning arcing across from one man to the other, only to be dashed ineffectually against the other's shields. The air was sharp and acrid, like the charged, moist stillness before a thunderstorm. The candles guttered wildly in the growing flux of energy. Energy howled and echoed in the rockbound chamber, coruscating around the heads of the two combatants like mad, misshapen haloes. A greater surge now blew out all the candles, and for a moment the wind moaned on in near-darkness.

Then the roaring of the wind increased in pitch, until the watchers could discern two voices—wordless, mighty, contending darkly in the abyss which had been opened by the forces locked in mortal combat. Their pressure grew, and the watchers tried to cover their ears, their eyes, their minds, against the not-sounds, not-sights, not-thoughts which barraged the senses from every angle.

Finally, the Michaeline staggered and let out a low, desperate cry, his eyes at last clearing from their trancelike stare as he reached out in desperate supplication and fell. Abruptly, all sound ceased, and the room was plunged into darkness. (*Camber of Culdi* 275-276).

The clash between Cinhil and Humphrey may be considered an informal Duel Arcane—so is Cinhil's defeat of Imre and Jehana's confrontation with Charissa. Because of the way informal duels come about—generally on the spur of the moment—one of the contenders is very apt to end up dead. We know from the beginning that if Cinhil wins, he will not spare Humphrey. Nor will the defeated Imre allow Cinhil the satisfaction of killing him, preferring to die by his own will. Jehana survives only because Charissa's killing strike is deflected at the last instant by Morgan and Duncan—an intervention that would not have been possible if the two women had been fighting under formal rules, in a warded circle.

We get only glimpses of what those formal rules might be in a proper Duel Arcane. We know that the contenders usually decide the stakes in advance and whether the fight will be to the death. We know that the Challenged has the right of First Strike in the testing spells that usually begin a formal duel—and that a man is expected to defer to a woman, even if he is the Challenged.

The Camberian Council, in its infancy, began to codify the rules governing Duel Arcane. However, one gets the distinct impression that these rules had begun to be regularized even before Camber's time, though it was for later incarnations of the Camberian Council to truly hone the ceremonial aspects—and eventually to allow the form to outweigh the substance. Based on what scanty knowledge we have to date, we might consider whether the Varnarites might actually have begun the codification process while still in Caeriesse. Perhaps the impetus came from the ranks of the Airsid, that ancient and mysterious Deryni brotherhood responsible for the building of the *keeill*. Whichever of these origins is correct—or even if none is—the Camberian Council did inherit increasing supervisory responsibilities in the decades after the death of Camber.

Unfortunately, we have seen the Council only in its infancy and in its decline, but we must assume that at some time during that two-hundred-year period it exercised a very real control over at least the blatant outward display of power by Deryni. Indeed, when Camber first broached the idea of a regulatory body to Joram, two major concerns immediately surfaced: (1) that the rulings of the body would have to be enforceable, and

(2) that the watchers themselves must be bound by the power they would wield, to prevent abuse.

We have not yet been told what censures the Council might have applied to punish transgressors in the early days, but by the time of Kelson, their threat was sufficient that Thorne Hagen certainly was intimidated, and even Wencit chose to observe at least the outward forms required by that august body. (And caught out by the real members of the Council, he dared not then deviate from the rules they had come to enforce.)

Charissa also seems to have been loath to transgress the rules of Duel Arcane. While her insistence upon such a duel with Kelson may have been partially motivated by vengeance—a desire to see the son of her father's slayer slain in the same way— it was not softness or pity for her intended victim that stopped her from killing him the same way she had killed his father, by stealth and ambush and the soft deadliness of drugs. One magical assassination might be denied, if the Council began asking uncomfortable questions, but two would be harder to explain. Making a blatant challenge by Duel Arcane was bold, but wholly within the rights of one Deryni mortally offended by another.

# CHAPTER ELEVEN

# Operative Magic II: Shape-Changing

Shape-changing is another Deryni talent with many facets. Over the centuries, it has been viewed mostly askance by many practitioners. Joram thoroughly disapproves of it on moral grounds, because it entails deceit. Rhys, though highly educated and intelligent, finds that he really knows little about it, other than to make an immediate connection with black magic when Camber pins him down about his beliefs.

Shape-changing. . . . He remembered a passing mention of it in an old volume of conjury, of how the conjuror superimposed the image of one person over that of another. The book had mentioned pentagrams and blood circles, and charges to keep evil influences out of the spell, but had not gone into any specifics as to how it was actually done. Another source—now he found himself able to scan his memory like a written index—another source had mentioned animal sacrifices and the assistance of demons. He counted that as spurious. Still another text had insisted that shape-changing was not possible at all—though that obviously was false in light of what Camber had just said. Searching through his memory, Rhys found that he could not pin down a single fact about shape-changing. He concluded that he was probably about to learn far more about it than he really wanted to know. (*Camber of Culdi* 149)

Of course, shape-changing is *not* black magic, though Camber concedes that perhaps it *could* be considered a bit grey around the edges:

> "a shade more dark than light, perhaps, because it *is* a deception; and deception is rarely used except for personal gain. At the risk of sounding hypocritical, I'll maintain that this is a fair example of the end justifying the means. The escape of innocents from danger not of their own doing is a generally accepted defense for all but the most rigid purists." (*Camber of Culdi* 147)

Here we have our situation ethics again: the end justifies the means. It appears to be sufficient rationalization for Camber, who sees things on a larger canvas than his sometimes inflexible son. But while Joram can reconcile himself to having his and Rhys' forms put on two of the family servants and to Camber taking on Alister Cullen's identity, he balks at the notion of taking away the identity of the innocent guard Eidiard, to place it on Davin. The others "just—happened. There was no premeditation. This is—cold. And your victim, there, has nothing to say about it. Before, all the participants were willing ones" (*Camber the Heretic* 245).

Joram's major objection, then, is that Eidiard has been given no choice in the matter and will never be able to return to his old life. Jebediah counters by reminding Joram that soldiers in a war serve in many different ways and this is Eidiard's—whether or not he has a choice. It must be done because it is nooooo0ary.

Our earliest exposures to shape-changing show no such moralizing or explanation, however. The very first shape-change we see is a result only, when Morgan and Duncan discover that a different shape has been placed upon the dead body of King Brion in his tomb. We can gather that Charissa or one of her associates must have been responsible, but we are never told exactly how this was accomplished. Later, we learn that Stefan Coram has regularly been taking the shape of the dead Rhydon of Eastmarch, though again, we are offered no explanation.

The first time we actually see the process is when Camber places the forms of Rhys and Joram on two of his servants, so that they can stand in at Cathan's burial and after, while the originals slip away to kidnap Prince Cinhil from his monastery. The procedure Camber uses to prepare the human Crinan, with a candle as a focus to facilitate rapport, is described several books later in greater detail, when he uses the same methodology to help Tavis O'Neill ease past the barriers that prevent their rapport.

"I'd like to show you an exercise that many Deryni children learn at a very early age," he said softly. "Joram and Jebediah learned it from their fathers, and I suspect that Niallan learned it from his. I, on the other hand, did not learn it until I was a Michaeline novice. The point is, I suppose, that it's never too late to learn something new. Now, this could come under the category of a spell, but it's time you learned that there's nothing to fear in a name." He held the candle a little closer to Tavis. "Put your hand over mine, so that we both hold the candle."

Tavis hesitated for just an instant, then obeyed. His fingers were icy cold, but Camber did not move—simply let Tavis settle for a few seconds, take a few deep breaths which finally began to have an effect.

"Good," Camber whispered, after a few more breaths. "Notice that *you* are the one who will be in control in this working. Your hand is over mine—I'm not holding you in any way. If at any time you begin to be afraid, or feel that you can't bear what we're sharing, feel free to withdraw as much as you need to. I won't be offended." (*Camber the Heretic* 428–429)

After initial reluctance to make the second contact with his stump, Tavis overcomes his squeamishness and self-consciousness and allows the contact. Camber continues to talk him through, soothing and reassuring, gradually shifting suggestion to compulsion.

"Good. Let's take a few deep breaths, then, and center down as if you're preparing to do a Healing. That's right. And when you're ready, *if* you're ready—some people never are— you can close your eyes for better concentration. The idea is to let the link form slowly, just a little at a time, so that each new meshing can be examined and digested at your own pace, with you controlling the depth of interaction, but passively— letting it happen, letting it flow.''

As he spoke, he could see the Healer's eyelids beginning to flutter, the gaze becoming less intense, more dreamlike, and he knew that Tavis was settling into his Healer's trance. The level of control was excellent.

"That's good," he continued. "Just let yourself float with me, as far as you want to go. And when you're ready, the spell will go something like this:

*"Join hand and mind with mine, my friend. And let the light flare up between our hands when we are one. Let the light flare up between our hands when we are one.*

"It's all a mental set, of course," he went on softly. "The words, of themselves, mean nothing. Their essence is what's important—that as our minds join, there will come a point when we are sufficiently in rapport to do useful work—and when that occurs, the light will flare between our hands, as an outward sign that that level has been reached. And it *will* happen. . . .''

Tavis was visibly nodding now, blinking very slowly, his breathing light and moderate. On one of the deep blinks, he did not open his eyes again. When Camber was certain that he was not going to, he closed his own eyes, beginning to reach out just a little across the bond of flesh to search for that other bond. (*Camber the Heretic* 431)

Using the candle spell for rapport with the resistant Tavis is far more difficult than using it on a cooperative human subject like Crinan, of course, or on an experienced Deryni subject like Rhys. And using it in tandem, first with Crinan and then with Rhys, the setup is easy—half spell and half para-hypnosis, as Camber bids Crinan hold a lighted candle, his hands on the squire's where they hold the first candle.

"Be not afraid," Camber smiled, his voice already lulling his subject to obey. "Thou hast but to gaze into the flame and let thy thoughts go slack. Relax and watch the flame, which blocks out thine awareness of ought within these walls. I shall not leave thee; thou art safe with me.''

Unable to resist, the squire did as he was bidden, staring deeply into the candle flame as Camber's voice soothed and silenced. After only seconds, Crinan swayed slightly, his head drooping lower toward the flame. Abruptly, Camber tightened his grasp on the man's hands and exerted control. Crinan's eyes closed as though in sleep.

"Good," Camber breathed, releasing the hands and looking across at Rhys. . . . blowing out the candle. . . . Then he held his left hand beside Rhys's darkened candle, fingers spread slightly. His eyes met Rhys's, calm, serene.

"Match hand and mind with mine, my friend, and let your candle flare when we are one."

With a solemn nod, Rhys touched his fingertips to Camber's, stilling his thoughts that the other might come in. His eyes slitted shut, the better to exclude the outer world, and then he was aware of Camber's palm pressed firmly against his own. In total calm and all control, he bade the light flare in his other hand, and felt the still, almost musical resonance he had come to cherish, as his thoughts meshed with those of the Master.

Then he was seeing through Camber's eyes, noting the candle burning steadily in his own left hand, his right pressed palm to palm with Camber's. He watched Camber's other hand rise slowly to rest on Crinan's forehead.

The Master's eyes closed, and there was only the crystal stillness, the peace, the all-pervading oneness of the bond they shared. Camber's voice was like the whisper of leaves rustling in a summer breeze, which no mere mortal may command; and Rhys knew that what Camber bade would be.

"Behold the light in thy mind's eyes," the Master said to him. "It is the essence of thine outward form upon the earth. Extend it now, and let it flow around the man here standing. His visage shall be thine until the need is past, as like to thee as any man may see."

And as he spoke, Rhys felt a soothing lethargy coursing through his limbs, a pulling of energy which tingled on his skin and centered in the hand that held the flame, which now ached to leap the void to Crinan's hands. None saw the mist which gathered round, or watched the flame flare from hand to hand. But suddenly Rhys knew the deed was done, the spell complete.

He staggered as the bond dissolved away, and looked to see his candle dark, the one in Crinan's hand ablaze with light. And as his gaze swept upward to the face, he gasped to see his own. (*Camber of Culdi* 152–154)

Thus we see the candle spell tailored for a shape-shifting operation, placing a Deryni's shape on a human. Placing a human's shape on a truly experienced Deryni subject is far easier, if a bit different, especially given time to perfect the Deryni subject's depth of trance and ability to hold the spell. Davin's assumption of the shape of the guard Eidiard is a case in point. Here, the procedure becomes a shorthand sketch of what was done before, between Crinan and Rhys. The entranced Eidiard is brought into a warded circle, where Davin changes clothes with him. Then the two are made to stand next to one another, Evaine taking command of the operation.

"Now, you understand how important it is that you open completely for this?"

"I understand."

"Good," Evaine replied, exchanging glances with Rhys as he came to stand behind Davin. "Because the deeper you can go, the wider you can open to me, the better image I'll be able to put on you. That's important, since you won't be able to do anything to help stabilize your shape for the first few weeks, while your abilities are blocked." She laid her hands lightly on his shoulders. "Now, take a deep breath and let's get started. Good. Now, another."

Davin obeyed, letting himself begin to sink into familiar trancing. The first stages were not difficult, but as he sank deeper and deeper under Evaine's subtle guidance, he could feel himself reaching new depths which were not easy to keep open in the smooth, passive widening which Evaine demanded, even though they had done it many times in the past week.

He drew in another deep breath, pushing himself down another level as he let it out, and then was dimly aware of Rhys's gentle hands slipping along either side of his head from behind, the Healer beginning to draw him even deeper, so that he lost track of his surroundings.

His eyes were closed now. He could not see with his vision, but his mental Sight was increasing with every breath—and those were becoming farther and farther apart, as his body settled into the relaxed, receptive state which Evaine guided and encouraged.

He was no longer master of his breathing now—though it did not matter, since Rhys guarded that function with his Healer's touch. Nor was he certain that his heart would have continued to pump, were it not for Rhys's Healing hands. His whole being was now contained between those other hands resting on his shoulders, now slipping up to touch his forehead. Something seemed to settle into place at that new touch—something which gave over, for all his present existence, the control of his destiny. Now, even if he had wanted to break the rapport, he was not certain that he could—and did not care.

Evaine's hands left him briefly then, and vaguely he sensed that Eidiard was being similarly prepared, that his pattern was being brought into the linkage. He teetered there on the brink of knowing and unknowing, precariously balanced between Rhys's two hands, until Evaine's touch once more glittered just behind his closed eyes.

*Hold steady now,* her mind whispered into his, as she poised between him and Eidiard on the balance point.

Then the energy began to flow, and he abandoned himself to its filling. He could sense the power tingling in his limbs, an eerie sensation like hundreds of tiny insects crawling all over his body—yet, oddly, not an unpleasant feeling—a vibrancy which permeated every part of him. He felt it as his own, and yet there was a part of it which was not his.

Suddenly it was over. His body was his own again, all strange sensation gone. As Evaine drew hand and mind apart from him, he felt himself surfacing from the place where he had been—swayed a little with the sheer giddiness of so rapid a return to normal consciousness. Rhys's hands steadied him, the Healer's mind withdrawing more slowly as functions were returned to Davin's control. When Davin opened his eyes, Evaine was gazing at him with a pleased smile on her face,

one hand resting on the shoulder of the still-entranced Eidiard. (*Camber the Heretic* 247–248)

As Evaine has indicated, Davin's shape-change is further
complicated by the fact that initially he will have no means of
reinforcing his new shape, for he must have his own powers
blocked for his initial foray into the Deryni-hostile society he
must penetrate. In this respect, he is far more vulnerable than
Camber was when he took on the shape of Alister Cullen—
though at least Davin had ample time for preparation. Camber's
shape-change was the decision of a moment, at the edge of a
battlefield. Had he been given time to consider all the possible
ramifications of what he was about to do—and especially, had
he been able to scry into the future to see what it held in store
for him—one wonders whether he would have gone through
with it.

But he did—and Gwynedd's history would have been far different, and likely far darker, if he had not. Camber obviously
has far greater background in shape-changing procedures than
just about any Deryni we have met so far. (Coram-Rhydon is
the only possible challenger at this stage of our knowledge of
such things.) It was Camber who determined to put Joram's and
Rhys' shapes on the servants after Cathan's funeral. And it is
Camber who decides to change places with Alister, against the
wishes of Joram—who is not at all convinced of the neutrality
of the magic involved, and was not convinced in the case of the
servants, either.

But Joram finally agrees. And he and his father use a variation
of the same process we have seen before, with Joram augmenting the link between his father and the dead Alister. This working is also different from the previous ones we have seen because
*two* shape-changes are involved; Camber actually switches
shapes with Alister Cullen.

Camber ignored the tears and leaned forward to touch
lightly the ring lying on Cullen's chest. At his touch, it began
to glow with a cool white light. Then Camber raised his left
hand and matched it, fingertip to fingertip, with Joram's right,
while his own right hand was laid gently on Cullen's forehead.
"Remember now," he murmured low, the bond of his love

forging the link between them as it had in a chapel at Caerrorie two years ago and more. ''Match hand and heart and
mind with mine, and join your light to mine when we are
one.''

He watched Joram's gaze waver, the flickering of his eyelids, trembling, closing, as he sank reluctant but obedient into
that calm, profound Deryni trance. Then he let his own gaze
drift to the ring between them, which glowed even brighter in
the ghostly twilight. After a moment, he let his own eyes
close, and concentrated on the crystalline oneness of the bond
that they shared. Joram was ready.

No still waters here, for Joram was not that—but rather, the
laugh of a sunlit spring dancing over stream-polished pebbles,
bright and jewel like, rare existence—and the cool and glim-
mer of deeper places, soft and silver-pure, into which Camber
now let his consciousness slip.

Joram was in control now; and if he had wanted to end
what was to be, he could have done it. But he did not. With
Camber's merging into union with his mind came the weight
of destiny and purpose which he now realized his father had
known long before, if only unconsciously, and of which Joram
himself had only dipped the surface.

No fearing now, but sharing, sureness, acceptance.

''Behold,'' Joram's voice whispered, green leaves floating
on gently welling waters. ''Behold the essence of thine outward form, O my father. Likewise, the outward form of him
who was our friend.'' He drew a steady breath. ''Let each
essence mingle now, in the cool fire which rests between you.
*Be* Alister Cullen, in all outward forming. And let the outward
form of him who was our friend become most like the Earl of
Culdi, thy dear face. Let it be done. *Fiat.* Amen.''

Camber's lips formed the words, but no sound came forth—
and Joram slitted his eyes open to watch with awe as a mist
seemed to shroud his father's face. As if through a veil, he
saw the familiar features shift, glanced quickly at Cullen's
face and saw similar changes taking place.

Then the signet ring flared brightly between them, so that
Joram flung up his free hand to shield his eyes. When he could
see again, it was not his father's form who knelt opposite him.
The visage of one who had been dead now opened pale, sea-

ice eyes to look at him uncertainly. And at his knees, his father's face slept the sleep of those who will never walk the earth again.

Joram swallowed audibly as he pulled his hand away from a stranger's touch. (*Saint Camber* 118–119)

The form Camber assumes is not really that of a stranger, of course. Alister Cullen was well known, both to him and to Joram, who assisted in the transformation, and they further had the advantage of having Alister's body present as a direct model—as, indeed, Camber had Rhys and Joram as models for the shapes he put on the two servants, and Evaine had Eidiard as a model for Davin's new form.

Evaine herself carries the process to yet another level, however. When she assumes the form of "Brother John" to divert Cinhil's attention while Camber is completing his assimilation of Alister's memories, there is no model present.

"Brother John" raised a young but bearded face to gaze at him with eyes of smoky black—not blue. Those incredible eyes flicked guilelessly to the king's for just an instant, forever establishing the differentness from any other identity which Cinhil might have suspected or even dreamed of, then dropped decorously under long black lashes. Lips far narrower than Evaine's moved hesitantly in the bearded jaw, speaking in a voice which bore little resemblance to any which Rhys or Joram could have foretold. (*Saint Camber* 189–190)

Indeed, not only are we left with the distinct impression that no such person as Brother John has ever existed, but the reactions of both Joram and Rhys suggest that shape-changing without a physical model and without assistance is at least highly unusual. "You shape-changed," Joram says accusingly. "How?"

"I managed," Evaine replies, before going on to explain that she reviewed the section of Camber's scroll on shape-changing as well as that on memory assimilation. "I thought it might help if we understood a little of how Father got the way he did. I must confess, I never thought I'd have to use the knowledge myself." (*Saint Camber* 192)

What neither she nor the men comment on, in their concern about everything else that happened, is that Evaine took on a male form. On reflection—which, fortunately, Cinhil never had cause to make—one must wonder just how far the shape-change went. Was it complete or only a matter of facial appearance? It must have been more than mere illusion, projected on the minds of those witnessing it, for Joram and Rhys saw it, too, and would have detected a psychic manipulation—as Cinhil himself might have done.

Real change does occur, then. As to how *much* change, we may, perhaps, gain some insight by recalling that when Camber needed stand-ins for Rhys and Joram, he chose servants close to their size and body types before working his shape-changing magic, just as Eidiard was chosen as the model for Davin's shape-change, specifically because of a general resemblance. Indeed, Camber muses on his own preexisting similarity to Alister Cullen as he settles into his new shape.

In fact, few changes had needed to be made, other than to face and hands, for he and Alister had been almost of a size, both of them tall and lean—though Alister had stood perhaps a fingerspan taller.

But height was easy enough to camouflage, if anyone even noticed so slight a difference. If the present Alister Cullen walked a trifle shorter, that could easily be ascribed to fatigue, to the new weight of responsibility which would befall him, now that Camber was dead.

Facial differences were no problem at all. Now that the initial transformation was accomplished, he could even, if he wished, change back to his own form occasionally, with little exertion involved. He had already taken the necessary steps to ensure that no conscious effort would be required to maintain his façade; it would remain even when he was asleep or unconscious. Of course, any enormous outpouring of power would probably necessitate his returning to his own shape for a time, but those instances would be few and, hopefully, in places of safety. Otherwise, only an act of his own will could let his new visage mist away. (*Saint Camber* 132–133)

All of this suggests that a major limitation to shape-changing is that of body mass and basic skeletal size. Placing the shape of a diminutive squire on a hulking warrior probably would not be possible. Nor would a blacksmith make a likely model for a slight and sedentary clerk. Superficial changes of eye color and hair color, type, and location obviously are possible, as is some fairly drastic rearrangement of body mass, as in remolding facial bones, but adding or subtracting body mass is not. (Shape-changing, alas, is not a Deryni substitute for dieting.) Nor can Tavis simply conjure himself a new hand when none is there—though he might be able to maintain the illusion of a hand, at least for some observers and for a short time.

As for Evaine's shape-change, we can gather that no such intention was in her mind originally. For the purposes of her initial disguise, whereby she gained entrance to Camber-Alister's apartments with Joram, she thought it sufficient to knot her hair tightly to her head within her hooded cowl, hiding feminine hands in the voluminous sleeves of her Michaeline habit. She was further muffled inside a Michaeline mantle when she first arrived, though she shed that before they began working. Quite probably she had bound her breasts as well, for Rhys notes nothing about her appearance that would have betrayed her to casual scrutiny, especially if one only expected to see a monk.

Evaine's face, then, would have been the overwhelming betrayer; it is likely that her face alone changed before she dared lift her eyes to Cinhil's. However, we must never forget Evaine's ingenuity. She had already chosen a man's face for her alternate persona. Had Cinhil persisted in his questioning, perhaps handing over ''Brother John'' to professional interrogators, who knows how far she might have been able to extend the illusion, and what they might have found beneath Brother John's Michaeline habit?

The other major limitation of the shape-changing spell, besides conservation of mass, is that the energy to maintain the spell comes from the subject. Hence, Camber has his human servants sleep a great deal of the time while they are shape-changed, to husband their energy. And of course, the death of the subject terminates the spell. Davin's return to his own shape at death is typical; it might also be argued that Camber's reversion to his own shape is an extension of the tendency, though a more likely explanation is that he needed all his available energy to attempt the spell to hold death at bay.

Another shape can be placed upon a dead body, of course, as Camber placed his own upon the dead Alister and Charissa placed a stranger's face on the dead Brion (adding a further spell to bind a part of the king's soul), but this involves a slightly different application of the procedure, with input of energy from the operator to maintain it. Accordingly, such shape-changes on the dead are not intended to last indefinitely. Camber and Joram are well aware that the Camber-shape on the real Alister Cullen will have slipped by the time the bishops are agitating to inspect the body, and Charissa would not have intended her shape-change on Brion to last beyond the coronation, when her death or Kelson's would render the matter academic.

## Preservation Spells on Bodies

In addition to maintaining the outward appearance of Camber, Alister Cullen's dead body was magically placed in a kind of suspended animation, decay and decomposition held at bay by a preservation or stasis spell that Rhys sets in place and maintains—obviously requiring considerable effort, in the heat of advancing summer, when one considers that the practical limit for preserving Archbishop Anscom's body, in a hot and humid September, was two days. In fact, eight days elapse between Alister's death at Iomaire and his funeral as Camber in Valoret, and presumably another two or three days by the time he is actually buried in the vaults at Caerrorie.

Such preservation from decay is a specific Healer function—less useful than actual healings on a living body, perhaps, but aesthetically comforting for survivors. The setting of the original spell generally lasts about long enough to cover the few days that usually elapse between death and burial. It can be extended, as we have seen, but energy requirements, somewhat affected by temperature, go up almost geometrically with the passage of time. Rhys died in winter, which helps explain why, even after a fortnight, his body showed no sign of decay, but there also were at least two Healers available who could pour out the energy required to keep a stasis spell in place: Dom Rickart, Bishop Niallan's personal Healer, and Tavis O'Neill, who felt partially responsible for Rhys' death, both of whom would have wished to spare Evaine's feelings as much as possible, when she eventually saw her dead husband's body.

And then there is Camber's own body, which does not decay—his preservation apparently a function of that more mysterious spell which perhaps holds death at bay; or perhaps it *is* a sign of sanctity, as his adherents claim. . . .

## The Forbidden Spell

One of the most mysterious spells—which hardly falls under any general category we have mentioned thus far—is a procedure to hold death at bay: a life-suspending spell of sorts, thought by most magical practitioners to be the merest stuff of legends, sometimes called the Forbidden Spell.

We first hear of this spell when Camber and Joram come upon the bodies of Alister Cullen and the Princess Ariella, and Camber recognizes signs of the spell having been tried. His first suspicions are raised by Cullen's sword, pinning Ariella's body to a tree, its pommel twisted and charred from transmitting enormous energy—a sight that makes him bless himself in awed acknowledgment of what Cullen must have done. So preoccupied is he by that thought that his initial approach to Ariella is almost an afterthought, as if her death is a foregone conclusion after taking the power that Cullen sent through the sword.

> But then he looked more closely at her hands and knew that they were not on the blade at all, sensed instantly what she had tried to do. The now-dead hands were still cupped together on her breast, the fingers still curved in the attitude of a spell believed by most to be impossible, merest legend. No wonder Joram had been so shaken. (*Saint Camber* 110)

The telling clue seems to be an attitude of Ariella's hands, cupped together at the breast as if to cradle something precious, not even trying to ward off the sword piercing her vitals. But as Camber runs his hands above her body, he realizes that she was not successful, that her life-suspending spell did not work. Later, as Camber resolves his reaction to watching his own funeral obsequies, he reflects that he thinks he knows why her spell failed, but he does not enlighten us.

By the time he is tempted to use it on Rhys, he is sure he knows how to succeed where Ariella failed, at least in theory, but he is not at all certain whether he has the right to make such a decision for another. And while he debates the pros and cons, Rhys dies.

From Camber's anguished soul-searching, however, we can surmise that the procedure may exact a heavy toll. Camber tries to rationalize that it is really "little more than the stasis that could be put on bodies to prevent decay—well, perhaps a *little* more, to keep a soul bound to a suspended body" (*Camber the Heretic* 411), but if that really was all that was involved, one can hardly believe he would have hesitated for an instant.

In the several weeks that follow, he obviously works it all out, however. For as he himself lies dying and must make the ultimate determination as to whether he dares to try the spell, he has gained additional insight. Now he does, indeed, know why Ariella failed and that he will *not* fail—and also that it would not have been proper for him to make the decision for Rhys. That is a decision that no man has the right to make for another soul.

But he *can* make that decision for himself: to take up the challenge that sometimes is offered to adepts of his stature, as they advance in spiritual maturity:

> not to die, for now, but instead to enter that other, twilight realm of spirit where one might serve both God and man in different ways—or were they different? And *he* had been given the knowledge whereby he might accept that challenge, might gird himself with the whole armor of God and labor on, in the service of the Light. (*Camber the Heretic* 481)

We do not know, for some time, whether Camber was successful. Shortly after Evaine discovers that he may, indeed, have attempted the spell, she and Joram debate whether it worked and the possible consequences if they cannot bring him back. Only gradually does Evaine alone come to understand the price Camber had paid, only partially to fail, and what will be the cost of correcting his error to release him to his intended purpose. From our taste of what Evaine experiences on the inner planes, as she bargains for her father's release, we gain just a glimpse of what must be ahead for Camber, when he takes his place among the great masters.

Ponderously, Evaine tried to comprehend, only gradually coming to fathom just what her father had done. His spell had worked—to a point. Camber had bypassed Death, but only at a terrible cost. In exchange for the freedom to move occasionally between the worlds, continuing in spirit the work no longer possible in his damaged body, he had forfeited, at least for a time, the awesome ecstasy of union with the All High. Had he been more canny with his spellbinding, he might have won both, at once free to come and go in the Sacred Presence and to walk in both worlds as God's agent and emissary.

But Camber had not fully understood the spell he wove, in that moment of imminent death. Death had not bound him, no. But he was bound, nonetheless. By the fierce exercise of his extraordinary will, he had sometimes been able to break through to the world and make his presence felt, but those times were rare indeed, and costly on a level only comprehensible to those who have glimpsed the Face of God—or been denied that glimpse. And until the balance should be set right, by the selfless sacrifice of someone willing to pay in potent coin, that Face might remain forever hidden from Camber Kyriell MacRorie. . . .

So she must release him to that joyful purpose beyond life, in which great adepts chose their work and eschewed the Great Return in preference for specialized assignments, teaching mankind to grow in the likeness of God. For herself, the choice would mean death of the body, for mortal flesh could not sustain the outpouring of energy she must make to send *him* on into that next dimension; but she had known the sacrifice was likely. Others had gone fearlessly unto death; so would she.

And there would be Rhys, waiting for her when her work was done, and her beloved Aidan—and other friends and partners in the Great Dance who had also fallen in the cause of the Light. It was not an ignoble end. Nor was it even an end at all. (*The Harrowing of Gwynedd* 412–413)

By the time Evaine completes her mission, we sense that her sacrifice has not been in vain, that it has, indeed, enabled Camber to enter fully into that new dimension of existence in which he may walk freely between the worlds. Does that make him a saint at last? Only time will tell. We have already noted that Deryni, with their talents, can mimic many of the things saints supposedly can do. How Camber continues to make his influence known in the Eleven Kingdoms will be a subject of continuing fascination and speculation.

# CHAPTER TWELVE

# Wards and Warding: The Guardians of the Quarters

According to Tiercel de Claron, wards are "a type of magical protection or defense." (*The Quest for Saint Camber* xviii). Warding, in the general sense, is simply the process of raising a protective energy barrier around the person or area being warded or guarded. Working wards can be practical indeed, like those Tiercel raises at the door of Duncan's study to prevent intrusion (*The Quest for Saint Camber* 128, 133), or the ones Camber-Alister raises around his quarters to prevent eavesdropping while he speaks with the delegation of bishops come to offer him the archbishop's mitre (*Camber the Heretic* 341)—shorthand wards raised with little fuss or ceremony by master adepts. Watch wards can be erected around a campsite to guard against both physical and psychic marauding while an army sleeps (*Saint Camber* 78–80), and permanent wards can be built into the walls of a room.

Creating a barrier is the key to warding of any kind, however. In terms of classic ceremonial magic, warding generally involves casting a magical circle to keep harmful or hostile forces *out*. By another reckoning, the circle is intended to keep positive and beneficial forces *in*. In either case, the magic circle is the bridge between the worlds, where those within the circle stand "outside time, in a place not of earth," in a literal as well as a spiritual sense. In the most basic ritual sense, it is the setting aside of sacred space for a working area.

In general, the Deryni understanding of the warding process tends more toward the classical interpretation, to prevent the penetration of the working area by outside forces and to protect those inside from same, though there is an aspect of containment as well. In nearly all ritual contexts, warding involves summoning the powers of the four elements—Air, Fire, Water, and Earth—as personified by the four great Archangels of the Quarters. While it is readily acknowledged that such entities have no true physical form, certain attributes have been assigned to each, more or less by convention, to assist the practitioner in a strong visualization to stabilize the concept in his or her mind. When this facilitates the appropriate connection being made on a higher plane, the practitioner will, indeed, See what he or she has called.

## The Archangels of the Quarters

Summoning the Archangels begins in the East, the source of Light—which prompts a brief digression on *orientation*. Indeed, the very term comes from *orior*, to rise up, especially pertaining to the rising sun. Solar religions, of which Christianity is one (Christ, the Light of the World, being described as the *Sun* of Righteousness as well as the Son), instinctively *oriented* their rituals and sacred spaces toward the East. (In the general sense, of course, orientation has come to mean any designation of an agreed-upon direction for focusing attention, usually for a group, the purpose being to aid in establishing a common mental-set. Some traditions "orient" toward the North as their primary focus; even in East-centered traditions, certain magical intentions relating specifically to particular elemental attributes are best oriented toward the Quarter associated with that element.)

Once specific buildings began to be set aside and even purpose-built for Christian worship, builders took great pains to site churches on a true east–west alignment, with the altar in the East. However, if space considerations precluded proper alignment, as occurs increasingly these days, the builder did the best he could and people agreed to designate "liturgical East" for the purpose of ritual focus. When necessary, this convention continues to be observed in modern esoteric workings.

Returning to the summoning of ward guardians, then. In the tradition revered by the Deryni, virtually all positive workings *begin* in the East—though the focus may shift otherwise for the working itself (as when Evaine must venture into the realm of the Guardian of the North). The Archangel of the East is Raphael, who rules the element of Air. He (though angels truly have no gender) is usually depicted in flowing, air-stirred robes of pale, golden yellow. Traditional Judeo-Christian symbolism associates Raphael with the mercy of healing and identifies him as the angel who stirred the waters of the well in Tobit—whence comes his common depiction holding a fish.

In classic esoteric thought, the element of Air is associated with thought, intellect, and hearing. Its symbol is the Sword, which perhaps was an arrow originally—an obvious Air attribute. In a working circle, the most common symbol of Air is incense smoke.

Second in the Archangelic pantheon is Saint Michael, Commander of the Heavenly Hosts, who rules the element of Fire in the South. Red is Michael's primary color, and he is usually depicted in armor, wielding a fiery sword—or sometimes a lance. In some traditions, it is he who guards the gates of Eden after the expulsion of Adam and Eve from Paradise. It is he who will wield the scales at the final Judgement. In conventional hagiography, he is most often depicted with sword or spear in hand, one foot on the neck of a chained, dragonlike devil he has just subdued; but artistic renderings by the Order of Saint Michael, whose patron he is, invariably depict him standing at ease but still on guard, gauntleted hands resting on the cross-quillons of the great sword whose point lies between his feet, his armor shining with the glow of molten red-gold, fiery wings folded along his back like a mantle of flame—the archetype of the heavenly Warrior of the Light. In that sense, he is also the patron of knights in general.

The element of Fire is associated with intuition and sight, but its weapon is not Saint Michael's sword but the wand—once a fire-hardened stick or staff, used in control of Fire, such as pokers or torches. Lighted candles are the symbols of Fire in the ritual circle, as well as the fire that burns the incense.

The third Archangel is Gabriel, Guardian of the West and Water, usually depicted in blues and aquamarines. By very solid tradition, Gabriel is the Angel of the Annunciation, who carried the tidings of Jesus' impending birth to the Blessed Virgin with the immortal salutation "Hail Mary, full of grace. . . ." Gabriel also is the angel of the Last Judgment, who will blow his heavenly trumpet to raise the blessed dead. By association, then, Gabriel is the heavenly Herald as well, and perhaps chief servitor of the Queen of Heaven—who is held in very high esteem by Deryni, perhaps as a reflection of the feminine aspect of Deity Itself.

Water is associated with feeling, love, and taste/smell, and its symbol is the Cup—originally the cauldron of immortality, the communal bowl whence comes sustenance. By this association, it also becomes the Holy Grail. The holy water used in aspersing the circle is the ritual symbol of Water.

Finally, the Archangel of the North is Uriel (Auriel, by some reckonings), who rules the element of Earth. In one of Uriel's aspects, he is the Angel of Death, though not in a morbid sense but as the agent of the natural cycle of birth, death, and rebirth. Though he is seen as stern and solemn, he also can be merciful; for while he separates individuals from earthly associations, he reunites them in the Nether World, after giving release from worldly suffering. Uriel alone has truly feathered wings, usually likened to the green-black pinions of ravens or magpies or the iridescent green of a mallard.

The element of Earth is associated with learning, sensation, and touch. Its symbol is the Shield or Pentacle, originally an early spade for scraping earth and planting seed, and thereby a link with sacred stones. The salt in the holy water used to asperse the circle provides the ritual symbol for Earth.

In some traditions, a fifth element of Spirit is invoked, often associated with the great Angel Sandalphon and the Earth Mother, the Planetary Being, linking and unifying the other four. We will have opportunity to learn more of all of these entities when we examine some of the ways they have been ritually invoked in the context of actual magical workings.

But if the presence of guardian Archangels is essentially a positive thing, summoned up by the visualization of those setting the wards, why ward at all? Would any sane practitioner deliberately call up something that might turn on one? Surely Archangels differ from demons, who in classic ceremonial magic practice must be summoned to a containing triangle to protect the operator from harm.

The answer is that though these mighty Beings *are* seen in a benign and protective context, the raw energy of their very presence is such that mere mortals might inadvertently be harmed by too close a contact. Hence, the circle is seen as a protective barrier to their too close approach, to keep them at a safe distance. The very real trepidation that Queron feels in *The Harrowing of Gwynedd*, as the Guardians of the Quarters are summoned before his induction as a member of the Camberian Council, illustrates how potent "mere" mental visualizations can be for the trained occultist. Queron waits outside the circle that already has been cast, temporarily protected inside a stasis spell set across the space between two pillars where he stands, but knowing that eventually he will have to leave that safety and ask admittance to the circle.

"By rites ancient and powerful have we prepared this place," Gregory said quietly, laying the fingertips of both hands on the sword again—though he did not pick it up. "Now, therefore, by ancient calling do we summon, stir, and call up the great archangelic hosts."

In the East, on cue, Ansel threw back his head and raised both arms in supplication, his young voice ringing with confidence.

"In the name of Light arising do we summon Raphael, the Healer, guardian of Air and Wind and Tempest," he said, "to guard this company and witness the oaths that shall be sworn. Come, mighty Raphael, and grace us with thy presence."

He conjured handfire as he spoke—a sphere of golden light that grew above his head and then, at his direction, arrowed across the darkness of the *keeill*'s vaulting to merge with the fire of the eastern torch in a white-gold flash.

Queron was stunned, for he had never seen such an effect before. Nor, shielded behind the veil of his stasis spell, could he sense the Archangel's coming immediately—though he saw, from the look on Ansel's face, that *he* was aware of it.

Gradually, however, Queron had the impression of a great

wind filling the *keeill*, groaning through senses that had nothing to do with hearing. It raised the hackles at the back of his neck, sending a shudder down his spine, ice-cold against the stone wall behind him, and he pressed himself harder into his protective niche, hoping he was invisible, as Ansel's arms were lowered and Joram's raised.

"In the name of Light increasing, we summon Michael, the Defender, Lord of Fire and Prince of the Legions of Heaven," Joram said, his voice echoing in the *keeill* as he threw back his head. "May he guard this company and give due witness to the oaths that shall be sworn. Come, mighty Michael, and grace us with thy presence."

Joram's handfire whooshed toward the southern torch with all the sudden alacrity of a lightning strike, heavenly fire returning to its true source, blinding-bright. When Queron could look at it again, blood-scarlet burned in the heart of the flame; and Michael's sudden and undeniable Presence was all but visual, as *he* loomed all at once in the shadows beyond Joram—fire bright, yet not thus to physical sight—which was all Queron had, veiled behind the stasis spell. But the Healer-priest would not allow himself to dwell on what was not possible, for Evaine was about to summon Gabriel, who was his own especial patron.

"In the name of Light descending," said Evaine, offering her own supplication, "we likewise summon Gabriel, Lord of Water, Heavenly Herald, who didst bring glad tidings to our Blessed Lady. May this company be guarded and our oaths witnessed. Come, mighty Gabriel, and grace us with thy presence."

The gentle, sea-blue fire that Evaine conjured was soothing balm to Queron's now shaky perceptions, and he gave quiet and humble thanks that he did not need to see with his eyes to know that Gabriel approached. Breathing silent prayer and welcome to that One, Queron closed his eyes briefly, feeling himself settle at last into something approaching peace, now that Gabriel was nearby to sustain him.

It was Jesse who summoned the final Witness to their rite—Jesse, youngest of them all and little-tried, but confident as he raised his hands in entreaty, somehow setting just the proper seal on what was being done.

"In the name of Light returning, we also summon Uriel, Dark Lord of Earth, who bringest all at last unto the Nether Shore," came Jesse's Call, quiet but assured. "Companion of all who offer up their lives in the defense of others, guard this company and witness our oaths. Come, mighty Uriel, and grace us with thy presence."

All at once, as Jesse's sphere of emerald green merged with the torch just outside Queron's niche, dark-feathered wings buffeted the other side of the stasis veil. Gasping, Queron ducked his head in acknowledgment of *that* One—to whom, he suddenly realized, he might well have to answer before the night was over. By now, he had been made most uncomfortably aware that the Camberian Council had access to knowledge and powers far beyond even the vast lore of Queron's Order—and Gabrilite training was usually accounted among the best available. Not only in symbol did his life hang in the balance tonight.

For a dozen heartbeats, he trembled in that realization, all too aware of the awesome Powers gathered in the space between the pillars and the circle's dome, watching the *keeill's* mortal occupants gather around the altar again, as the immortal Ones loomed outside the circle.

And he must pass among *them*, in order even to beg admittance to the circle's sanctuary! Small wonder that he had been left behind the safety of the stasis veil—and what was he going to do when it was lifted? (*The Harrowing of Gwynedd* 75–78)

The above scene is probably the most graphic example to date of a formal summoning of the Quarter Guardians and certainly illustrates the reason for a protective circle. But sometimes this function can be incorporated into a ritual itself. When Cinhil sets out to empower his sons with the Haldane potential, Camber and his kin inform the king of basic forms to be followed in casting the magical circle and actually triggering the empowering process, but *he* must direct it. Cinhil's first attempt to establish the Presence of the Elemental Forces is sketchy, for he does not know the formal words for what he wants to do, so he speaks from the heart, trusting that Those Who listen will recognize his good intent. We can contrast these invocations with the more involved ones used in the previous passage, both in language and in what is requested.

> "Saint Raphael, Healer, Guardian of Wind and Tempest, may we be guarded and healed in mind and soul and body this night. . . .
> "Saint Michael, Defender, Guardian of Eden, protect us in our hour of need. . . .
> "Saint Gabriel, Heavenly Herald, carry our supplications to Our Lady. . . .
> "Saint Uriel, Dark Angel, come gently, if you must, and let all fear die here within this place." (*Camber the Heretic* 77)

But as the ritual proceeds, Cinhil apparently becomes unsure whether he has set the visualizations of the Elemental Guardians strongly enough, for he augments his first effort as he begins preparation of the cup that will be the trigger for his sons' empowering. The king couches the words of his invocation in the pattern of a Eucharistic prayer that would have been familiar and comforting to him, and his Deryni allies pick up the pattern and reinforce it in Cinhil's chosen imagery. Note, also, how each element manifests in some tangible sign of Its presence.

> As they took their places once more, Joram to his left and Alister to his right, he [Cinhil] drew strength from his own resolve. Impassively he took the cup from Alister and turned to face the altar, raised the cup slightly with both hands in salute to the Divine Presence.
> "O Lord, Thou art holy, indeed: the fountain of all holiness. In trembling and humility we come before Thee with our supplications, asking Thy blessing and protection on what we must do this night."
> He turned to face his son, lowering the cup to extend his right hand flat above the rim.
> "Send now Thy holy Archangel Raphael, O Lord, to breathe upon this water and make it holy, that they who shall drink of it may justly command the element of Air. Amen."
> A moment more he held his hand motionless there and forged his will, his heart pounding in the unbreathing silence

of the warded circle. Trembling, he let his right hand slip down to support the cup with its mate, felt the ring beneath the water vibrating against the snow-white glaze.

A breeze stirred his robe, a lock of hair, wafted a curl of incense smoke past his nostrils, beginning to circulate with increasing force within the confines of the circle. He saw the wild look in his son's eyes as the breeze became a wind, a vortex which snapped robes tight to bodies and whipped hair against faces which did not flinch or turn aside.

Evaine's hood was swept from her head, her hair coming down in a cascade of tinkling golden pins which showered the carpet at their feet. Yellow and iron-grey hair stood out like living, writhing haloes on Joram and Alister, but they did not move—only stood with hands crossed still on blue and purple-clad breasts, serene, implacable, though the bishop did close his eyes briefly, Cinhil noted.

Then, suddenly, the storm was past. Almost before anyone could react, the wind had captured more of the incense smoke and coalesced in a tight spiral centering over the cup which Cinhil still held. He was aware of all their eyes upon him, of an eddy of surprise that he had called up this imagery for the work they did. But there was an undercurrent of acceptance, too—of acquiescence to this approach—and he knew that they would follow his lead.

He watched as the breeze subsided to a tiny, controlled whirlwind hovering above the cup, did not dare to breathe as the funnel sank and touched the surface of the water, stirring it slightly and then dying away.

When all movement on the surface of the water had ceased, when all that stirred was the renewed shaking of his hand, Cinhil closed his eyes briefly and passed the cup to Joram. Joram, apparently unmoved by what he had just seen, bowed solemnly, grey eyes hooded and unfathomable. Holding out the cup beside the entranced Alroy, he extended his right hand over the rim as Cinhil had done.

"O Lord, Thou art holy, indeed: the fountain of all holiness. We pray Thee now send Thy holy Archangel of Fire, the Blessed Michael, to instill this water with the fire of Thy love and make it holy. So may all who drink of it command the element of Fire. Amen."

A moment, with his hand held over the cup, and then the hand was drawn a little to one side, though still it hovered close. Fire glowed in the hollow of his palm, growing to an egg-sized spheroid of golden flame which hung suspended but a handspan from the cup. The flame roared like the fire of a forge, filling the warded circle with its might.

After a few heartbeats, Joram turned his hand slightly downward and seemed to press the fiery sphere into the surface of the water. Steam hissed and spat for just an instant, then ceased as the flame subsided to a cold blue which brooded, barely visible, on the surface and around the rim.

Carefully, reverently, Joram turned toward his sister and extended the cup to her. She tossed her wind-tumbled hair back from her face with a quick, graceful gesture and took the cup, held it close against her breast for just a moment while she gazed into the water.

Then she raised it high in supplication, her eyes focused on and through the glow of flame.

"O Lord, Thou art holy, indeed: the fountain of all holiness. Let now Thine Archangel Gabriel, who rules the stormy waters, instill this cup with the rain of Thy wisdom, that they who shall drink hereof may justly command the element of Water. Amen."

For an instant there was silence, a growing electric tension in the air. Then lightning crackled in the space above their heads, and thunder rumbled, and a small, dark cloud took form above the cup.

Cinhil gasped, his resolve shaken at what Evaine had called, but the others did not move so neither did he. Evaine's face was suffused with radiance, her blue eyes focused entirely on this thing she had called.

Thunder rumbled again, lower and less menacing this time, and then a gentle rain began to fall from the little cloud, most of it falling into the cup but a few drops splashing on those who watched. Cinhil flinched as the first drop hit his face, restraining the almost irresistible urge to cross himself, but the rainfall ended almost as soon as it had begun. Abruptly, the cup in Evaine's hands was only what it had been before, though fuller by perhaps a fingerspan than it had been. The outside of the cup ran with water beaded on the glaze, drip-

ping a little on the precious Kheldish carpet as Evaine handed
it to Alister with a bow.

Cinhil drew another deep breath as Alister glanced into the
cup and raised it to eye level with both hands, focusing his
attention on the point above their heads where the cloud had
manifested itself seconds earlier.

"O Lord, Thou art holy, indeed: the fountain of all holiness. Let Uriel, Thy messenger of darkness and of death,
instill this cup with all the strength and secrets of the earth,
that they who drink hereof may justly command the element
of Earth. Amen."

Instantly the cup began to tremble in Alister's hands, the
ring inside to tinkle against the cup, the water to dance so that
it threatened to spill over the rim. At first Cinhil thought it
was Alister's hands which shook, as his own had done; but
then they all became aware that other things were rattling and
trembling, that the very floor was vibrating beneath their feet.

The tremor increased, until Cinhil feared the very altar
candles must be toppled from their places. But then the shaking subsided, as quickly as it had begun. Alister raised the
cup higher and inclined his head in acknowledgment of the
Power which had been manifested through his hands, then
lowered the cup and turned his gaze on Cinhil, extending the
cup to him.

"The cup is ready, Sire," he said in a low voice. "What
remains is in your hands." (*Camber the Heretic* 79–82)

It certainly is clear by now, even to Cinhil, that the circle's
Guardians are very real and fully present. Just *how* present and
real only becomes evident when the ritual itself is done and the
soul of the transformed Cinhil prepares to pass through the gate
Joram has opened to the Nether World.

Then Cinhil was moving through the gateway, his face
transformed by a shining light which grew around him. Dimly,
past the slowly receding Cinhil, Camber thought he could see
others standing and reaching out to Cinhil—a beautiful young
woman with hair the color of ripe wheat, two young boys who
were Cinhil's image, others whom Camber could not identify.
In a rush of wind and the illogical impression of wings,

four Presences seemed to converge around Cinhil then—
*Beings* with vague shadow-forms and sweeping pinions of
raw power which somehow sheltered rather than threatened.

One loomed massive and overpowering, vibrant with the
hues of forest tracts, feathered green-black wings shadowing
the entire northern angle of the room as it passed over an
apparently oblivious Evaine and Rhys. Another seemed to
explode silently into existence right before the altar, bursting
either from the gold-glass gleaming of the eastern ward candle
or from the altar's open tabernacle, shining like the rainbow
fire of sunbeams caught in prisms, so bright Camber could
hardly bear to look, even with his mind.

The third was winged with fire and sighed with the roar of
infernos, the heart of the earth, though its great sword of flame
was raised protectively over Cinhil's head as he stepped outside the circle without a trace of fear. And from the fourth
Presence—a shifting, liquid form of blue and silver shadow—
a shimmering horn of quicksilver seemed to take form.

A soundless, mind-deafening blast of titan resonance as-
sailed Camber's senses, reverberating in every particle of his
being; and suddenly he could feel the circle beginning to
fragment around him, as if the horn sounded some note which
the fabric of the circle's dome could not withstand. He *heard*
the energies which rent the dome asunder—knew that all that
saved him from eternal, mindless madness was the ciborium
with its consecrated Hosts, resting on the table close beside
him.

Then, even as the shards of shattered circle were still falling
to the tile, there to disperse and melt away like flakes of snow,
Cinhil and his ghostly Escort began to recede, slowly at first,
but then faster and faster until nothing remained but a shrinking point of rainbow light suspended between Camber and
the altar candles.

Then, even that was gone. (*Camber the Heretic* 95–06)

From the universal reactions of dismay expressed by the survivors of this particular magical operation, we can conclude that
this was *not* the usual way of dispersing a circle. However, it
certainly serves to illustrate the very real sense in which non-
mortal Witnesses may attend when They are summoned.

So wards provide a very practical and sometimes quite dramatic function in protecting those within from too close an exposure to forces beyond mortal enduring. Besides their purely protective functions, however, wards *can* serve as a device for concentrating positive energies, as in a scrying operation or a working intended to make a psychic link or communication with someone outside the warded area. Examples of this latter function include the wardings done before scrying with the Haldana necklace, before placing a shape-change on Davin MacRorie, and before Morgan and Duncan attempt to seek out Kelson and Dhugal via psychic links. But whether the wards are intended to be protective, containing, or both, they can be set by ritual, by triggering a certain mind-set, or by using Ward Cubes.

# CHAPTER THIRTEEN

# Ward Cubes I: Basics

Ward Cubes are a physical aid to erecting magical protections, though, in fact, no such physical accoutrements are really necessary for a competent practitioner. As Tiercel tells Conall, "Eventually, you'll learn to use them in conjunction with working other spells. It won't always be necessary to use a physical matrix to set the wards, but these will help, in the beginning" (*The Quest for Saint Camber* xviii). Indeed, we have already seen how short-term wards can be erected or banished around an area by a merely psychic operation, though usually they are keyed in with some physical cue such as a hand gesture. (Tiercel, of Duncan's study, *The Quest for Saint Camber* 128, 133; Camber, of the sacristy in the village church, after Cathan's funeral, *Camber of Culdi* 144.) Wards also can be built into rooms and lie dormant until called into operation. We see such a room in Dom Emrys' working chamber at Saint Neot's (*Camber the Heretic* 176) and Rhys' and Evaine's bedchamber at Sheele (*The Deryni Archives* 34).

So, what are Ward Cubes, specifically? In short, they are a convenient symbolism on which to hang certain mnemonic keys that, when activated, trigger very specific psychic processes and result in the channeling of energy into a "dome" of protection.

Their physical appearance has become quite standardized. In general, Ward Cubes come in sets of four white and four black cubes, about the size of dice but without spots. In fact, as Tiercel remarks to Conall, when teaching the latter how to use Ward

Cubes, the early ones might have been dice—"or could have been disguised to look like dice, once it became dangerous to be Deryni. I've seen spotted ones, and they work just as well." (*The Quest for Saint Camber* xix) Indeed, Derry seems convinced that Morgan's cubes are really just strange dice (*Deryni Rising* 120–121).

The traditional and most usual materials are ivory and ebony, the organic nature of both substances probably facilitating the patterning that must be placed on a new set of cubes before they can be used for the first time. (Indeed, the first set of Ward Cubes known personally to the author were cut from half-inch balsa wood stringers, half of the cubes blackened with India ink. Subsequently, this original set was replaced by black-and-ivory-colored plastic—aesthetically less than optimum, perhaps, but they *look* like ebony and ivory, and the symbolism is better than painted wood, since at least the color is uniform throughout.) Ultimately, the actual material matters little, so long as the colors of the two quarters contrast sharply, to symbolize the notions of light and dark, positive and negative, male and female, and a balancing between these pairs of opposites—for the only real function of the physical Ward Cubes is to cue a particular mind-set.

Still, one of the very deeply rooted traditions of esoteric ceremonial is that one's magical implements should be the best quality one can afford—though cubes made of the humblest woods, lovingly cared for and dedicated will work just as well as the most expensive cubes cut from semiprecious stone. Indeed, quartz, marble, and white opal have been suggested for the white cubes, and obsidian, Apache tear (a clear, smoky black), black opal, and even malachite for the dark of the set. Tiercel's are described as "the white ones yellowed like old ivory . . . the black ones more a charcoal grey than true ebon or obsidian" (*The Quest for Saint Camber* xix). When activated, all the white cubes universally seem to glow milky white or an opalescent white. Both Tiercel's and Morgan's black cubes are described several times as taking on a green-black color, but Camber's are a "dark, blue-black glitter of darkest opal fire" (*Camber the Heretic* 318).

We also know that Ward Cubes acquire a "psychic signature" with use, peculiar to their owner, which can facilitate or impair use by another practitioner, depending on the relationship of the persons involved. We might even surmise that some sets of Ward Cubes could be psychically imprinted so that they would not work at all for anyone besides the owner or someone he or she approved, though we have seen no examples of this as yet.

Our first actual glimpse of Ward Cubes occurs in *Deryni Rising*, when Morgan uses a set to erect Wards Major around the sleeping Kelson. By Morgan's time, the use of such cubes appears to be limited to the protective function employed by Morgan. Indeed, he and his contemporaries appear not to know of any Ward Cube function except that of erecting Wards Major around something.

Yet we are told that most Deryni children begin their formal training with Ward Cubes. In fact, Ward Cubes may represent the first really serious accoutrement of ritual magic that most young Deryni encounter in their formal training—and perhaps the first real magical "implement" acquired. Camber taught Joram about them as his very first spell (*Saint Camber* 308). Tiercel de Claron seems quite bored at the prospect of teaching their use to Conall—though he takes heart considerably when Conall proves a quick study (*The Quest for Saint Camber* xviii–xxiii).

We shall not dwell on Tiercel's teaching of this skill, other than to point out that he lets slip several interesting points that may help us to understand the Ward Cubes' function. The colors of the cubes, light and dark, appear to symbolize the balance that must be achieved when juggling the powers harnessed by the cubes for the warding function. Indeed, balance seems to be a vital part of all Deryni magic. When Tiercel has Conall change the white and black cubes to opposite hands, Conall senses a difference—perhaps the polarity of right and left, light and dark, positive and negative that we see reflected later on in *Harrowing*, in the imagery of the cube altar beneath Grecotha. There, the cubes are rearranged horizontally to form the Pillars of the Temple, with the body of Orin laid along them as the Middle Pillar, Man in balance with the forces of Severity and Mercy.

# Wards Major

The key to actually using the cubes for warding, however, is well-focused concentration—which is the reason Tiercel had Conall practice centering all winter. Naming the cubes in the appropriate fashion triggers a particular mind-set in the operator, focusing the power and establishing certain balances, the achievement of which is signified by the named component beginning to glow. First the four white cubes are placed in a square, all touching, with the black ones set at the four corners, diagonal corners touching. Then the cubes are designated by their names, or *nomena*, each cube being touched in turn as the operator pronounces the *nomen* of that particular cube. (The *nomena* come from the eight defensive moves of the sword—yet another link with the sword-defense symbolism so highly regarded by the Michaelines.) We may regard the *nomena* as mnemonic triggers for initiating the mind-set necessary for manipulating and balancing the energies that make up a ward matrix.

The white cubes are named first, in the following order, holding the positive energies in focus. Each glows white from within as it is activated.

1—*Prime*
2—*Seconde*
3—*Tierce*
4—*Quarte*

Next the black cubes are named, shifting balance to the negative poles—and not just negative in a vague, general sense, but the negative balance of the white cubes already named.

5—*Quinte*
6—*Sixte*
7—*Septime*
8—*Octave*

Now the named cubes must be balanced, each pair harmonized not only within itself but in reference to the other three pairs. Keeping this in focus, the operator now matches the white cubes to the black, in the following order, and gives each pairing its *cognomen*. These *cognomena* are balance mnemonics to trigger psychic processes taking place in the operator's mind.

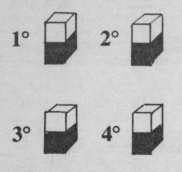

Prime to *Quinte* = *Primus*
Seconde to *Sixte* = *Secundus*
Tierce to *Septime* = *Tertius*
Quarte to *Octave* = *Quartus*

The union of opposites produces four silvery-gray "rectoids," or double cubes, which Tiercel refers to as ward components. "Some magical systems equate the ward components with the Elemental Lords and their Watchtowers, or the Archangels of the Quarters. Some prefer the symbolism of the pillars. All are valid conventions" (*The Quest for Saint Camber* xxi).

What follows, however, is the true magic of the procedure. For now, after placing the four activated "towers" around the person or area to be warded, the operator must trigger the final processes that will link those towers in space and time. The actual shape of the field projected by the towers will be determined by their placement—usually as four points on a circle or ellipse, with the first designating East. The field usually is contained at the horizontal by the floor—which means that, in theory, danger might be able to approach from below—but the field *can* extend in a matching shape below the horizontal as well. (See Gregory's completion of the circle in the *keeill*, before Queron's induction as a member of the Camberian Council, when it becomes clear to Queron that the dome of the circle has been drawn below them as well as above—*The Harrowing of Gwynedd* 75.)

Activating the wards, then, is the final part of the Deryni balancing act, though the physical part of the procedure is quite simple. The operator simply points to each of the towers in turn, calling them by cognomen—*"Primus, Secondus, Tertius, et Quartus"*—and ends with the simple command: *"Fiat lux!"* Let there be light! If everything has been done correctly, the Light immediately Is. After that, if the operator wishes to revise the position of the ward, he has only to move the towers in or out, or to direct the energies inward or outward with the focus of the palms of his hands. Activation can be done from inside or outside the area to be warded, but normally, only the operator who raised the wards can control or eventually dispel them.

As an important side point, it should be noted here that the rotation for naming/numbering the cubes (and rectoids) does not follow the strict clockwise rotation from the eastern starting point that one might expect, but rather the Z or "lightning flash" configuration analogous to the route of progression on the Tree of Life, or the path of the sun from East to West. It also corresponds to the order for naming heraldic quartering on a shield.

Hence, the activated "towers," *Primus* through *Quartus*, are moved to the nearest Quarter, so that *Primus* represents East and *Secundus* South, as expected, but *Quartus* goes to the West and *Tertius* to the North. And for the final setting, they still are named by *cognomen* in the proper order, *"Primus, Secundus,*

*Tertius, et Quartus, fiat lux!''*—not the order corresponding to more usual Quarter invocations.

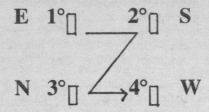

Dismantling or "banishing" the Wards Major is far simpler than erecting them—so simple that this procedure was not demonstrated until *King's Justice*, where Morgan banishes the wards he has used to protect him and Kelson while he formed a communication link with Duncan.

Shaking his head to fend off further discussion until he was done, Morgan blew out the candle set on the camp table between them and put on the signet ring he had just used as a focal point for concentration. All around them, barely discernible against the redder glow of a lantern hanging from the tent pole, the dome of the warding he had raised to shield them glowed a cool, gentle silver. It pulsed briefly brighter as he raised both arms to shoulder height on either side, empty hands upraised, and drew a slow, centering breath.

*"Ex tenebris te vocavi, Domine,"* Morgan whispered, slowly turning his palms downward. *"Te vocavi, et lucem dedisti."* Out of darkness have I called Thee, O Lord. I have called Thee, and Thou hast given light.

*"Nunc dimittis servum tuum secundum verbum tuum in pace. Fiat voluntas tua. Amen."* Now lettest Thou Thy servant depart in peace, according to Thy will. Let it be done according to Thy will. . . .

As he lowered his arms, the doming light faded and died, leaving only four pairs of dice-sized polished cubes set tower-like, white atop black, at the quarter-points beyond their chairs. Two of the four sets toppled as Kelson leaned down to retrieve them, too precariously perched, on the straw matting of the tent's floor, to stand steady without the balancing effect of magic. Morgan sat back in his chair and sighed, wearily rubbing the bridge of his nose between thumb and forefinger, as Kelson stowed the Ward Cubes in their red leather case. (*The King's Justice* 96)

Incidentally, though I did not know this at the time I first mentioned Ward Cubes in *Deryni Rising*, there apparently is a real-world equivalent to Wards Major, using blue and white candles instead of black and white cubes. Briefly, protection is invoked as the candles are blessed, bound in pairs with red silk thread, lighted, and set at the edges of the area to be warded. The protection lasts as long as the candles burn.

On a note even closer to home, I have been told by several readers who work with Tarot cards that setting up Ward Cubes on the table where a reading is to be done reduces interference from outside energies and helps reinforce a calm, centered mindset conducive to better readings.

## Alternative Matrices

Of course, as we know from our perusal of the magic of Camber's time, Wards Major are not the only use to which the cubes can be put. When Camber first does a partial demonstration of one of the variations for Joram (*Saint Camber* 309–311), underlining the possible connection he has made between the small Ward Cubes and the large cubic altar under Grecotha, it is clear from the context that he is well along his way to trying at least several other permutations—a notion that appalls the conservative Joram. This particular demonstration begins with the standard starting arrangement for the cubes—four white ones in the center and the four black ones set at the corners. Then, though one would next name the cubes in the usual fashion, if one was actually going to work this variation, Camber switches *Prime* with *Quinte* and *Quarte* with *Octave*.

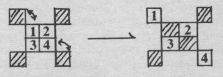

Then Camber proceeds to stack the cubes, working from the outside in, rather than from the inside out (as is done when setting the more common Wards Major), in the following order and with the indicated end result:

*Prime* on *Quinte*
*Sixte* on *Seconde*
*Septime* on *Tierce*
*Quarte* on *Octave*

Joram finds it difficult to make the connection at first, but Camber persists until his son reaches the desired conclusion.

"I see—a cube made of eight alternating black and white cubes," Joram finally whispered. "And the—altar is also made of eight black and white cubes." His eyes sought his father's. "Are you saying that the altar cubes are part of a giant Ward Major matrix?"

Camber sighed and scooped up the little cubes in his palm, letting them fall, one by one, back into the black velvet bag. He did not look up or speak until he had retied the bag and tucked it back into his tunic.

"That I don't know. I don't think it's a Ward Major matrix, but I'm beginning to suspect that it *is* a matrix. At very least, I think the altar may be symbolic of the cubes we use. In fact, the very appellation of 'Ward Major cubes' is probably a misnomer. I've found sketches of a full dozen additional cube matrices already, and there are literally dozens more possibilities. Unfortunately, I haven't yet figured out what any of them do, including this one—which appears to be the only one worked in three dimensions, by the way."

"A dozen different matrices!" Joram whistled low under his breath. "Have you tried any of them yet?"

Camber shook his head. "I'm afraid to. I haven't a notion what might happen. This one especially." He laid his hand on the altar once more. "And if the altar is symbolic of the power of the particular spell being invoked by this pattern, which I think highly likely, then it must be powerful indeed—

perhaps at the very heart of our Deryni abilities. We already *know* that there was great power associated with this altar, if we can still detect its traces after hundreds of years. Who knows what we might unleash if we go experimenting without suitable preparations? We've time to go slowly.'' (*Saint Camber* 310–311)

# CHAPTER FOURTEEN

# Ward Cubes II: Advanced Permutations

In the next decade, Camber and his kin obviously summoned up the courage to try at least a few of the potential permutations that Camber has mentioned—as, indeed, they located the physical premises, begun by the mysterious Airsid but never completed, which were taken over as a meeting place for what became known as the Camberian Council. (How they discovered the theoretical existence of a Portal within the legendary complex and managed to summon up the courage to dare a blind Jump to a Portal never seen by any of them is a story in itself, which probably will be told one day.)

In any case, recovered knowledge continued to accumulate over the next ten or twelve years, so that by Davin's death in late September of 917, at least one additional cube permutation had become a regular and unremarkable part of procedure within the Camberian Council, to raise and lower a black and white cubic altar (very similar to the one beneath Grecotha) set in the center of the *keeill*, the Council's ritual chamber. As word of Davin's death spreads and the members of the Council congregate, Camber uses the process of raising the altar as a focus for getting his own grief under control.

Camber took a deep breath and made his conscious mind block out what the archbishop was saying, laying a finger on the white cube in the upper left on the square before him before projecting its *nomen*.

*Prime!*

He had not spoken the word aloud, but immediately the cube lit from within, glowing with a cool white light.

*Seconde!*

The upper right cube gleamed like its companion.

*Tierce!*

So followed the cube below the first.

*Quarte!*

The last cube's activation made of the four of them a single, softly glowing square of white light, whiter than the slab on which they lay. A moment Camber paused to shift his perception to the other side of Balance, from white to black, then touched the black cube next to Prime. Jaffray's voice was a meaningless buzz as Camber formed the first black's name:

*Quinte!*

The touched cube sparkled to life, a dark, blue-black glitter of darkest opal fire, as he moved on to the next.

*Sixte!*

The fire seemed to leap instantaneously from the first black cube to Camber's finger to the one so-named, and to follow as he touched the remaining black cubes in rapid succession.

*Septime! Octave!*

As the fires stabilized in the heart of the last cube, Camber drew a deep breath and let his conscious resume its attention to Jaffray's words, wincing a little as what he had blocked now came through in full force, filling in the gap of his brief psychic absence. . . . With a shake of his head, Camber flung up his shields again and blocked out Jaffray, taking but an instant to balance between black and white as he placed his first two fingers on Prime and Quinte and shaped the *phrasa*.

*Prime et Quinte inversus!* He switched the two cubes' positions and felt the energies warp slightly.

*Quarte et Octave inversus!* Again, the change of place, an intensification of the weaving, the stranding, of the power being harnessed. He laid his fingertips on Septime and the transposed Prime.

*Prime et Septime inversus!*

And *Sixte et Quarte inversus!* The final *phrasa*, suiting action to words.

The cubes lay in a saltire configuration now, one diagonal

glowing a deep blue-black and the other gleaming white on white against the marble slab, their arrangement and the working he had done steadily drawing in more energy and laying in new strands to be commanded. He came back to the others, their words of the past few seconds flooding into his consciousness and making him wince with the intensity of accompanying emotion. . . . Gradually he gained everyone's dazed attention.

"This will be a new working for some of you," he said, voice steadying as discipline displaced the flux of mere emotion. "Ansel, Jesse, you're about to see one of the few second level configurations we've had the nerve to try—and one of the even fewer that we've gotten to work. It seems to have limited application, so far, but we're still learning. We have Evaine's research to thank for it."

As Evaine smiled weakly, Camber carefully picked up the cube named Septime and placed it on Quinte, black on black.

*Quintus!* he spoke in his mind, feeling the energy lick up around his fingers for just an instant before he moved on to Quarte, stacking it on Seconde, white on white.

*Sixtus!*

"More energy, twining with the first," he murmured, gesturing for them to sense it for themselves.

He felt their support and Ansel's and Jesse's increasing curiosity as he set Prime atop Tierce, Sexte on Octave.

*Septimus!*

*Octavius!*

He did not know whether the words themselves were important—he suspected not—but the mental energies behind them were, and he could feel them woven among his fingers as he held his hand above the cube he had formed. *The pillars of the temple*, Joram had called the configuration, the first time he saw it. It reminded them all of the shattered altar beneath Grecotha.

Carefully, Camber got his feet under him, ready to stand, then let his right hand rest squarely on top of the cube. . . . Then he activated the energies.

He could feel them tingling in his hand and all up his arm, even tickling at the edges of his mind, as if hand and cubes had fused in one vibrant unit. As he wrapped his mind around the strands of energy and wove the grid, he could feel the potential building, so that by the time he began slowly to lift his hand, the cube rose, too—and also the marble slab, soundless save for the faint whisper of polished stone in passing.

The slab continued to rise, as effortlessly as if it were feather instead of marble, supported by four large cubes, white and black alternating. Camber stood . . . his upper body still bent over the smaller cube whose power he had harnessed. A second course of black and white cubes began to appear, these set in opposition to the first course, finally revealing a black base of the same size as the *mensa* on top. Pillars the size of a man's arm stood at the four corners of the cube thus revealed, alternating black and white like the broken ones under Grecotha.

When the black slab had risen to the same thickness as the top one, the entire mass stopped. Camber, with a slight sigh, withdrew his hand out to the side of the small cube and flexed his fingers experimentally, then glanced at his intrigued audience as he scooped up the wards and returned them to their pouch.

"Its own weight will take it back into place when we're done," he said matter-of-factly. "One only need the cubes to raise the things." (*Camber the Heretic* 317–321)

The passage certainly gives a graphic description of the sort of working going on—if mere words can suffice to describe psychic processes—but we can benefit from breaking out the steps in this particular working.

1. The cubes are set up in the traditional manner, white ones in the center and black ones at the corners.
2. The cubes are named as usual.
3. The first two pairs of black and white cubes are switched, as Camber did in his earlier demonstration, to appropriate *phrasae*:

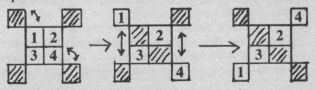

*Prime et Quinte inversus!*
*Quarte et Octave inversus!*
    and then, unexpectedly:
*Prime et Septime inversus!*
and *Sixte et Quarte inversus!*

This gives us the distinctive saltire configuration described, from which Camber constructs the "Pillars of the Temple" by the following moves, outside to inside:

*Septime* to *Quinte* = *Quintus!*
*Quarte* to *Seconde* = *Sixtus!*
*Prime* to *Tierce* = *Septimus!*
*Sexte* to *Octave* = *Octavius!*

As a further comment on Ward Cube configurations, we should consider the variation that Queron discloses, only gradually pieced together from an almost forgotten Gabrilite practice. From seeing it worked on an ordinary altar (that is, the bluestone cube in the chapter house at Saint Neot's), Queron had been led to believe that it is a purification ritual only. But when applied to a black and white cubic altar, it is found to be much more. Queron's memory of the working is triggered as Evaine prepares to share information *she* has recently gleaned from her own researches.

"This new material seems to deal with advanced warding techniques," she told them, laying out the four white and four black cubes that made a set of Wards Major. "A lot of it was veiled in allegory, as these things so often are, but I think I've isolated at least one new configuration. Now, most Deryni with any training at all know the basic spell for constructing Wards Major."

She had been moving the four white cubes into a solid square in the center, and now set the four black ones at the diagonals. "This is the starting point for it—and for half a dozen other configurations of varying complexity, the most powerful of which, as we know, can raise this altar slab to reveal the black and white cube altar that supports it.''

"What we've usually called the Pillars of the Temple," Joram said.

"That's right." Without bothering to name the cubes or activate them magically, she placed her first and second fingers on the first white cube and the black one at its diagonal and switched them, then did the same with the two diagonally opposite, so that the central square ended up checkered black and white, with cubes of opposite colors at the four corners.

But when she would have gone on to the next step, Queron suddenly seized her wrist.

"Wait! Don't do that yet!"

"Why? What's wrong?"

"Just wait!"

"Queron, the cubes aren't even activated," Joram murmured, stealing a startled glance at Evaine, whose wrist Queron still held. "Nothing's going to happen."

"I know that."

Queron's voice was strained, intense, forbidding further conversation, and both Joram and Evaine fell silent, only watching as the Healer-priest continued to stare at the cubes. When, after a few more seconds, he softly exhaled and released Evaine's wrist, he looked a little sheepish, and brushed a hand self-consciously across his eyes.

"I'm sorry. I certainly hadn't expected *that* memory to surface."

"Can you tell us about it?" Evaine asked quietly.

"I—that's what I'm not sure about." He swallowed uncomfortably. "Good God, I never really thought I'd be put into a situation where I'd seriously consider violating my vows."

Joram cocked his head curiously. "Your priestly vows or the seal of the confessional?" he asked.

"Not exactly either." Queron drew a deep breath and exhaled it as fully as he could, as if steeling himself for something either unpleasant or dangerous. "This—ah—has to do with that—ah—other tradition besides Gabrilite, that we talked about, some time ago. You'll remember that I mentioned in passing that I hoped I wouldn't have to make a choice."

"You don't have to tell us," Evaine said.

"No, I think I do," Queron said. "That's just the point. Something that never quite made sense before, that was part of that earlier tradition, suddenly took on a whole different perspective as you started to move those cubes around. There was a piece of ritual that the Master used to do, several times a year, at morning meditations. We were always taught that it was symbolic—exactly what the symbol was, was never made quite clear—and I never questioned that. But—well, let me show you a part of it, and see whether it makes any sense to either of you. If I don't actually work the spell, I don't suppose I'm technically in violation of my vows—and if it doesn't mean anything to you, we can just drop the whole thing."

"Queron, this really isn't necessary," Joram began.

"Yes, it is, at least this far," Queron replied. Drawing a deep breath, he picked up the four cubes at the outer corners of the black and white square formed in the center and placed them on their opposites, forming the familiar checkerboard of the cube altar.

"Now, there's a proper ritual procedure for what I just did, of course, but the result was to end up with this configuration, which mimics the cube altar underneath this slab."

Evaine nodded. "The actual arrangement of the cubes is quite logical, of course. Father always suspected that there was an actual working that went with it, but we never found enough evidence of one to risk trying anything."

"Well, I'm not certain what the intention was," Queron said, "but what the Master used to do was to set up this configuration in the proper sequence, then recite a particular prayer while he held his hands over the checkered cube—sort of cupped, as if he were consecrating the Eucharistic elements. After a while, energy washed outward from the cube, all the way to the edge of the altar." He cocked his head thoughtfully. "Actually, I suppose I always thought the working was to purify the altar. But now that I think about it, he only ever did it on the cubical altar in our Chapter House—never the oblong one in the sanctuary—and the cubical altar was only ever used for meditation."

Evaine nodded. "I remember Rhys telling me about that altar—a cube of bluestone, wasn't it? And Father recognized it as a power nexus of some sort. In fact, he even wondered if there was some connection with the black and white altar under Grecotha.''

"I wonder what Queron's Master would have done with a black and white altar," Joram mused. "And if it was only for purification, why was it never done on the regular altar?''

Raising an eyebrow, Evaine cocked her head. "Now, there's a thought—if you would agree, Queron.''

"Try it on a regular altar?" Queron said.

"No, try it on a black and white altar." She patted the white slab beside the piled up cubes. "Try it right here.''

Queron looked uncomfortable with the thought at first, but then his expression turned more speculative. "I wonder if I *could* do it. And what hidden meanings was I missing in my youthful ignorance? Thinking back, the symbolism was *not* just that of purification, though it was part of it.''

"I thought we were looking for a stronger warding spell," Joram said uneasily. "Besides, what you're talking about obviously was intended to be kept secret from those not of your Order.''

"I can *do* a stronger warding," Evaine said, a little impatiently. "That's what I brought you here to show you. But a new purification spell might also be useful—if that's even what it is. It doesn't seem to be dangerous, in any case.''

Queron nodded half reluctantly. "You're right on both counts, Joram. However, I'm not sure that hidden part of my Order even exists anymore—and we do seem to have some rather special needs. Besides that, I confess I've aroused my own curiosity as well. God, I hadn't thought about that in years.'' He grimaced. "I suppose I *am* still a little uneasy about working this outside the Order, but—never mind. I'm going to do it. The oaths I've exchanged with the two of you are at least as solemn as anything I swore to the Gabrilites. Let's try it.''

"You're sure?" Evaine said.

"Yes, I'm sure." Deftly Queron dismantled the little cube matrix and reset the individual cubes in their original starting places, the four white ones forming a square in the center, with the four blacks set at the diagonals. He twined his fingers together and flexed them backward briefly until the knuckles cracked, then disentangled them and wiggled them briefly while he ordered his thoughts and Evaine and Joram crouched to either side of him.

"I think I'll raise the altar first," Queron murmured, poising his right hand over the cubes. "The Master always did the special working from a standing position. I don't know that it would make a difference, but I think we ought to duplicate the original conditions as much as possible."

"I agree," Evaine said, as Joram glared resigned disapproval.

"So, I'll name the components. *Prime!*" he said, touching his right forefinger to the white cube in the upper left of the square and speaking its *nomen*. (*The Harrowing of Gwynedd* 271–275)

The cubes are activated in the usual way, observation being made about the nature of the balance achieved in the saltire configuration:

one black and one white diagonal, Might held in balance by Mercy. And carrying the operation to its conclusion would create the Pillars of the Temple, but in three dimensions, with the balance of the altar itself firmly established as the Middle Pillar, the mediating force which could facilitate even greater things. (*The Harrowing of Gwynedd* 276)

Queron proceeds as we have seen, forming the specified pillars, and raises the altar. He then proceeds with the second part of the operation—which finally will result in a miniature altar cube configuration, of which much speculation has been made over the years.

"So far, so good," Evaine murmured. "I assume you have to start again now. This is an end point, so far as anything *I* know."

Sighing again, Queron nodded, dismantling the little cube and setting up the small cubes in their original configuration, white cubes forming a solid square in the center and the black ones set at the corners.

"You're still sure you want to do this?" Joram said.

Queron nodded. "I certainly do. I know a lot more now

than I did as a novice. I'm curious as to what the old Master *did* intend, when he used to do this working. I remember that it was always at the Quarters and Cross-Quarters, and the novices were encouraged to keep an all night vigil in the Lady Chapel the night before—though that wasn't required. Odd, that—because otherwise, we were rarely offered such options.''

He drew another breath, as if shaking off the weight of long-ago memories, then held his hand briefly over the cubes.

''Very well. It starts the same way the other variation did, by naming the eight components. I remember that the Master never spoke the *nomena* aloud, because he thought it interfered with the proper mind-set. So I'll do as he did.''

Not pausing for their reaction, he brushed his forefinger quickly over the eight cubes in the same order as before, beginning with the four white ones and then naming the four black ones. Each sparked to life as he touched it, and Evaine and Joram followed his progress easily, *Prime* through *Octave*.

''The first half of the next part also goes the same,'' Queron whispered. He set his first and second fingers on Prime and Quinte and intoned the familiar *cognomen* as he changed their places: *''Prime et Quinte inversus!''*

Quarte and Octave followed, their *cognomen* also almost sung.

*''Quarte et Octave inversus!''*

When he had switched the second pair, they were left with a central square of black and white alternating, with a cube of the opposite color at each outer corner. And now, instead of transposing Prime with Septime and Sixte with Quarte, as he had done before, he picked up the white Prime from the upper left diagonal and set it carefully on Quinte, the upper left black cube, with a *salutus* sung in one of the eerie Gabrilite plainsong chants:

*''Primus est Deus, Primus in aeternitate. Amen.''*

Touching his right hand to his breast, he made a profound bow to the altar, then picked up black Sixte, setting it gently on white Seconde as he sang the next *salutus*:

*''Secundus est Filius, Coaeterus cum Patre. Amen.''*

Again he bowed profoundly before picking up black Septime to place in on Tierce.

*"Tertius est Trinitas: Pater, Filius, et Spiritus Sanctus. Amen."*

Another bow before picking up the final cube, Quarte, to set it on Octave and complete the checkered cube.

*"Quattuor archangeli custodes quadrantibus sunt. Quattuor quadrant coram Domino uno. Amen."*

The completed cube glowed with the soft, opal fire of its original components, a jewel-like miniature of the larger cubes of black and white marble that supported the white altar slab on which it rested. Queron raised his clasped hands to his lips, closing his eyes briefly as he gathered his concentration to continue, then drew his hands apart at chin level, palms turned toward one another, and began to chant.

*"De profundis clamavi te, Domine: Domine, exaudi orationem meam. Adorabo te, Domine . . ."*

He turned his hands over the cube as he prayed, palms cupped gently as if in blessing, fingertips slightly overlapping. All of them could feel the power gathering—a taut, tingling sensation that began at the crown of the head and quickly permeated to the toes.

*"Fiat lux in aeternam. Fiat lustratio, omnium altarium Tuorum,"* Queron murmured. Let there be light in eternity. Let there be purification of all Thine altars . . .

Light began to glow beneath Queron's hands, emanating from the cube matrix. As he tipped his palms apart and raised his arms, light fountained upward between them—a miniature pillar of fire centered over the matrix, as thick and high as a man's forearm. He brought his hands briefly to cover his eyes as he continued to sing, then crossed them on his breast and bowed profoundly.

*"Quasi columna flammae me duces, Altissime, in loca arcana Tua . . ."* Like a pillar of fire Thou shalt lead me, O Most High, into Thy secret places . . .

The pillar remained as his psalm ended, hovering in the stillness. Fearlessly Queron stretched out his right hand toward the top of the pillar, lowering it onto the flame.

*"Gloria in excelsis Deo . . ."*

But the flame did not appear to burn, and gave way beneath

his touch. The pillar fattened as he compressed it, pooling wider and wider out from the cube matrix as his hand descended, living light washing over the surface of the altar all the way to the edges and then brimming over in a cascade of luminance that was swallowed up by the black edges of the base slab. Queron's hand touched the top of the matrix as the light reached the corners of the mensa slab—and gave at the pressure, the entire altar beginning to sink, the light continuing to glow across its top and sides.

"Sweet *Jesu*, where's it going?" Joram whispered.

"Back into the dais," came Evaine's awed reply, "though somehow, I don't think the Master's spell ever did *this*."

Queron expression suggested that it most certainly had not, but he kept on singing the *Gloria* and the altar kept sinking—and kept sinking even when the white mensa drew level with the floor of the dais, becoming flush with the level of the dais, sinking beyond that, until even the now-kneeling Queron could no longer keep his hand on the small cube. It did not stop until the top of the mensa had sunk its height and half again below the top level of the dais, just as Queron's singing ended. Evaine and Joram were also on their knees, peering uneasily into the hole made by the altar's retreat.

"Why did it do that?" Joram murmured, as Evaine conjured handfire and sent it into the opening.

Queron gasped as the light revealed an extension to the opening, stretching back toward the north, and dropped onto his stomach to lean down for a closer look as the other two also peered down.

"There's a passageway and what might be stairs leading down!" (*The Harrowing of Gwynedd* 276–279)

After exploring the empty chamber that lies below, Evaine speculates further on the possible significance of the working Queron has just done.

". . . when your Master worked the spell, you *did* say that he always did it at the bluestone altar in your chapter house?"

"That's right."

"And he did it as a meditation and ritual purification of the altar. Also correct?"

Queron nodded.

"Suppose the ritual had come down from a much earlier tradition that used a black and white cube altar rather than a bluestone one," Evaine said, "and suppose that the ritual not only purified the altar, but also operated the mechanism for opening the way to another, more secret inner sanctum."

Joram nodded emphatically. "And if the original tradition had been transmitted incompletely, as sometimes happens, no one would have been any the wiser. Or maybe the additional meaning got lost in melding the different strands of discipline that made up the Gabrilite tradition."

"That's certainly possible," Queron agreed. "But if there *was* a tradition of secret chambers under black and white altars—good God, what about the altar down in the ruins? It's right in the middle of *ancient* remains! Maybe there's another chamber under *it*. What if *that's* where the Varnarites hid their most important archives?" (*The Harrowing of Gwynedd* 280– 281)

In addition to what this passage shows and hints about the Gabrilites, it is clear by the end that what Queron has shown is at least one way of working the cubic altar configuration on which Camber and Joram speculated so many years before. And by the time Evaine takes her father's cubes and merely stacks them in two towers of four, black on the left and white on the right, as a glyph for the very Pillars of the Temple themselves, we know that at least this Deryni has come full circle, returning to a point where physical accoutrements are no longer necessary.

So. Before her was a glyph of what she had to do, childish in its simplicity—a symbolic rendering of the task for which all the rest had been but prologue, carefully crafted to bring her to this moment.

For by the power of her will alone, and for the sake of the man who had trained her to use that power of will, she now must make of those tiny, symbolic pillars the very real and solid Pillars of the Temple—the temple of the Inner Mysteries, whose corridors communicated with Divinity Itself and life and death, at levels only rarely given to mortals still bound by physical form.

Between these Pillars she must pass, in a very real sense, and even beyond the Purple Veil itself, if she had any hope of bringing that man back. . . .

Drawing a deep breath and settling even deeper into the Otherness requisite for these sorts of workings, Evaine returned her attention to the Pillars, seeing them swell and grow, pushing toward the ceiling—certainly to the limits of the circle—stabilizing as the circle contained them. In the shadow world to which she now turned her concentration, she knew the Pillars to be as substantial as the floor under her feet, solid with a power that transcended the mere time and space of the physical world. A mist seemed to have intensified between the Pillars, even as the Pillars themselves solidified, and she stood up in her astral form to look more closely, rising out of the body that sat so quietly behind her. (*The Harrowing of Gwynedd* 404, 408)

# CHAPTER FIFTEEN

# Healers and the Healing Function

When we speak of Healers in the Deryni context, we are not referring to mere physicians but to individuals who, by the power of will and mind, can catalyze and accelerate the body's natural inclination toward wholeness and health. This healing function appears to be a very specialized subset within the general spectrum of abilities available to all Deryni. That is, not all Deryni are Healers, but virtually all Healers are Deryni (or miracle-workers or saints—for some few humans, such as Warin de Grey, also can heal).

Unlike other Deryni abilities that gradually surface and unfold from fairly early childhood, the healing talent normally does not begin to manifest until puberty—though occasionally, in response to acute need, the full-blown talent may surface spontaneously at an earlier age. Such need brought Rhys Thuryn's healing powers to usable levels at age eleven—quite unexpectedly, since nothing in his ancestry suggested that he might be a future Healer—and somewhat early even if the healing potential *had* been anticipated (*The Deryni Archives* 24). Some twenty years later, Rhys was able to identify the same potential in two of his children, almost from the moment of conception. We do not yet know how Jerusha will carry the healing gift, but Tieg, at least, has already proven unusually precocious even among Healers—though having healing power manifest at three and a half would have been of little use without his mother's ability to direct it. Evaine herself was not a Healer, but long experience working with Rhys gave her the skill to focus Tieg's power (*Camber the Heretic* 451–453). Had she been present as Rhys lay dying, who knows whether she might have been able to tap and focus his power as well, perhaps saving his life?

Very early detection and/or confirmation of Healer potential is not necessarily the norm, however. Even in children whose background suggests possible Healer potential—a Healer parent or grandparent—the usual age for formal screening is between six and eight, when personality patterns have begun to form—for success as a Healer is not determined solely by mere potential. (The Varnarite-trained Tavis speaks of a former classmate, the collaborator Ursin O'Carroll, as being a failed Healer, and the Healer's novice Ulric is said to have broken under the strain of his Gabrilite training.)

## The Healing Gift Sex-Linked?

One interesting characteristic of Healers is that the vast majority are male. We hear of few female Healers. Rhys, shortly before the birth of his Healer daughter Jerusha, can name only four others alive at that time and tells Camber that "the male line carries the gift more easily than the female" (*Camber the Heretic* 219). Similarly, we know that though Evaine experienced "twinges" when carrying Tieg—reactions to his *in utero* perception of others' healing needs and pain—Jerusha's sensitivity was even greater, such that Evaine had to leave the room when Rhys was dealing with Tavis' amputated hand.

These observations suggest several speculations about Deryni genetics as they relate to the healing abilities. First of all, whatever genetic factors combine to produce the startling array of talents that makes a Healer, at least some of the factors unique to Healers must be sex-linked, since "the male line carries the gift more easily than the female." Furthermore, since Healers do come in both genders, this would tend to suggest that at least some of the factors governing healing potential are carried on the X-chromosome. Whether the double-X configuration of a female simply intensifies negative aspects of the Healer legacy normally carried on the X-chromosome, or the negative effects of one X-chromosome are modified by factors carried on the Y-chromosome, we do not know—only that more male Healers are born than females.

In addition, because non-Healer parents can produce Healer children, we know that at least part of the healing legacy must be recessive. As in Rhys, who had no known Healer lineage, the Healer potential can skip generations, carried via male or female lines, by Deryni who display no healing abilities themselves. It is when these recessive factors combine to produce dominant characteristics that a Healer is produced—usually male.

The paucity of female Healers seems to suggest that the double-X Healer configuration may well potentialize a lethal genetic linkage, resulting in the miscarriage or stillbirth of many or most female Healer fetuses. This represents the ultimate failure of the female line to carry the gift. While the lethal gene theory cannot be proven either way, it does provide a reasonable working hypothesis to explain the rarity of female Healers. In fact, the male-linked factors may form lethal combinations, too—male Healer fetuses may well abort with greater frequency than normal male Deryni fetuses do—but the vast preponderance of male Healers suggests that the overall survival rate of male Healer fetuses is higher.

In a somewhat related line, I often have wondered whether female Healers might have fertility problems as well, based partly on the speculation that difficulty in combining Healer factors properly in the double-X configuration might well result in gene splits and reproduction problems even if the woman was fully functional in every other way.

Certainly this is not always or even usually the case. Rhys and Evaine evidence no apparent concern that their Healer daughter might be barren, thus suggesting that probably most female Healers *can* produce viable offspring and that Rhys anticipates no complication in this regard. However, it also can be argued that Rhys has other things on his mind besides the likely fertility of a daughter not yet born. Evaine, too, has more pressing concerns in the short time she gets to spend with her infant daughter.

What also tends, indirectly, to support the notion of possible impaired fertility—and this must be inferred almost as much from what is *not* said as from what *is* said—is that as widely

reputed and competent a Healer as Rhys knows of only four
female Healers, and can *name* them. Given the restrictions
placed upon "respectable" women in his society—ladies of
gentle birth may be daughters, wives and mothers, or sisters in
a religious order—it is not likely that Rhys would know the
names of any but the latter, for daughters, wives, and mothers
would not be permitted to employ their healing abilities outside
the household or family.

And where would female Healers get their training? Convent
schools might provide some of the direction needed by a fledgling Healer, but most Healers—and most teachers—are men.
Coeducation is not an institution in the Eleven Kingdoms. Indeed, any kind of education for gentlewomen beyond basic reading and writing, simple ciphering, and domestic management
is almost unheard of. (We may recall what measures Camber
had to employ for Evaine to be permitted to sit in on the occasional university lecture. Readers familiar with Robert Bolt's
film *A Man for All Seasons* may well note the similarity between
Sir Thomas More's favorite daughter, Margaret, and Evaine
MacRorie—both women their fathers' darlings and educated far
beyond the level usually accessible by women of their times.)

Only within the framework of a religious community might a
woman really achieve a positive notoriety outside the confines
of home and hearth, her good name and person protected by the
Church rather than father or brother or husband. Granted, the
monastic vow of chastity would preclude even attempting to pass
on the healing potential, but if female Healers were apt to have
difficulties in childbearing anyway, what better place than a convent to turn a possible liability into an asset, healing other wom-
en's children and devoting oneself to other good works in an
atmosphere of honor and respect for one's God-given vocation?
In an age when being barren could be grounds for annulment of
a marriage, when women often sought the cloister after being
put aside for childlessness, a female Healer fearing the stigma
of sterility might well choose the veil, preferring the dignity of
the religious life and the safe freedom it offered to pursue her
healing vocation. The rarity of female Healers would make one
welcome in any religious community—a jewel in the abbey's
crown to be cherished and favored, given the finest private tutelage and facilities, her name a watchword of mercy and charity

to be invoked outside her abbey's walls. The names of such women would have been well known to Rhys.

Besides Rhys' and Evaine's infant daughter Jerusha, we know of one other female Healer by name: Jodotha, the great Orin's disciple. We also know that both disciple and master were members of some kind of religious order. One day we will learn more about them, their order, and their interaction with King Llarik Haldane and his sons. It remains to be seen how Jerusha Thuryn eventually will handle her healing legacy and whether she carries the healing potentials untainted.

Male Healers had far more options. Despite the reputation and high profile of Gabrilite Healers, and the apparently large number of Healer-priests gathered under one roof at Saint Neot's, we must remember that the Gabrilites were the *only* all-Deryni order specifically geared toward Healer training. (There were Healers among the Michaelines and other mixed human-Deryni orders, but nearly all ecclesiastical Healers spent at least a year under Gabrilite discipline.)

Outside the walls of Saint Neot's, however, most Healers chose to work in a lay capacity and, in fact, were encouraged *not* to enter the religious life but to pursue their healing vocations in a secular context, eventually marrying and producing children—for only thus would the healing lines be perpetuated. (Gabrilite Healers observed a celibate life-style, and were greatly respected, but only those Healers in whom the vocation to the religious life burned even brighter than the healing vocation were permitted to make Gabrilite vows.)

## Human Perceptions of Healers

Healers enjoyed a far more benign reputation than Deryni in general. To humans, Healers were the least threatening of all Deryni, and few were ever seriously accused of misusing their powers, even during the darkest days of the Festillic Interregnum. But the Haldane Restoration, though it restored humans to rights and privileges and power suppressed during the Interregnum, did it at the cost of the Deryni—*all* Deryni. After a brief period in which some Healers were forced to collaborate with the regents, sometimes betraying not only their own kind but their very healing vows, even Healers fell under the general opprobrium being applied increasingly to all Deryni. In the aftermath of the Restoration, with the concomitant breakdown of the great Deryni institutions and the advent of increasingly vicious anti-Deryni persecutions, formal training of Healers and, indeed, all Deryni virtually ceased. No Deryni power might be used legitimately, even to heal. Individual Healers may have been able to keep their art alive for a few generations of students, training successors under simple apprentice arrangements carried out in secret, but with no central coordinating bodies to preserve the wider body of knowledge, to test proficiencies, and to maintain standards, the bulk of specialized knowledge accumulated over a span of centuries gradually died out and was lost. Only generations later, when pressure began to diminish on Deryni as a whole, could the healing talents begin to surface again in wild-card Deryni such as Morgan and Duncan, to be wielded instinctively at first, adding to their knowledge by trial and error, without training or guidance or even understanding of the potentials they carried.

Not only Deryni in general but even Healers were already well into decline in Gwynedd by the time of King Cinhil's death in 917. Because of the former importance of the several institutions of Healer training such as the Gabrilite Saint Neot's Abbey and the Varnarite School, and the prominent roles played by certain individual Healers in the immediate post-Interregnum history of the kingdom, it is tempting to assume that Healers still were reasonably available.

But by the time of young King Alroy's coronation, as Deryni of all sorts were being systematically expunged from positions of influence and authority, it is significant that, even in the face of a royal summons, only the relatively inexperienced Oriel was immediately available to come to deal with Tavis O'Neill's hand amputation. At least a few other Healers must have been resident in the city at this time, for the archbishop's secretary recommends several, but they cannot be located readily. Perhaps they were busy already on call-outs, their services spread thin because of their declining numbers, or perhaps they simply made an excuse not to answer a call to the palace, where their services were becoming less and less appreciated.

Yet another possibility is that the guards sent to find a Healer simply ceased further inquiries once Oriel had been located, disinclined to overexert themselves over an injured Deryni, even to please their young prince. Surely a few more Healers must have remained in residence in a military capacity—for even the regents were not yet so blind as to reject the usefulness of Healers for treating battle injuries.

On the other hand, the guards were men with experience of battle injuries, who had a fair notion of what even a Healer could do. Such men would have realized the probable futility of trying to reattach a severed hand to a burned stump. Why bother, only to end up with a Healer with only one hand? A Healer unable to heal was only another Deryni—of which there were far too many to suit these men already!

Deryni status continued to deteriorate after that, of course, even for Healers. Soon both Healers and ordinary Deryni were being actively and forcibly recruited for the regents' purposes, as they conceived the notion of using collaborators to further their own aims. And anti-Deryni legislation soon closed the loopholes that had allowed even the regents' ''pet'' Deryni to continue to use their powers. The regents' blind hatred of what they could not understand or control caused the destruction of untold numbers of men, women, and children in the ensuing decades, whose only crime had been to be born with gifts not shared or understood by the rest of humanity.

## The Healing Mechanism

Stripping away philosophical differences of orientation in the way Healers are trained, we can establish several common premises regarding how healing works. First of all, healing requires physical contact. The Healer must touch his patient, preferably close to the wound or site of injury. This requirement tallies with the many biblical references that link healing with the laying on of hands, several of which emerge in Tavis' tearful exchange with Rhys as to why he will not be able to heal anymore, with his hand cut off. ''What good is a Healer with only one hand?'' Tavis demands.

''Why, the same as one with two hands,'' Rhys began puzzledly.

"No!" Tavis croaked. "The balance won't work, don't you see? I'm flawed, defec—"

"Tavis!"

"No! Listen to me! Even the scriptures—"

*"Tavis!"*

"The scriptures agree: 'They will lay *hands* on the sick, who will recover.' *Hands*, not *hand*! And the *Adsum* confirms it. *Cum manibus consecratus*—with consecrated hands, make whole the broken. . . ."

"The *Adsum* also says, *Tu es manus sanatio mea*—thou art my healing *hand* upon this world," Rhys interrupted, thinking fast. "And all your arguments and self-pity to the contrary, there's nothing in scripture to suggest that *two* hands are necessary to heal. Jesus put forth His *hand* to heal the leper—"

"*No* . . ." Tavis wailed, near hysteria.

"Tavis, stop it!" Rhys snapped. "Stop dwelling on what you *don't* have, and think about what you *do* have. You're still a Healer. It wasn't your mind that was affected by what happened to you today—only your hand!" (*Camber the Heretic* 217–218)

The Healer's powers of mind are the key, then—and the *balance* of those powers as *symbolized* by the Healer's two hands. But a symbol is only that: a symbol; a convenient hook on which to hang a mental set. If, as Tavis maintains, *old* balances no longer work—if the old symbolism no longer is applicable—then *new* balances can be learned, once Tavis comes to terms with his limitations and gets on with his life—which, eventually, he does.

Certainly there will be *some* limitations. Having only one good hand means that occasionally Tavis will be hampered in the physical manipulations a Healer needs to effect a proper healing—as, indeed, occurs when he brings the injured Ansel through the Portal to the Michaeline sanctuary in *The Harrowing of Gwynedd* and must call for other Healers to come and assist him—but *any* Healer would have needed help for such an emergency. One does the best one can, in the given circumstances.

Healers often worked with non-Healer or even human assistants to help with tasks not requiring a Healer's specialized abilities. Evaine worked regularly with Rhys, to the extent that she eventually was able to direct her Healer son's healing power, though she was not a Healer herself. And the first assistant that we see with Rhys, a manservant called Gifford, is not even Deryni. Even an able-bodied Deryni such as Dom Sereld, the royal Healer called to tend the hamstrung Rhys, engages non-Healer assistance.

> "[Don't move] yet, son. I want to make sure I've gotten any clots before you move that leg much. Of course, something like a hamstring's a little tricky to manage on oneself," he went on, bending Rhys' restored leg at the knee and stroking his Healer's hands lightly over the area where the wound had been. "I had to have Lord Camber help me with the physical manipulation. Healing's much easier if you can get injured bits back in the general area where they belong, before you start. Hard to heal across a handspan of empty space when you're trying to reattach two cut ends." (*The Deryni Archives* 25)

*Any* Healer may need additional physical assistance at some point, then. Tavis simply may need it sooner or more often than a Healer with both hands. But his handicap will be minimal, so long as he learns to maintain his balances and can enlist physical assistance when he needs it. The hands themselves are not the real issue—though one may speculate that a Healer without hands at all might encounter more than usual difficulties in exercising that particular gift.

This said, we should not move on without noting that a Healer's hands do have an additional significance that probably did not occur to Tavis consciously at the time of his loss, but certainly would have registered at some unconscious level. This also may help to explain his near-hysterical reaction. For at the height of Deryni ascendancy and influence, the hands of a Healer, as the most apparent instrument of his power, had come to be held in almost the same reverence as a priest's hands, which are consecrated at his ordination with holy chrism to make them worthy to handle the elements during the Eucharistic sacrifice. Indeed, the Healer's vocation was perceived as so closely akin to that of the priest, in sacredness of calling, that at a Healer's final matriculation and commissioning, his hands were anointed and consecrated in a manner almost identical to that employed for a priest's. We have seen Sicard MacArdry's revulsion at what was done to Duncan's priestly hands during torture (*The King's Justice* 227) and Loris' justification of the action on the grounds that Duncan, as a Deryni, had profaned with those hands the very sacrifice he dared to offer. We should also recall Rhys, contemplating what *his* hands have done and can do as he considers the new ability he has discovered, of blocking the very powers that give him his abilities.

> "They are a Healer's hands, consecrated to the service of mankind—human as well as Deryni. I pledged that service in my Healer's oath, many years ago. I have often held life itself between these hands—sometimes *your* lives. Now it appears that I have been given not just the lives of individuals, but of our *race*—here, in the span of these two frail hands. . . ." (*Camber the Heretic* 147)

Tavis would have sworn that same Healer's oath, and both men would have had their hands consecrated in solemn ritual. Small wonder, then, that Tavis' loss of a hand is so devastating.

Moving on, then. Physical contact with the patient is essential for healing, preferably with two hands, but possible with one. Next, the Healer must be able to visualize very precisely just what it is he is trying to accomplish. This means an intimate knowledge of what the normal, healthy human body is supposed to look like *before* it was injured. From this we can surmise that Healers acquire a basic knowledge of normal human anatomy and physiology during their training, just as human physicians and battle surgeons must do. In the case of gross injuries such as broken bones or even most lacerations, healing visualizations will be relatively straightforward. They can become more involved and more difficult as injuries become less apparent or involve more complicated structures such as internal organs, whose working is less well known.

Straight surgical procedures, as distinct from the healing of injuries, comprise another definite if limited area of Healer ability. Our primary example of this kind of healing is that of the

Healer Simonn, some sixty years after we saw him as a young Healer novice at Saint Neot's, removing a tumor from young Gilrae d'Eirial's forearm (*The Deryni Archives* 46–76). Additional surgical applications might include opening and draining of abscesses, removal of foreign bodies such as arrowheads, and possibly even cesarian sections.

The principal limitation of such healing would be the ability to visualize the patient's body restored to health. (Obviously, anything affected at a microscopic level, such as the metastasizing of cancerous cells, would be beyond a Healer's ability.) That Simonn is able to recognize a possibly malignant growth on Gilrae's arm, to determine that nerve pressure from that growth probably is responsible for the young man's loss of function in the arm, and to carry out the appropriate surgery under field conditions—anesthetizing his patient, excising the tumor surgically, and then healing the incision—tends to confirm that he, at least, was able to continue his Healer training after the Gabrilite dispersion of 917. Simonn's ongoing presence near the ruins of Saint Neot's suggests that perhaps other Healers also returned to Gwynedd after the initial fury of the regents' persecution had peaked, part of a secret missionary underground that may have extended cautious tendrils all over Gwynedd. (His invitation to Gilrae to join him at an unstained altar implies that some offshoot of the old Gabrilite Order must still survive, even if humans now are admitted as well as Deryni.)

Anatomical knowledge is a key to Healer success, then, but unfortunately it does not address the general area of medicine and disease mechanisms—an area in which the most accomplished Healer has little edge over a well-trained human physician. A connection between contamination of wounds and infection has been observed, and cleanliness of wounds and of a patient's environment is judged important by both human and Deryni physicians, but germ theory will not really be developed for many centuries. A standard pharmacopeia of simple medications for treating symptoms is available to medical practitioners of all persuasions, with Deryni additionally having access to a few Deryni-specific drugs, but other than the observed healing properties of natural substances such as sphagnum moss and a bluish powder that appears to be a penicillinlike mold, the Healer's pouch is relatively sparse when it comes to actual promotion of medical healing. Healers cannot cure the common cold or any of the other troublesome ills that have plagued mankind through the centuries.

Other Deryni powers not specific to Healers alone also can be used in a healing context. The ability to "knock out a patient painlessly before working on him . . . [is] a blessing, no matter where the ability comes from," Dhugal observes (*The Bishop's Heir* 25) after Kelson has assisted him in suturing a wounded soldier in a postbattle situation. Indeed, forced sleep is one of the most useful tools of the Healer—that and the blocking of pain—and both abilities generally are available to all Deryni of any training whatsoever.

To a certain extent, most Deryni also can learn to control bleeding—essentially a simple application of psychokinetic principles, though one must know when and where and for how long to exert the appropriate pressure to avoid doing more harm than good. Blood loss itself cannot be remedied by Deryni magic, however—as the distraught Kelson had cause to know all too well, watching Sidana's life pump from beneath the frantic hands of Morgan and Duncan. If the patient expires through loss of blood, he or she is dead and cannot be revived, even if the trauma that caused the blood loss is healed. (Camber would have known this from long association with Rhys, so he must have worked his life-suspending spell *before* he bled to death.)

A Healer cannot produce new blood to reinflate the circulatory system, either; nor does the protoscience of the Eleven Kingdoms yet extend to blood transfusion. Conventional medicine *is* conversant with the basic concept of replacing lost fluids by mouth and feeding the patient food and drink likely to promote the production of new blood, but such a measure is not always enough. The patient must be alive to eat and drink. Healers may be "miracle workers" and hold death at bay for a while, but they do not have absolute power over life and death.

Non-Healer Deryni who work regularly with Healers often learn other quasi-medical procedures as well, such as monitoring and regulation of respiration and heartbeat—safeguards also useful during the performance of certain magical workings involving very deep trance, in which the operator might lose touch with his or her own body functionings and forget to breathe.

Some degree of body temperature control also is possible, though mostly limited to minor adjustments connected with environment rather than fever-associated conditions. Camber is able to lower his body temperature just slightly as he waits to go to his episcopal consecration (*Saint Camber* 285–286), but when Nigel asks about temperature control before the setting of his Haldane potential, Duncan informs him that it would take energy they will need for other things. "Besides, *you're* not Deryni." (*The King's Justice* 43).

Healers can work in nonphysical modes as well. The mind can be a source of ills no less serious than the body. Indeed, in this particular area of healing, non-Healer Deryni often can function nearly as efficiently as those with the full healing gift—as psychic psychiatrists, as it were. A Deryni counsellor, able to distinguish between truth and falsehood and even to read the mind of a patient, often can bypass unconscious resistance and succeeding levels of artifice and sometimes gain direct access to the roots of psychological disturbances. We see examples of this kind of work in Rhys' and Joram's attempt to help Cathan deal with his grief and guilt (*Camber of Culdi* 70) and in Oriel's work with the broken Declan Carmody in *The Harrowing of Gwynedd*. Queron states that the technique he uses for projecting Guaire's memories is a useful tool in treating certain mental illnesses as well.

In the area of pastoral and spiritual counseling, both Healer and non-Healer Deryni have a distinct edge over human physicians of the soul. Indeed, this may account in part for some of the hostility of the institutional Church toward Deryni clergy—for a Deryni confessor's ability to discern precisely what is in the heart of a penitent can make him far more effective in his spiritual counseling than a human priest might be.

On the other hand, what protection has a poor, defenseless human, lured by the supposed confidentiality of the confessional, against the wiles of a Deryni priest who can *force* disclosure of information that the penitent otherwise might keep even from a confessor? The Deryni know better than most that no truly conscientious priest, human *or* Deryni, would ever violate his sacred vows by breaking the seal of the confessional, even under pain of death, but the human-dominated hierarchy of the Church, especially after the Haldane Restoration, has increasing suspicions about the Deryni. After all, Deryni methods of meditation sometimes appear to produce levels of religious fervor and ecstasy not easily accessible to mere humans. Perhaps the Deryni have a closer link with God! And even if they do not, how dare they claim to do so? And do the Deryni religious orders not celebrate the rites of the Church in slightly different ways? Perhaps the Deryni do not even ally with God at all! And these fears do not even begin to address the nonreligious fears that grow in minds poisoned by jealousy and closed by lack of understanding. Healer-priests? They are no better than any other Deryni after all!

## Blocking Deryni Powers:
## A Healing Subspecialty

Before moving on to look at Healer training, we should briefly examine the ability to block Deryni powers. Based on a sample of four individuals able to do this, we may theorize that the blocking ability probably is a subspecialty of the healing gift.

In fact, we should not be surprised that power-blocking turns out to be a subset of healing, for what better tool for a Healer than to be able to remove resistance in a patient too injured or ill to give active consent for treatment? Granted, the ability is even more open to abuse than many other Deryni powers, but that does not detract from its usefulness as a healing tool. Indeed, the very first appearance of this particular gift occurs when Rhys is working in deep trance to heal the injured Gregory of Ebor, perhaps in response to Gregory's earlier bout of powers running amok because of his head injury. This is a spontaneous and initially instinctive defense on Rhys' part against further lapses that might cause Gregory to do real injury to someone next time.

Whatever the catalyst in Rhys, it touches a trigger in Gregory as well, "switching off" his powers. Fortunately, the highly trained Rhys is able to retrace his footsteps and locate where the process had occurred—and reverse it—but this sets the stage for high-level speculation as to the implications, for no one is certain whether Gregory's powers would have returned in time, without Rhys' further intervention.

Nor, despite considerable desire and motivation, is Rhys able to teach this procedure to others, whether Healers or simply other Deryni adepti. He knows where the process takes place in his own mind and can show that location to others, but he does not know *how* he does it. Only by chance does Tavis stumble on the knowledge that the talent even exists, while Rhys is at his mercy, and seek out the ability in himself—to find that he, too, has the gift. Unfortunately, Rhys is killed before he and Tavis together can explore the implications of that discovery, leaving Tavis to make the leaps of self-healing and maturing that will enable him to offer his talent for the use of Rhys' kin who remain.

Finding the next person with the ability is equally fortuitous and haphazard—and finding another is essential if development of the Baptizer cult is to proceed as Rhys had planned. Since only Healers are known thus far to manifest the ability—Rhys and now Tavis—Queron postulates that the next person to be identified probably will be a Healer as well.

And where is the highest concentration of Healers in the Eleven Kingdoms, now that the Healers of Saint Neot's are dispersed? Why, they are among the steady stream of refugees funneling through Gregory's new manor of Trevalga. To enable Tavis to screen them, Queron has Gregory and Jesse devise a procedure for channeling the Healers through the Michaeline stronghold, a few at a time.

So, why was Sylvan O'Sullivan not discovered earlier? After all, he is Gregory's household Healer and battle surgeon. He had been accustomed to working with Rhys in the past, before Rhys discovered how to block. That Rhys was even working on Gregory on the day in question was due to Sylvan's services being required elsewhere. We might expect that his close proximity to those making things happen would have led to him being screened fairly early in the game—except for the fact that less than a month has elapsed since Tavis learned the ability and Rhys died.

In addition, as Gregory's household Healer, we can assume that Sylvan will have continued to have heavy responsibilities within the household, especially with so many refugees filtering through. When Gregory brings him through with Dom Aurelian, in response to Tavis' cry for help, their prompt arrival suggests that Gregory pulled the first two Healers he could lay his hands on and thought about screening them only after they already were there and working on Ansel. Dom Aurelian probably would have been brought in the usual course of things, but Sylvan might have been overlooked for some time simply because he *was* such a familiar and vital fixture at Trevalga.

The discovery of Tieg's ability to block falls into another category altogether. Little Tieg Thuryn, not yet four, is full of surprises. He illustrates very aptly the complications that can arise when Deryni abilities surface at too early an age, before the individual has learned control, judgment, or depth. Fortunately, as we have already established, ethical considerations permit placing binding controls on such a young child to keep him from running amok with his talents before he learns discretion and control; but we can appreciate Evaine's concerns for her son as she considers the implications of a child having this ability. At such a tender age, his healing talents alone have been cause for mixed joy and consternation. His first venture at blocking could have had disastrous effects, had Evaine's fears been realized and the unblocking limited to the one who placed the block.

Tieg's ability, now known, will never be discounted, though, and of all the Deryni remaining in the Michaeline haven, Evaine and perhaps Joram know best how ruthless one sometimes must be in the service of what is perceived as a just cause. She herself has performed ruthless acts in the interests of their greater goals and will do more ruthless things to come. If it was decided that no other way remained but to use Tieg and his blocking talent, then Tieg would be used. The thought is *most* sobering.

But, enough discussion of what essentially is an aberrant talent—for it neutralizes the very powers that enable it to exist. Let us return to Healers and the training thereof.

# CHAPTER SIXTEEN

# The Training of Healers I

Healer training, up to the time of the Haldane Restoration, had become reasonably standardized, while still allowing for differences of philosophical approach within the various schools. Institutions like the Gabrilite *schola* at Saint Neot's dealt a heavy dose of esoteric theory and practice with their Healer training. Varnarite training was more pragmatic and tended to produce highly competent battle surgeons but often shortchanged students in the spiritual aspects of the healing vocation. As Camber-Alister notes (*Camber the Heretic* 428), the Varnarite-trained Tavis would have learned the "standard Healer's approaches" for establishing rapport for the first time but "not the secondaries."

Various smaller, independent *scholae* such as those at Llentieth, Nyford, and the one reported burned near Barwicke, just after Cinhil's funeral, employed their own training systems, though all Healers entitled to wear the green mantle eventually went through an examination process by no less than three established Healers, culminating in a school matriculation and a religious service of consecration and commissioning. Some few Healers did acquire their training by studying with individual master Healers outside the *schola* network, in a classic apprentice bonding, but this was looked upon as a disadvantage if it was the sole source of training.

Gabrilite Healer's training was probably the finest institutional training available. Indeed, so highly valued was the Gabrilite imprint on future Healers that virtually all ecclesiastical Healers and even a vast majority of secular ones spent at least a term or two in residence at Saint Neot's toward the end of their studies, regardless of what particular healing work they intended to pursue after matriculation. The Gabrilites believed in education of the whole Deryni, the spirit as well as mind and body—and not only those Deryni with the healing gift. Though sworn against violence themselves, the Gabrilites nonetheless recognized that warriors in the service of the Light must be equipped to meet violence with violence, if necessary. As a result, ethical training in martial pursuits was part of the curriculum for most young Deryni who came to Saint Neot's, whether or not they were called to a healing vocation, as Camber-Alister observed on his first visit to the Gabrilite abbey.

They moved along the students' cloister walk until they came upon a group of young boys sitting under a tree in the cloister garth, their plain white tunics identifying them as students. A youngish looking man in the habit and braid of a Gabrilite priest was lecturing them softly, though his voice did not carry to where Camber and Emrys paused to watch. Camber wondered whether this was by design.

"These are some of our ten and eleven year olds in general training," Emrys murmured. "They have been here only about four months. Dom Tivar is a weapons master, among other specialties, but so far he has not allowed any of them to even touch a weapon. First they must learn to sense an opponent's moves through their Sight—even a Deryni opponent. But of course, you Michaelines have much the same kind of schooling in this regard."

"Yes, we do."

Even as he replied, the boys were scrambling to their feet at some unknown signal and pairing off to practice, closing their eyes and beginning to move slowly through the routine of a fighting exercise, swaying and dipping and blocking each other's blows with hands and forearms which seemed almost to sense the movements by themselves. Camber had done similar exercises as a young man, and his dual awareness as Camber-Alister could appreciate the training even more than he alone.

"Ah, yes, I remember that one—though we did it a little differently at Cheltham," he added. "Do you remember the bruises, once the exercises were brought up to speed? Or, do Healers receive the same martial training?"

"I did not, but many do." Emrys smiled. "Come and I'll show you some more direct Healer's training, if you'd like. This will be very familiar to Rhys, I'm sure." (*Camber the Heretic* 174)

Camber's reference to Cheltham underlines Alister Cullen's training in the Michaeline warrior tradition—though we should remember that even Michaeline training was not geared solely toward battle. A slight digression is in order here, since much of the training did overlap. We are told little in specific about the nonmilitary aspects of Michaeline training, but we know that the Michaeline school at Saint Liam's Abbey could boast of such luminaries as Father Joram MacRorie and Lord Rhys Thuryn among its former pupils.

We can surmise an active spiritual life as well, both from the general spirituality of particular Michaelines and from specific examples of devotional practice, such as the mention of meditations focused on a flame or the Sword of Saint Michael. In addition, it should be recalled that the Michaeline manner of celebrating Mass within the order was in several ways different from ordinary practice. In particular, King Cinhil Haldane was to discover that Michaelines received communion under both species—a practice normally reserved for clergy only (*Saint Camber* 87). We may infer other differences as well, perhaps perceivable only to Deryni—yet another reason for fear and jealousy to arise among non-Deryni clergy, who worry that Deryni might have a more direct link with God.

Alister Cullen's training, then, probably was *solely* in the Michaeline tradition—unlike Camber's, which came from more eclectic sources. We know, for example, that Camber had felt an early call to the priesthood—an entirely appropriate occupation for the third son of an earl—and attended seminary for several years at Grecotha with the future archbishop Anscom of Trevas. Given the prominence of the MacRorie family as well as Camber's own academic prowess, it is very likely that the

Honorable Lord Camber MacRorie would have become a bishop in due time, had his ecclesiastical career not been cut short. We can speculate that Camber would have entered junior seminary early in 856, before his elder brother died later in that year and moved Camber one place up in the succession, and that his stint at Grecotha ended no later than the end of 862, on the death of his remaining brother. Camber would have been sixteen when he returned to Caerrorie to take up his filial duties—a future priest no more, but heir to the Earl of Culdi.

Somewhere along the way, Camber also would have received intensive training in the use of his Deryni powers, at least some of it before he went off to university and seminary—though certainly his Deryni education would have continued there as well. Similarly, as an earl's son—even though he was not then likely to succeed to the title—the young Camber would have been taught the more practical disciplines of riding, swordsmanship, and basic estate management appropriate to any son of the nobility. Reading and writing would have been mastered at a very early age, and it is likely that the tutors responsible for this part of his education recognized his academic bent from the start and encouraged it—an interest that was to sustain the young Lord Camber even when his religious vocation must be put aside and he must assume his duties as his father's heir.

Perhaps Camber had personal exposure to Michaeline military training after his return to Caerrorie. Certainly his father would have wanted to ensure that the young Camber had the best possible preparation to carry on after him, and the Michaelines were simply the best. In addition, the more worldly Lord Ballard MacRorie was fully aware of the dangers inherent in life at the Festillic court, himself well accustomed to moving in the rarefied atmosphere of Deryni kings and princes. Further, he may have seen Camber's seminary training as too soft, when weighed against the harsher demands of secular life. Michaeline martial and legal training would whip his son into shape—from secular Michaeline Knights rather than clergy.

Whoever had ultimate responsibility for Camber's further education, they apparently dealt very well with Camber's mind, for it must have been during the nine years between his homecoming and the death of his father that Camber gained most of his education in the law. Legal training must have stood him in good stead, because he served two Festillic kings at very high levels—and retained sufficient scruples that he declined to serve a third. If Michaelines were responsible, however, we can gather that Camber absorbed very little of their increasingly activist political ideas.

Despite growing apprehension about Michaeline politics, Camber apparently still thought enough of their education to send Joram and Rhys to the Michaeline-run Saint Liam's Abbey for their primary schooling—and presumably Cathan as well, though we are not told this directly. Nor did he stand in the way when Joram eventually announced his intention to become a Michaeline, even though this remained a source of frequent argument between father and son for some time. It is perhaps one of the more appropriate ironies of Camber's life that, in taking on the identity of Alister Cullen, he was forced to become a Michaeline himself—which led to a hitherto unexpected sympathy with the order and the reasons it had acted as it did in the past. Indeed, without the Order of Saint Michael, even the Haldane Restoration might not have taken place.

However, the Michaelines do not train Healers specifically, though there are Healer members of this essentially martial order, as one might expect. If any one order is primarily responsible for Healer training, it is the Order of Saint Gabriel—though it is clear, from comments of the order's last abbot, Dom Emrys, that the Gabrilites draw their members from many, many traditions. At one point, Emrys discloses that his earliest training was in another tradition than either Gabrilite or Michaeline and that it is sandalwood oil which takes him back in memory to those early days—not the cedar oil familiar to most other orders. Later on, Emrys remarks that he did not receive even the refined sort of martial training usually given Healer candidates at Saint Neot's—one of several indications that yet another tradition exists, even more spiritually oriented than the Gabrilite discipline, in which nonviolence plays an even more important part in the philosophy. (Yet it was Emrys who put an arrow through the heart of an amok Healer novice who had killed a master with magic—of which more later.)

Another specific approach to Healer training is that given by the Varnarite School at Grecotha, though Deryni trained in other disciplines appear to regard Varnarite training as deficient in some areas. Camber, though not himself trained as a Michaeline, can draw heavily on Alister Cullen's memories of Michaeline training after living with those memories for more than twelve years, and he has the rest of his own training to draw upon as well. His first really close contact with Tavis, as Alister Cullen, illustrates one view of Varnarite deficiencies.

"I'm afraid I have you at a slight disadvantage, Tavis. We Michaelines are trained in the old rituals, the formulae for contacts, as are Gabrilites, and we sometimes assume, erroneously, that all others of high training are, too. But your Healer's training wasn't Gabrilite, was it? And it certainly wasn't Michaeline."

Tavis shook his head sheepishly.

"Varnarite?"

"Yes."

"Ah, that explains much. Their approach tends to be more pragmatic than philosophical—an acceptable variation on the art of Healing," he added, at the beginnings of a defensive expression on Tavis' face, "but it often ignores some of the more subtle nuances which would be useful in a situation like this. Let's see, you would have learned the standard Healer's approaches, but not the secondaries. Correct? You see, after many years of working with Rhys, I am somewhat familiar with the terminology." (*Camber the Heretic* 428)

From Tavis' reactions, Camber also deduces that the young Healer has been hurt at some point during his training. One almost gets the impression that training injuries are not that uncommon among the Varnarites. Certainly, in learning any new skill one must expect the odd bump or bruise—Camber-Alister remembers the bruises *he* got, learning fighting movements being demonstrated in the Gabrilite yard—but permanent scarring, whether physical or psychological, ought not to be the norm. When this occurs, provided the student has given an honest effort, the teacher generally has misjudged the student's level of ability. If it happens with any regularity, there may be a problem with the teacher or the method of teaching itself.

Camber makes no outward judgment about such a practice,

for only further positive experience can balance out whatever negative experiences may have marred Tavis' training, but one may gather from the context of this scene that such experiences are not condoned by most other Deryni *scholae*—much as modern educators might scorn the practice of rapping students across the knuckles to make a point or throwing a child into the deep end of a pool to sink or swim.

A similar reasoning lies behind the penance Archbishop Hubert assigns Prince Javan for disobeying him in *The Harrowing of Gwynedd*. Though Hubert promises that Javan will not be scarred, neither will the punishment be a light one, for Hubert intends the lesson of obedience to be learned. The monks administering the penance have many years' experience disciplining young monks and will attempt to gauge their strokes by what they believe Javan should be able to endure without crying out, but if Javan *does* cry out, a stroke will be added for each occurrence, potentially raising the twenty-stroke sentence to forty.

Fortunately, Javan manages to hold his tongue—and is surprised when the monks commend him for bearing his punishment manfully. "I'm surprised you didn't keep on until I *did* cry out," he says. "Wasn't that the whole purpose?"

"Only to a certain point," the man said frankly. "The true purpose was to test your self-control, to bring you right to the brink, but not to break you. The penalty should be sharp enough to hurt a great deal, to the very edge of what one can bear, to impress the seriousness of one's error, but not enough to humiliate or do permanent harm. You'll remember this lesson, I think—and the fact that you tested yourself beyond what you thought your limits were. That builds character rather than tearing it down." (*The Harrowing of Gwynedd* 354)

Learning to gauge the abilities and limitations of the student is one of the marks of the master teacher, then—and in this regard, even Hubert's monks prove themselves most adept. (Indeed, whatever we may think of the man behind them, the thoughtfulness of *these* men in dealing with Javan—their quiet hints on how best to endure what must be faced—gives one hope that perhaps there is still a shred of decency in at least a few of the men recruited for this order founded to destroy Deryni.) The fact remains that the master teacher knows when the student is ready to take the next step and will not assign a task beyond a student's capability. As Tiercel remarks to Conall when asking him to use a Transfer Portal for the first time, "Have I asked you yet to do something you weren't ready to do?" (*The Quest for Saint Camber* 126)

This ongoing evaluation and testing of the student is an important facet of any kind of training, gradually increasing the challenges to strengthen the student's developing abilities. Another purely Deryni application of this principle is connected with the mind-muddling drug called *merasha*—which was *not* discovered by Charissa, as the untrained Morgan believed, but had been developed well before the time of Camber to control Deryni.

We know from various sources that most Deryni fortunate enough to receive formal training will be exposed to the drug in the course of their studies. *Merasha* disruption is not something to which any young Deryni looks forward, but learning to recognize and minimize its effects is a valuable part of Deryni education. We might expect Healer training in this regard to be even more exhaustive than for ordinary Deryni, since Healers may be called upon to administer the drug to others, alone or in combination with other medications, and to deal with the results. We know that Camber's children and Jebediah already were quite familiar with the drug's properties when they agreed to take it during testing of Rhys' power-blocking talent, and that the young Denis Arilan, trying to find a way around the doctored sacramental wine before his ordination, had some prior experience of the drug's effects. And we have seen Kelson's and Dhugal's first exposure to the drug, under very closely supervised circumstances, so that they, too, will be able to minimize the trauma, should they encounter it in the future. We would hope that few Deryni have to discover *merasha*'s effects the way Brion did.

Returning to Healer training, however, as epitomized by the Gabrilites. The *schola* at Saint Neot's takes Deryni of both Healer and non-Healer potential, but concentrates on the former, mostly in a secular capacity. (As has previously been mentioned, religious vocations among Healers are not actively encouraged, for if the best of them eschew marriage and children, the quality of Healers gradually will decline and the lines eventually may fail altogether. Healer-priest candidates undergo an extremely rigorous testing of their vocation, along with the already exacting training of Healer candidates.)

Healer students generally enter at about age twelve, as soon as the potential has begun to manifest, and begin by working through a broadly based curriculum to bring the general Deryni talents to full potential, though some development of the Healer talents also begins. By about age sixteen, emphasis has shifted to primarily Healer-oriented training, with generalized development continuing on a secondary basis.

It is at this time that Healer students from other institutions are permitted to rotate through Gabrilite Healer training for a specified period. We know that Rhys spent some time there. After beginning his schooling with Joram at the Michaeline-run Saint Liam's—remember that he was Camber's ward after the deaths of his parents and probably received some of his basic Deryni training from Camber himself—Rhys went on to Camber's old university at Grecotha, gaining the bulk of his Healer's training at the Healer's Schola there, including the Varnarite School, before spending what would amount to his senior Healer training in residence at Saint Neot's.

We have caught a glimpse of a part of Healer training in *Camber the Heretic*, when Camber, as Alister Cullen, goes to Saint Neot's Abbey for his historic meeting with Dom Emrys and Dom Queron (*Camber the Heretic* 174–175). There we observed an unnamed Gabrilite Healer working with a boy called Simonn, who is learning to control his own body as a preparation for learning to control others'. Let us now expand on that incident and find out a little more about the Gabrilite way of making a Healer.

# ''First Session''

The boy was nervous, as was only to be expected, but oddly graceful for thirteen. The dossier that Dom Emrys had forwarded on the lad when assigning Dom Kilian his crop of new junior novices for the Easter term indicated that the boy had exceptional promise. Dom Kilian sized up his newest charge with something approaching approval as the lad peered hesitantly around the door jamb and then entered, at Kilian's impatient gesture.

"Don't stand there gawking, boy," Kilian muttered, though his faint smile softened what otherwise might be taken as rebuke. "I've never yet bitten the head off one of my students—though if you tell anyone that, I'll thrash you for a liar and a knave. Your junior masters tell me you might have the makings of quite an adequate Healer."

The boy flushed a little at even so restrained a compliment, daring a quick, surreptitious glance around the tiny training room, with its stark cot and the white-robed Gabrilite Healer sitting on a stool at its head. He came dutifully enough to kneel at Kilian's feet and bow his head for the customary blessing given by a master to a new student at their first meeting. In fact, what was about to be asked and given was far more than a blessing, as both Kilian and the boy knew full well.

"My name is Simonn de Beaumont, Domine," the boy said strongly, reciting the words he must have rehearsed many times in preparation for this moment. "I have felt the call to a Healer's vocation and I joyfully obey. I ask that you take me as your pupil to teach me the healing arts, and I promise to be faithful and diligent in my studies. To that end, I submit me to your tutelage and discipline and place myself unreservedly in your hands."

The words were a paraphrase of the simple vows the boy would have given Dom Emrys on entering Saint Neot's as a Healer candidate. Kilian did not remember Simonn's profession specifically, but he was well familiar with the pattern. In return, the abbot would have pledged himself and the order to assist Simonn in any way they could, to develop and refine the healing gifts already identified at the time of the boy's entrance examination. Kilian's personal ratification of that pledge would cement a specific contract between the two of them, to endure throughout Simonn's training, giving Kilian license to pursue whatever means were necessary to bring Simonn to his full potential as a Healer.

The boy did not start or flinch as Kilian's hands came to rest lightly on his head. Nor did he resist as Kilian's psychic probe came easing gently along the link thus formed by their physical contact and quested lightly against his shields. Unexpectedly, those shields rolled back with a smoothness the Healer-priest had not often encountered in one so young, laying bare the boy's most immediate thoughts and memories and promising access to further depths if required—exactly as was intended in a contact of this sort, though the ideal was not often achieved, especially at first.

Pleasantly surprised, Kilian closed his eyes and delved into those further depths of Simonn's mind, finding and binding the control areas customarily given over to a new student's principal teacher. Such a binding had not always been necessary, but it was standard practice now. Everyone at Saint Neot's knew of the tragic Healer's novice Ulric, but a few years older than Kilian himself had been at the time, who had broken under the pressure of his training and turned on *his* mentor. The distraught Ulric, his powers out of control, had killed the novice master in a forbidden Duel Arcane and had injured several masters and even a few students before Dom Emrys' timely arrow put an end to the mayhem and, alas, to the unfortunate Ulric.

Emrys had been but newly elected abbot then, and the incident had touched him and the order in ways that no one present that day would ever forget. The Gabrilites intended to lose no more fledgling Healers as Ulric had been lost—or to force any of their brethren into the unenviable position of having to take a life.

So now Kilian bound the controls that would prevent such a recurrence—less an active interference with the free will of the individual than a safety valve, only rarely needful of being invoked. This reassurance he planted firmly in young Simonn's mind, along with the usual triggers set in all Healer students to facilitate training. He bypassed reading any details about Simonn himself, for he preferred to become acquainted with his students through more conventional methods of interaction.

Finally, to finish the outward form of what had just occurred, he invoked a verbal blessing, using a formula hallowed by many centuries of Gabrilite use.

"The Lord Thy God hath ordained: Thou shalt be a Healer and a soother of the hurts of humankind. He shall give His Angel charge over thee and shalt prosper thee in His service. Be thou blessed in the Name of Him Whom thou shalt serve: Father, Son, and Holy Spirit, Amen.''

As he lifted his hands to trace the sign of blessing over Simonn's bowed head, the boy sketched a quick echo of the movement, then looked up with unbidden tears shining in his brown eyes as he seized Kilian's hand and kissed it.

''Thank you, Domine,'' Simonn whispered. ''I shall try to prove worthy of your teaching.''

''I am confident that your trying shall be adequate to the challenge,'' Kilian replied, keeping a look of bland patience on his face as he gave the boy both his hands and raised him to his feet—for it was not done, to let a student know too soon that he had very much promise. ''Now, suppose we find out just how much you know already. Lie down here and we'll begin. How well have you learned to monitor your own body functions?''

Looking both apprehensive and eager, Simonn sat in the middle of the cot and swung his legs up, lying back with his head toward Kilian's end.

''Dom Alvis was satisfied with my progress, Domine,'' he said, craning his neck to look back at the Healer. ''But I'm not sure how much he expected of a prenovice.''

''Well, you're a junior novice now, and we expect rather more of juniors than we do of prenovices, so I'll direct you,'' Kilian replied, shifting his stool so that he faced the head of the cot more squarely. ''Settle yourself and close your eyes, and we'll start with the basic relaxation exercise that you were taught when you first came here.''

He set his hands on Simonn's shoulders and waited until the boy had obeyed before also closing his eyes. ''That's fine. Now, I shan't do anything at first; I'll only monitor. I want to see what you can do. Take a deep breath and relax as you let it out. That's right.''

As Simonn complied, settling readily into deep relaxation, Kilian nodded slowly to himself and eased his hands from Simonn's shoulders, raising them to either side of the boy's head, close by the temples but not touching.

''Very good. Another deep breath and let it out slowly. And with every breath you take, you become more and more relaxed, more and more centered. Think just in passing about your breathing and let each breath take you deeper . . . and deeper . . . and deeper . . .''

He became aware of someone peering through the latticework of the door—Dom Emrys and several others, Healers but for one—but he did not allow their observation to distract him from his work.

"That's good, Simonn. Relax every muscle. You know how. Very good. Now, center in and let yourself slowly become aware of the blood whispering through your veins. Feel the pulsebeat. Now be aware of your heart pumping that blood. It's beating a little faster than it needs to, but you can slow it if you really want to. Give it a try . . .

"No, you're trying too hard, son. Relax. Don't *make* it happen; *let* it happen. Now take a deep breath and let it all the way out. Again. Now you're getting it. That's right. This is the way every Healer has to start—learning to control his own body before he can control others'. Good. Now let's slip a little deeper and go on to other awarenesses. Deeper . . . deeper . . .''

Lightly he let his fingertips touch the boy's temples, gently questing with his mind for the proper triggers, directing young Simonn's awareness to the center that controlled his heart rate—sending his approval as the boy found the control and made it his own, gradually moderating the rhythm to a slow, steady pace more in keeping with his deep trance state.

"Excellent," Kilian breathed, barely even speaking the word, only dimly aware himself that his unseen watchers had withdrawn and gone on about their own business.

"Now let's turn our attention to your left hand." As he spoke, Kilian quietly slid his own left hand down his subject's shoulder and left arm to circle the boy's bare wrist. "Be aware of my touch at your wrist and think about the blood supply to that area. Know that you can control the flow of blood to that hand—and now exert the force of your mind to restrict that flow."

He began the process himself, but felt his student pick up and echo the response almost immediately, instinctively exerting the proper controls himself. Now truly pleased, Kilian withdrew his own controls and opened his eyes, easing to his feet to stand at Simonn's side, the boy's left hand still lightly clasped at the wrist. Much of the color had gone out of the hand, and now Kilian drew two fingers along the back.

"Well done, Simonn," he murmured. "Now restrict the nerves as well, to block the sensation of pain. You know that the nerves follow the same general paths as the blood vessels. Feel them compressed at the wrist and lose all sensation in this hand."

As he stroked the hand again, helping the boy focus, he reached out another part of his mind to a small shelf at the foot of the cot, calling a razor-keen scalpel to his right hand, though he laid that out of sight at Simonn's side as he bade the boy open his eyes.

"Good. Now, hold what you've done. You've restricted the blood supply to your hand and you've blocked sensation to it. *You've* done this, not I. Examine exactly how it feels now, so that you can do it again at will. Look at it physically, if that will help you hold the images. Have you got it?"

The boy was deep in trance, his eyes only slowly coming to focus as he raised his hand from Kilian's grasp to flex the fingers experimentally before his face. Kilian watched until the blue gaze shuttered briefly before circling the wrist again.

"Do you think you've got it all sorted now?" he prompted, stroking two fingers across fingertips and palm and then across the back again, to reengage his attention.

Dreamily the boy nodded, his hand completely relaxed in Kilian's. "Aye, Domine," he murmured.

"Good," Kilian replied, pinching up a fold of skin on the back of the boy's hand and giving it a sharp tweak. "Feel anything?"

"A—slight feeling of pressure, Domine," the boy said softly. "No pain."

"Do you think you can hold that?"

"Yes, Domine."

"What if I were to do something a bit more painful that would also tax your control of the blood supply?" Kilian insisted, glancing sharply at the boy's eyes as he brought the scalpel into view and set the blade lightly against the fleshy bulge at the base of the thumb. "I won't ask you to heal what I do—I'll do that when we're done—but can you hold the pain and bleeding?"

Simonn blinked rapidly several times and took a deep breath, then let it out with a slow sigh, once more firmly in control.

"I think I can, Domine," he said.

"I *know* you can."

Without further preamble and watching Simonn very closely, though he pretended not to, Kilian jabbed the blade into the flesh to half the depth of his little fingernail. Simonn's gaze flicked away for an instant, just as the scalpel moved, but he neither flinched nor bled.

"Very good," Kilian breathed. "I've seen men many years your senior go absolutely white when I did this. May I take the lesson a little farther, to reinforce? I have no doubt that you can handle it."

Drawing another deep, slow breath, the boy Simonn nodded, watching this time as Kilian drew his blade downward, trebling the length of the original incision. The cut gaped as Kilian withdrew the blade, but it only seeped a little, certainly not bleeding.

"Here, hold this," Kilian said with a smile, putting the scalpel into Simonn's uninjured hand as he prepared to turn his own healing powers to the wound. "Actually, do you want to see what the inside of your hand looks like before I heal it?"

The boy glanced at the incision, suppressed a queasy grimace as he flexed the hand slightly and felt some sensation that made him uncomfortable, then turned his brown eyes on the master Healer in silent plea.

"I—think I'd just as soon you went ahead and healed it now, Domine," he whispered. He was trying not to show his growing uneasiness, but Kilian saw it in the death grip the boy had on the handle of the scalpel, over where he thought the Healer-priest would not notice.

"And so I shall, my son," Kilian murmured, though he could detect no sign of pain in his pupil, even when he brushed the boy's forehead with his free hand. "The wound isn't hurting you, so that can't be what's causing you distress. Can you tell me what it is?"

The boy seemed to draw strength from Kilian's words, but he stiffened and then made a visible effort to settle as the Healer turned the wounded hand upward and pressed at the sides to make the wound open.

"It just—feels odd," Simonn admitted, not letting himself look directly at what Kilian was doing. "I know that a cut like that should be throbbing and bleeding like a stuck pig—but none of that is happening."

"And what *is* happening?" Kilian insisted, reading the edge of Simonn's distress but deciding not to delve deeper.

"I—when you move the wound, so that it gapes," Simonn whispered, "it—feels like a—a mouth, where no mouth should be. I can feel your touch as a—a faint pressure and the coolness of the air in the wound, which should be warm. I can't really explain it very well."

Kilian smiled reassuringly, for he thought that Simonn had explained it very well indeed.

"We'll examine those perceptions in our next session," he promised. "For now, I think it's time to heal this wound. Suppose you release the bleeding just a little now, to make sure it's clean. I'd rather not risk a possible infection in one of my better students."

The oblique compliment had its intended effect. The relieved Simonn was able to release his control of the bleeding and at the same time maintain his control of the pain, not even batting an eye when Kilian thrust a little fingertip gently into one end of the now-blood-filled wound and drew it through, drawing healing with it as the wound closed smoothly and without a mark to show for it. That done, the Healer-priest set his fingertips over the closed wound site for several more seconds, finishing his work carefully so that Simonn should have no vestige of discomfort from what had been done, then withdrew completely, moving unhurriedly to the foot of the cot to wash his hands in the basin set there for that purpose, aware of Simonn's respectful gaze upon him. When he had dried his hands, he returned to wipe off the small amount of blood remaining on Simonn's palm.

"Let's have normal circulation and sensation now," he said quietly, passing his hand across Simonn's before reaching out to brush the boy's forehead in further cue to return to his normal conscious state. "You've done a good morning's work here today. I'm quite satisfied. How does your hand feel?"

Simonn blinked and slowly began to grin, propping himself up on his elbows to survey his left hand with pleased satisfaction.

"It feels perfectly normal. And what I did—it really wasn't that hard. I know I can do it again!"

"And so you shall," Kilian said, briefly clasping the boy's

shoulder in reassurance. "And what's more important, you shall learn to do it for others. But for now, you should go and rest for an hour before the noon meal. This will have taken more out of you than you realize."

"But I'm not tired, Domine—"

"You will go and sleep for an hour," Kilian repeated, guessing that it would not be necessary to reinforce the order by using the controls he had placed earlier. "You are *very* tired, but you will awaken refreshed after an hour's sleep, with good appetite for your noon collation, remembering everything you've learned and eager to progress." He tossed aside his soiled towel and smiled as Simonn yawned, a good-natured look of resignation coming upon the young face.

"That's more like it," Kilian said. "I shall expect you tomorrow morning at the same time."

The above is typical of the sort of training young Healers receive at Saint Neot's, at least in the early stages. It is reasonable to surmise that further training continues to draw on the student's ability to control his own body functions, with gradual expansion of this control to the bodies of others—both of fellow students and, in advanced training, of the masters and brethren themselves. As skills increased, clinical experience would follow, under the supervision of experienced Healers, much as a modern-day medical student or intern would work under the supervision of senior physicians.

More conventional medical training also would be involved, for a Healer's function is not so very different from that of a human physician; the Healer simply has resources not available to his non-Deryni colleagues. The training received by human battle surgeons closely parallels that part of Healer training, so far as it goes, for both human and Healer battle surgeons must learn to deal with sudden trauma, shock, and minor surgical procedures for putting patients back together. (In fact, human physicians of promise sometimes are allowed to study at Saint Neot's, learning what they can.) The human surgeon has a small pharmacopeia from which to draw basic sedatives and painkillers, he learns simple suturing, and he may have knowledge of certain herbs and molds that seem to retard infection and even aid healing. The Healer functions within the same basic parameters, but uses his healing power to close wounds rather than needles and silk sutures. Neither sort of physician has much advantage over the other when dealing with actual diseases, though the Healer may be able to assess his patient's condition and symptoms with greater accuracy.

What *is* important to both sorts of physicians is a knowledge of anatomy. This is particularly crucial to the Healer, since his ability to repair damage with his healing powers pivots on the ability to visualize the body as it ought to be. A certain amount of external knowledge can be gained by studying one's own body and those of one's colleagues, but internal information can be gained only from observation of a body's innards. Some of this can be accomplished by watching master Healers at work, on an as-available basis, but much can be gained only by detailed study and dissection of human cadavers, just as is done in modern medical colleges.

We take this phase of medical training for granted today, but we should remember that even in the last century, dissection of human remains was restricted to the bodies of executed felons. Supply rarely met the demand, nor was the condition of such bodies always of a quality to facilitate much learning by the time they reached the dissection table. Horror tales of grave robbers digging up freshly buried bodies for sale to anatomists and body-snatchers stalking the streets of London in search of fresh cadavers (and sometimes hastening their demise) are not mere products of the writer's craft, but reflected actual practice throughout most of "civilized" Europe.

The reasons for the prohibition of human dissection are several, and hardly credible in light of our present attitudes about the human body, but they were important points of philosophical belief for our forbears and those of the Deryni. Adherents of all sorts of religions in both worlds had quite adamant arguments against such practices.

For if the human body was the temple of the soul, it ought not to be violated after death. This was sacrilege. Furthermore, the Church taught (and still teaches, according to some beliefs) the literal resurrection of the body at the Last Judgment. This also accounts for the prohibition against cremation until quite recently—for how could a body reduced to ashes be reassembled at Judgment Day?

Of course, this argument does not take into account those bodies that never receive burial, through no fault of their own—lost at sea and eaten by fish, or devoured by wild animals, or utterly consumed in fires, or whatever—or even the apparent impossibility of reconstituting a body that has gone through the normal cycle of decay associated with burial, in which even the bones eventually go back to dust and become part of the soil that grows plants that feed animals that are eaten by people who reproduce more of their kind, *undoubtedly* using some of the same atoms and molecules . . . *Reductio ad absurdum*.

On the other hand, if God *can* physically resurrect bodies on the Day of Judgement—and being, by definition, omnipotent, presumably He can, if a totally spiritual Being should choose to resurrect physical bodies for His creatures—then presumably He can find a way to reunite all the specific atoms and molecules of any given individual to accomplish His plan, regardless of the degree of physical destruction.

Is a warrior slain in battle to be denied resurrection because his body has been mangled by enemy weapons, then? What of the victim of mutilation? Surely God will not decline to resurrect such individuals simply because of the damage inflicted on their bodies. Far less would He turn His face from those on whom a respectful dissection is carried out, so that physicians may learn more about the body's structure and healing.

The Gabrilites' attitude reflects this kind of rationale, even if the institutional Church may have frowned upon dissection of the dead. Behind Saint Neot's walls, it became common and relatively open practice to delay the burial of a deceased brother until a senior master could dissect the body for the instruction of selected Healer students. This was looked upon as no sign of disrespect for the dead, but rather a final service that the deceased could perform for his community, in offering his body for the edification of the next generation of Healers.

Our Dom Kilian would have benefitted from such instruction—though one of his earliest exposures to this part of his training was marked by one of the most profound tragedies in the history of Saint Neot's Abbey.

# CHAPTER SEVENTEEN

# The Training of Healers II

## ''The *Examen*''

The mortuary theater was hushed as young Kilian MacShane and another almost latecomer entered and hurried to their places, though there were twice as many students ranged along the tiered seats as Kilian had ever seen at the usual *examen*. The events of the day before had stunned everyone. Now every senior novice who could wheedle a place was present, along with a handful of upper juniors like Kilian and nearly every master Healer in the school.

Expectant silence deepened in the circular chamber as the newcomers settled, abruptly replaced by the shuffle of sandal-shod feet and a faintly audible whisper of white habits and student tunics, the crisper green of lay masters' mantles, as everyone rose for the abbot's arrival. The white-clad Dom Emrys was accompanied by two of his most respected master surgeons, one of them in secular green, but both of the men remained by the doors as the abbot continued into the room.

White drapes covered what lay on two waist-high white table slabs dominating the center of the chamber. Emrys kept his eyes averted as he passed between them, but one pale, colorless hand brushed the edge of one of the drapes where it spilled over the lip of the nearer table and lingered in trembling caress of the polished stone.

No one needed to say in words what lay beneath that drape, least of all Emrys. Less than twenty-four hours ago, the Abbot of Saint Neot's had put a hunting arrow through the heart of the occupant of the table—a deliberate and calculated act on the part of a man who had vowed never to take human life. No one questioned the *necessity* of the killing, or the extenuating circumstances that justified it, for Emrys' victim already had slain the man on the second table and might have taken countless other lives if not stopped quickly, beyond any chance of further mayhem, but that would not relieve Emrys of the burden of reconciling his action with his conscience and his broken vow. Small wonder that Emrys' confessor, the brilliant Dom Queron Kinevan, watched the abbot's every move and expression with such concern, standing among the senior Healers ranged along the topmost tier.

If Emrys was aware of Queron's scrutiny, however, he did not show it. With hands now folded in the sleeves of his immaculate white habit, the abbot mounted the two shallow steps to the lecture dais with his usual serenity and bowed his head, the pale hands shifting to an attitude of prayer, clasped palm to palm before his breast—visual cue for the waiting assemblage to bow their heads as well. After a moment the white-clad shoulders shifted as Emrys drew a slow, deliberate centering breath and let it out.

Then the abbot was lifting his head to thrust joined hands toward heaven, silently invoking the Sacred Presence and entreating blessing as his arms swept gracefully to either side and back to center, gathering the psychic strands of their group attentiveness. Peace washed upward and outward with his gesture, settling like the quiet of a new snowfall as he bowed briefly over folded hands again and then signed himself in more conventional blessing. The soft rustle of others repeating the sacred sign whispered through the chamber and died away as he looked up at them again.

Nothing in his expression or his psychic aura betrayed whatever inner turmoil he must be enduring, about to embark upon the *examen* of the man he had killed. His sparse gesture bade the assemblage take their seats, in another whisper of woolen robes and leather soles. The pale eyes scanned the faces above the robes without emotion, waiting patiently until everyone had settled and silence once more filled the theater.

"Anyone expecting dramatic disclosures this morning will be well advised to return to his cell to meditate instead," Emrys said quietly without preamble. "I will tell you only that Death Readings were carried out on both our late lamented brethren last night, as our statutes require, and I am satisfied with the results. In the matter of our dear brother, Dom Calvagh, I wish to assure you that he died in a state of grace. Nor ought any blame be attached to him for any part of yesterday's proceedings, lamentable though they may have been.

"In the matter of Brother Ulric—" Here Emrys' voice faltered just a little, and he had to take a deep breath before continuing. "Regarding our dear son in Christ, it is my fervent prayer that he, too, died in a state of grace, though temporarily without control of all his faculties. The full reasons for this lapse are being investigated, and appropriate remedial action will be taken."

As Emrys signaled the two surgeons to join him, Kilian realized that there was going to be no further explanation of what had happened.

"Accordingly, we will now proceed with the final *examen* of our departed brethren," Emrys went on, his voice resuming its accustomed briskness. "This evening, following a solemn Requiem Mass, their mortal remains will be consigned to a hallowed resting place, as is our custom. For this morning, Dom Turstane has the rota for those who have been selected to assist Lord Dov and Dom Juris. If your name is called, please come down to the floor for specific assignments. If your name is not called, please remain where you are until we can determine how many closer places have become available."

To Kilian's surprise, he heard his own name called among the four assigned to assist Lord Dov—though it was only to hold a tray of instruments. An upper senior named Thomann would provide any real assistance Lord Dov might require. Still, Kilian had not expected to be named at all. He had been on the floor twice before, but only to conjure and control handfire to light the working field—the traditional first assignment for lower juniors finally allowed participation in an *examen*. Holding instruments usually was a senior prerogative. It entitled Kilian to stand directly at the master's elbow, giving one of the best possible views of what went on.

Pleased, Kilian collected his instruments and fell in at Dov's side, though his stomach did a queasy little flip-flop, quickly suppressed, when he realized that Dov was leading his assigned team toward the table on which Ulric's body lay—Ulric, who had been a classmate, albeit several years Kilian's senior.

*I will not disgrace myself,* he told himself. *I will remain detached. I will not disgrace my masters.*

"I shall place only one restriction on this *examen,*" Dom Emrys said in a low voice, startling Kilian by his sudden appearance at the head of the white-draped table. "I myself shall be assisting Lord Dov and I alone will touch the subject's head. The reason for this, in case some of our less experienced brethren have not deduced it for themselves, is that Death Readings among our order are taken under the Seal of the Confessional. Residuals invariably linger. Given the—unfortunate circumstances of our dear Brother Ulric's passing, outside apprehension of these particular residuals would be singularly inappropriate. Lord Dov, you may begin."

With a little bow in Emrys' direction, the dark-haired Dov motioned for the assisting Thomann to help him fold back the drape covering the body, exposing it to the waist. The other senior novice suppressed a little shudder as he glimpsed the face of his slain classmate. He and Ulric had been close. The other junior went very pale and swallowed noisily.

Kilian himself gave a little start at seeing the stump of Emrys' arrow still protruding from Ulric's motionless chest—a far more poignant reminder of what had happened than the unmarked body of Dom Calvagh, being similarly exposed by Dom Juris and Dom Turstane on the table behind them. For Calvagh had been blasted by magic—no less fatal a weapon than the arrow that had claimed Ulric's life, but the more insidious for leaving little physical evidence. With no outward trauma to investigate, Dom Juris had already begun opening Calvagh's chest, gesturing for his two junior assistants to conjure handfire and bring it nearer.

"To begin this *examen,* I have chosen to focus on the death wound," Lord Dov was saying, falling into a familiar lecture mode as he fingered the stump of the arrow and scanned the observers in the tiered galleries. "I shall use it to demonstrate how a similar wound might be dealt with in a living patient. The battle application of such a procedure should be obvious, though I will grant before starting that this particular wound would have been almost instantly fatal, no matter if a skilled *team* of battle surgeons had been able to attempt treatment immediately—as, in fact, was the case, but sadly, to no avail. After we open the chest, we will study the extent of internal damage and physically confirm—as was already learned from Healer's Reading yesterday—that the arrow pierced the heart and partially severed the great vessel called the aorta—damage far beyond our skills.

"Now, for the battle application." From the tray Kilian held, Dov picked up an intact hunting arrow and displayed it for all to see. "This arrow has a head identical to the one we are about to remove. It carries a flat, broad-headed hunting barb that is very similar to the usual war arrow you're likely to encounter in the field. Because of the backswept barbs, neither sort can be withdrawn without significant additional trauma to the patient." He demonstrated by pulling at the arrow in the circle of his closed fist.

"In fact, if the wound is embedded in a fleshy part of the body—an arm or a leg, something not life-threatening in itself—you may be ahead, in some instances, to guide the arrowhead out the other side, going *with* the direction of the barbs instead of against them." After illustrating *this* procedure with the arrow and his fist, he replaced the arrow on Kilian's tray and surveyed his enthralled audience again.

"Unfortunately, the through-and-through technique is not suitable for most body wounds, for obvious reasons—and since the trunk presents a much larger target than an arm or a leg, you can guess how the battle statistics are going to fall. This means cutting out most arrowheads—one hopes with as little additional trauma to your patient as possible.

"This morning, therefore, I should like to demonstrate the standard field procedure for surgical removal. For purposes of the demonstration, we shall assume that the location is *not* fatal—or at least not *immediately* fatal—and that you've already put your patient to sleep, blocked his pain, and are competent to continue monitoring for shock, which is the most immediate danger in an injury such as this. If you're quick and lucky, sometimes you'll even manage to mend a potentially fatal wound before your patient expires. Handfire, please."

At the command, the junior and senior assigned to that task conjured two spheres of softly glowing white light, sending them to hover above and to either side of the arrow stump, but not in Dov's way. Nodding his approval, the master surgeon selected a scalpel from the tray Kilian was holding and used it to extend the lower edge of the entry wound by a finger's breadth, deftly thrusting his left forefinger close along the path of the arrow shaft while his right hand tested at the stump.

"Now, to give myself more room to work, notice how I've made a small incision to slightly enlarge the opening," Dov continued, his eyes going a little out of focus as he relied on touch and his Deryni senses to probe into the wound. "The object here is to ease one finger along the arrow shaft until I can locate the barbs—which may necessitate just a little more room." The scalpel flashed again as he extended his original incision by half. "That's better. Are there any questions, to this point?"

"Enlarging the wound, master," one junior novice called from the middle tier. "Isn't that dangerous?"

"Yes and no," Dov replied, thrusting deeper with his finger as he continued to probe. "It does mean you'll have more to heal. But not getting at the barbs is far more dangerous—and healing a cut is far easier than healing a tear, if you try to force things. Incidentally, keep in mind that a living patient would be bleeding all over what you're trying to do, so you won't be able to depend much on physical sight. That isn't much of a factor in an *examen*, since we drain the blood beforehand, but—a-ha! There's one corner of the barb—and the other one."

After dropping his scalpel on Kilian's tray, Dov exchanged it for a blunt, flattish probe, using it and his finger like retractors as he began easing the arrow out of the wound.

"I'm handling this as if the situation *is* life-threatening, where speed is important," Dov explained, still not really looking at what he was doing. "If you have the luxury of time, there are special, grooved instruments that can help you shield the barbs while you back the arrowhead out, but you must know how to do without. As it is, these particular barbs are rather deeply embedded. I'm having to shift my fingertip from one side to the other as I ease them free, relying as much on physical dexterity as I am on my ability to assess the damage with my Sight—hardly much advantage over a human battle surgeon in this case, I'm afraid. There.'' He permitted himself a faint grimace of satisfaction as the barbed arrowhead came free—though he left his forefinger deep in the wound. ''A nasty item, as you can see.''

He exhibited the barbed arrowhead on its broken stump for their inspection, then passed it to Dom Emrys with a glance that betokened something more than mere wood and metal passing between them. Emrys stared at the bloody implement in numb fascination, then clenched it in his fist and bowed his head over it briefly.

''Meanwhile,'' Dov went on, not missing a beat as he circled the wound in the angle of his right hand, ''as I've been physically manipulating the arrow out of the wound and using my Sight to guide me, I've also been monitoring my patient's condition and preparing to Heal. If I'm good enough, I may even have begun sealing off bleeders and making preliminary repairs as my finger went into the wound. And I can certainly leave healing in my wake as I slowly draw my finger out of the wound and have it close behind me—at least in a living patient.''

He had suited action to his words as he spoke, smoothly withdrawing his finger from the now-empty wound, but it remained a dark, teardrop-shaped hole—for even a Healer's power could have little effect on flesh from which the life force had faded and certainly not after so long a period as a day. His finger was lightly stained, but the color was like the pale brownish red of a butcher's hands after cutting meat, not the bright gore of the surgeon's hands.

All at once Kilian found himself wondering quite clinically what happened to the blood that was drained from the bodies of the dead. He had known it was done, but he had never really thought about it before. Why, there must have been bucketfuls from yesterday alone! Where did it all go?

He was suddenly horrified to find Dov looking at him thoughtfully as he put his probe back on the tray, apparently catching the question. He was even more horrified when Dom Emrys cleared his throat and spoke to the question instead, laying aside the bloodstained arrowhead and gently drawing a clean towel over Ulric's face.

''It occurs to me,'' Emrys said softly, ''that a few among you may not be aware of what happens to the blood of our beloved dead when they are being prepared for *examen* and burial.'' Instantly, every eye was on the abbot, causing Kilian to suspect that he had not been the only one to wonder.

"I know," Emrys said, raising one white eyebrow. "Most of us have heard the assertion at some point in our lives, usually offered in sniggering taunt but unfortunately believed by some, that we Deryni require blood in our magical workings. We also are alleged to kidnap and sacrifice young children for our nefarious purposes—or so the Willimites and other enemies of our race would have it.

"Ridiculous, of course, but some humans are willing to believe anything about those they do not understand and therefore fear. And because we are an order that guards certain mysteries particularly pertinent to those of our blood, and possibly not even fathomable by those who are of our blood but not of our order, we are seen as hiding something. By their reasoning, hiding something means that it must be wrong.

"Add to this the fact that there are those outside these walls who regard any tampering with the bodies of the dead as sacrilegious, who would begrudge the final bequest that every Gabrilite in residence at the time of his death makes to this Order— the bequest that makes an *examen* like this possible, so that future Healers may learn.

"We do not believe it sacrilege, of course. While we reverence the body as the temple of the spirit during life, we reverence more the soul and intelligence that once inhabited that body. And if that body can provide some lasting instruction to those who remain after the soul has departed, to the greater glory of God and the healing ease of His creatures, what finer memorial to the soul that occupied it?

"As for why we drain the blood at all," Emrys went on, almost as an afterthought, "this is a matter of expediency, both to retard decay and to provide a bloodless field in which to demonstrate anatomical structures. In thanksgiving for the life lived, we return the blood to the earth, as ultimately would occur if the bodies themselves were buried in the earth—though they are not, at Saint Neot's, as those of you familiar with our crypts and catacombs can attest. In a consecrated chapel deep within those catacombs, there is a special drain set aside for this purpose, cut into the living rock, very much like the *piscinae* used for cleansing the holy vessels in the sanctuary. As the body also is a holy vessel, we feel it appropriate that the blood once contained by that vessel should be returned to the earth in this fashion."

The explanation reassured Kilian greatly—not that he had *really* suspected any nefarious purpose behind the custom—and it apparently relieved a number of observers as well. Some of the others were *not* relieved when Lord Dov casually selected a short, sharp blade from Kilian's tray and, without any preliminary warning, began blithely opening the dead Ulric's chest from throat to navel, about a handspan left of center.

Kilian forced himself to stay detached from this part of the procedure, keeping his attention firmly on the tray he held until the surgical field looked less like a human being. He had seen a chest opened before, but never on someone his own age, whom he had known. It helped that Dom Emrys had covered the face before Dov began, but the junior novice charged with maintaining handfire got very pale, and his senior partner earned a sharp glance from Dov when faltering concentration made the handfire flicker. The novice Thomann remained cool and unflappable throughout, even when called upon to suction out blood that had pooled in the chest cavity.

"I should like to draw your attention to the heart now," Dov said when the organ had been exposed. "After we've concluded this part of our discussion, you'll all have a chance to come down for a closer look."

Work stopped on the adjoining table as Turstane and Juris came to look on, bringing their assistants with them, and the observers in the galleries sat forward a little on their benches.

"Unfortunately, I've added to the damage considerably in removing the arrowhead, so you'll want to have a look at the other specimen as well," Dov went on, easing one hand under the heart to lift it slightly so he could pass a probe through the entrance and exit wounds. "Here is the path of the arrowhead through the heart, and beyond you can see the damage to the aorta as well—all but severed, as our preliminary readings indicated, and which accounts for the large amount of blood we found in the thoracic cavity.

"The single most important point about this particular wound is that it cut off the blood supply to the brain and caused virtually instantaneous unconsciousness,'' Dov said, metal chiming against stone as he tossed his probe onto the marble slab beside the body and boldly lifted his eyes to scan the galleries. "Without wasting time that might have seen additional mayhem and death done, it bypassed the uncertainty of trying to deal with psychic powers gone amok by rendering the subject instantly incapable of further lethal action. That death followed within seconds was an unfortunate side effect of stopping the mayhem. He did not suffer,'' he added in a slightly lower tone, looking deliberately at Dom Emrys, who stood with his own head bowed, clutching the table edges to either side of the dead Ulric's head, one thumb locked over the broken stump of arrow and barb that had killed the boy.

No Gabrilite would have dared to say what Dov had said—not with the man who had done the deed standing over the boy's now-mutilated body, the killing implement at hand, obviously guilt wracked that he had violated his vows by taking a life, even if the taking of that life *had* safeguarded precious other lives. However, Lord Dov was not a Gabrilite but a secular Healer, though Gabrilite trained, attached to Saint Neot's teaching faculty by different loyalties than the brethren under vowed obedience to their abbot. Under the master surgeon's steady if faintly challenging gaze, Emrys slowly raised his eyes. Kilian, still standing at Dov's elbow, could feel the energy surging between the two men, but could not seem to make his feet take even one step back to move out of range.

"I know he did not suffer,'' Emrys said softly, as if he and Dov and the dead Ulric were the only ones in the chamber. "I knew, when I loosed the shaft, that he would not. I also knew—with my mind—that killing him then and there, as quickly and as cleanly as I could, even in violation of my vows, was infinitely better than allowing him the chance to destroy even one more precious Healer.''

A faint shudder went through his shoulders as he glanced down at the ruined heart by Dov's bloodstained hands and then let his gaze focus on something else that only he could see.

"I knew it with my mind, Dov,'' Emrys whispered. "I know it now. But my heart mourns the stark necessity, dear friend. Oh, how it mourns. You must give me time to heal *my* heart, no less sundered than the one whose physical wounds you have pointed out so ably.''

With that he closed his eyes tightly and choked back a silent sob, swaying a little on his feet, so that Dov instinctively reached out one bloody hand to steady him, heedless of the russet smear he left on the snow-white habit. But before anyone else dared to intervene, Emrys drew a deep breath and squared his shoulders, declining further assistance with a faint grimace and a shake of his silver-white head, lifting his eyes unflinchingly to meet Dov's.

"Thank you, Dov," he murmured. "I'll be fine—now. But I think we should continue with the *examen*, don't you?—and you as well, Turstane, Juris." In an act of personal courage such as Kilian had never seen, the abbot lifted his gaze to the awestruck assemblage as well. "We have young Healers who must learn from their elders—and elders who have already learned from their juniors."

Almost magically, Dom Emrys' words seemed to return the mortuary theater to its usual atmosphere of relaxed but respectful attentiveness. After Dov had dissected out the lungs and given a short discourse on function and general anatomy, Emrys himself traced out such thoracic circulation as had been exposed and spoke to the general topic of the body's circulatory system, grilling his rapt listeners at the dissection table and in the galleries with customary thoroughness before deferring to Dom Turstane for a discussion of the digestive organs.

While Turstane lectured, illustrating on the structures already exposed in the *examen* of Dom Calvagh, Dov proceeded with the formal *examen* on Ulric. Kilian had his moments of personal difficulty, whenever he let himself think too much about the face underneath the towel at the head of the table, but mostly he let himself become engrossed with serving the surgeon Dov and observing all he could. Gradually he found he could distance himself from the physical identity of the body before him, so that eventually even the spectacle of Ulric's internal organs fanned out across the open body cavity conveyed an awe-ful beauty rather than any revulsion, each structure exquisite in the stark artistry of its former function. *This* was what healing was all about and what Kilian and every other man in the chamber had pledged himself to serve.

When all the trunk dissections had been completed by the master surgeons, and the observers up in the tiered galleries had been given opportunity to file past and study the work, new teams of senior novices were rotated in to dissect the limbs.

Under close supervision, the student surgeons laid bare the basic structures of musculature, major blood vessels, and nerves, with accompanying commentary by Emrys and Juris. Though custom generally included head and neck dissections, the faces of Calvagh and Ulric remained covered, and no one questioned the omission. The afternoon was devoted to more academic review of the morning's work, with some of the senior masters bringing in twos and threes of younger students to view the final result.

Finally, when all had been learned that reasonably might be expected, all the extra students and even masters were given leave to depart, that final preparations for interment might be carried out. Kilian found himself drafted with Thomann to fetch basins of warm water and towels and baskets of bandage rolls for Dov, as the senior surgeon and Emrys set about the business of restoring Ulric's body to a seemly appearance for the Requiem to follow. Juris and Turstane ministered to Dom Calvagh's body, assisted by two more novices retained for the purpose. The reverent silence of the four senior Healers was an all but tangible thing, conveying a tenderness so poignant that Kilian almost felt he was intruding by his mere presence, even though he had been asked to stay.

Gently the bodies were reassembled as well as could be done, the blood washed away, the internal organs set back in place, the chests and abdomens firmly bound with turns of clean white bandage. The limbs received a similar swathing, until only the heads were still exposed.

When that was done, what remained of Brother Ulric was dressed in the full white habit of a Gabrilite, even though Ulric had never taken his final vows in life, denied only the Gabrilite Healer's badge of the green hand pierced by a white eight-pointed star that graced Calvagh's habit.

Healer Ulric had been, however, if never consecrated so, and they spread a Healer's mantle of deep, forest green in his coffin before gently laying him upon it, lovingly drawing the fine wool around his shoulders so that the more commonly known badge of a Healer was exposed—the white hand pierced in the palm by a green eight-pointed star, the reverse of the Gabrilite badge. It was Ulric's right, for he *had* been a Healer—and one of great promise . . .

# CHAPTER EIGHTEEN

# Dark Magic

Humans who do not know better tend to believe that all Deryni magic is Dark, its power coming from satanic sources, its motivation from diabolical persuasions. Those with firsthand knowledge and experience of magic, whether human or Deryni, know that this is not the case—that power derived from magic is no more good or evil than power from any other source; that it is the use of power that determines its place in the moral hierarchy. As Morgan explains to Dhugal:

"Magic simply has to do with harnessing power which is not accessible to most people. The power itself— Let me try to put it to you another way. Power exists. Correct?"

"Of course."

"I think you'll even grant me that many *kinds* of power exist—that power can come from many sources. Yes?"

Dhugal nodded.

"Good. Let's take fire as just one example of power, then," Morgan went on, rubbing his hands together briskly and holding them toward the cold hearth as he glanced back at Dhugal. "Fire can be used for many beneficial purposes. It can give us light, like those torches on the walls," he gestured vaguely with his chin, "and it can warm a room."

A mental nudge sent flames springing up bright from the kindling already laid, and Dhugal scrambled to a sitting position to stare.

"How did you do that?"

"I think it's sufficient for now to acknowledge that I did it," Morgan replied, "and that providing light or heating a cold room are good things. But fire can also be destructive when turned to evil use. It can burn down a house—or heat hot irons to take a man's sight. . . . Does that make the fire good or evil?

"It isn't either," Dhugal replied carefully. "It's how the fire's used. The same hot iron that cost your friend his sight also could have been used to cauterize a wound."

Morgan nodded, pleased. "So it could. And what does that tell you about power in general?"

"That it isn't the power—it's how the power's *used* that makes it *con*structive or *de*structive." Dhugal paused for an instant. "Are you saying that magic is the same?"

"Precisely the same."

"But the priests say—"

"The priests say what they have been told to say for the last two hundred years," Morgan returned briskly. "Deryni have not always been persecuted, and not all 'magic' has been anathema until fairly recently. *Black* magic—extraordinary power applied to destructive or selfish ends—has always been condemned by the righteous. But those who could harness extraordinary power for the aid of man—for healing and defending against the abuse of power—traditionally have been called miracle workers and saints. They were also once called Deryni."

"But there *were* evil Deryni!" Dhugal objected. "And there still are. What about Charissa and Wencit?"

"They were Deryni who used their gifts for evil. The gifts themselves . . ." Morgan sighed. "Do you think I'm an evil person?"

Dhugal's face went very still. "No. But they say—"

"They *say* *what*, Dhugal?" Morgan whispered. "And who are *they*? And do *they* ever give an accounting of what I've *done*, or is it all because of what I *am*?" (*The Bishop's Heir* 247–249)

It seems clear, then, that motivation and the *use* of power are what determine the morality of such use. Still, spells there are that even the Deryni are not sure about. We have already mentioned Joram's uneasiness over the subject of shape-changing, because it entails deception. Far more questionable, however, are the truly dark spells.

## Binding Souls

When Deryni speak of souls being bound, they are not referring to the classic selling of one's soul to the Devil in exchange for worldly gain. Binding souls has to do with preventing the departure of a soul from its dead body, blocking its passage into the escort of the astral Forces that will convey it beyond the Gates of Death to the Nether Shore, ultimately to stand before the Sacred Presence.

We are not told how someone *does* this, but we see several instances of Deryni perceiving that it has been done and taking steps to reverse it. Duncan recognizes "a definite impression of evil" when he inspects the shape-changed body of King Brion. His experience reversing the spell tends to confirm at least negative intent, even if the spell itself might not be evil per se.

Duncan took a deep breath, exhaled slowly, then gingerly placed his hands on the forehead of the corpse. After a few seconds, his eyes closed and his breathing became more shallow, strangely harsh in the gloom. . . .

Duncan's breathing was even faster now, and droplets of cold sweat dotted his brow and the backs of his hands, even in the icy cold of the crypt. As the boy and Morgan watched, the features of the body beneath Duncan's hands began to waver, flicker, blur before their eyes. Duncan finally gasped and stiffened slightly, and in the same instant, the features of the corpse stabilized into Brion's familiar face. Abruptly, Duncan removed his hands and staggered back from the casket, his face drawn and pale.

"Are you all right?" Morgan asked, reaching across the coffin to steady his kinsman.

Duncan nodded weakly and forced his breathing to regularize. "It was—bad, Alaric," the priest murmured. "He—wasn't entirely free, and the bond was powerful. As I released

him, I felt him die. It was—unspeakable." (*Deryni Rising*
154)

Duncan's reaction and comments might lead us to wonder
whether being bound may be not merely a passive state of limbo
but a more exacting level of awareness wherein the victim is
compelled constantly to relive his or her death, over and over
again, until the binding is released and the endless loop of recall
is severed. It is a fate the vengeful Charissa might have wished
upon her mortal enemy, who slew her father to retain the throne
that should, by rights, have been his and then hers. In fact, given
the thoroughness of Charissa's planning, it is altogether possible
that some preliminary binding was on Brion from the moment
he drank her potion, subtle and insidious, enabling her to stop
the functioning of his physical body but leaving intact, at least
for the moment, some lingering vestige of spiritual and/or psychic life.

In this sense perhaps Brion was not truly dead at all when he
seemed to expire in his son's arms on the field of Candor Rhea.
Perhaps at that time he only lay suspended between life and
death, perhaps even vaguely aware of what was going on around
him as his loved ones prepared his funeral obsequies—aware,
but helpless to make his plight known.

Duncan might have recognized what was happening, had he
been permitted access to the body, but Jehana forbade it because
of Duncan's associations with the hated Morgan. She did permit
the court physicians to examine her husband's body, but they
merely reiterated the original diagnosis of heart failure—which,
as Nigel points out, *is* the ultimate cause of all deaths. Given
the haste with which Brion was buried, as well as the prevalent
attitude toward any potential desecration of a dead body, we
may assume that his body probably was neither embalmed nor
autopsied—a definite reassurance, since we do not know how
much sensory input might remain to a victim in such a state.

So Brion might have remained for several days—trapped im-
mobile in a body that would never live again, deaf and blind,
but aware at some deep level—until Charissa herself came to
visit him in the night, perhaps while his body still lay in state
before the High Altar of Rhemuth Cathedral, there to fray the

silver cord beyond any hope of rejoining properly, forever bar-ring his return—but not enough to let him escape into death.

And then, after Brion's interment in the royal crypt beneath the cathedral—of which he might have been aware, at some level, as the lid of the sarcophagus closed over him in smoth-ering darkness—there would have been another visit from Char-issa, to alter his physical form as well, so that even when the one person returned to Rhemuth who might have the nerve to investigate and find out what had really happened, it would be too late.

A horrific scenario and, alas, quite in keeping with what little we know of Charissa. It also coincides with what Evaine fears about *her* father, as she and Joram debate whether he could have managed to work the infamous Suspension Spell. (For that mat-ter, was Charissa far more adept than we have even considered? Could *she* have known how to work the Suspension Spell and used that to hold Brion's body until she could sever and bind his soul? If so, she was not constrained by the scruples that ham-pered Camber, as he agonized over whether he should use the spell on the dying Rhys and whether he had the right to make such a decision for another soul. The ramifications of this spell extend to many different levels and contribute to the many reasons it has also been called the Forbidden Spell.)

In any case, Evaine and Joram are well aware of the impli-cations if Camber's spell *has* worked and he merely lies sus-pended, not dead—and if he should come out of it spontaneously. Says Joram:

> "I can't imagine anything much more terrifying than re-gaining consciousness in a tomb and realizing you'd been buried alive."
>
> "I can," Evaine murmured, not looking at him. "Being bound to a body that really, truly, *is* dead—decaying." (*The Harrowing of Gwynedd* 5)

If this *was* a factor in Brion's binding, presumably it has not yet become a factor in the only other case we see of soul binding, for Camber and Joram find the dead Alister Cullen within an hour of his death at Ariella's hands. Still, the binding *is* treacherous. A chill sweeps through Camber as he kneels by the slain Alister and lays his hands on the dead man's forehead.

> Cursed be whoever had done this, for Cullen both was and was not dead! His body had been slain, but some essence of his being remained—isolated from his body beyond all reunion, yet caught still in some vicious bond which had endured even beyond the death of his assailant. There could be no return of that essence to its body in this life, for the silver cord had been severed, the bond of soul and body broken. The body was already past all animation, the vaults of memory fading with the body's warmth. (*Saint Camber* 108–109)

Unlike Brion's case, we are not left with the impression that Cullen continues to suffer. We sense none of the urgency to release him that Morgan and Duncan felt about Brion. Though obviously deeply troubled by what he discovers there in the clearing at Iomaire, Camber takes the time to investigate the cause of Ariella's death, to enlist his son's aid in what he decides to do, and to assimilate Cullen's memories for later integration before tackling what must done to free Cullen entirely.

> . . . He quested outward one more time, this time to touch those other bonds—grim, slimy chains—which lingered, part of Ariella. Those he loosed with the strength of his affection, as he had loosed others before—vestiges of arcane battle, which did not always kill cleanly, as Joram had pointed out. The very air seemed to lighten around him as the last of the spell was neutralized, and he bade a final farewell to Cullen: former adversary, fellow conspirator, intellectual sparring partner, friend, brother. He opened his eyes to find Joram staring at him.
> "Is he . . . ?"
> "He's at peace now," Camber said gently. (*Saint Camber* 116–117)

Cullen's condition was inexorably bound up with Ariella's, though—and Ariella died by as convoluted an application of Deryni power as did Cullen. "We Deryni do not always slay cleanly," Joram tells his father. "[Cullen] and Ariella fought to the death—and Ariella fought even beyond.'' (*Saint Camber* 109)

Earlier we saw what Cullen actually did—willing all his remaining strength into his consecrated sword with one last, desperate prayer before flinging it point-first at Ariella. We do not know, at the time, whether Cullen succeeded, or whether he stayed conscious long enough to know. We see the eventual outcome through Camber's almost clinical appraisal.

Ariella lay slumped against a tree, her slender form transfixed by a sword, its cross-hilt swaying slightly in the breeze of his arrival. As he knelt in disbelief, drawing more handfire into being, he could see that the sword was Cullen's Michaeline blade, sacred symbols engraved on the steel, its pommel twisted and charred by a force which had all but destroyed it.

He blessed himself—not at all an empty gesture, in light of what had happened here—then turned his attention to the woman. . . . At first he thought she had only tried to escape the pinning blade—the dead fingers were near the steel, and she would have struggled long before she died, with vitals thus pierced.

But then he looked more closely at her hands and knew that they were not on the blade at all, sensed instantly what she had tried to do. The now-dead hands were still cupped together on her breast, the fingers still curved in the attitude of a spell believed by most to be impossible, merest legend. . . .

He took a deep breath and ran his hands lightly above her body, not touching it as he extended his senses, but then he breathed a sigh. Here was no arcane binding of life to ruined body. The life-suspending spell on which she had spent her dying energy had not worked. Power and life were gone. Ariella, unlike Cullen, was truly dead. (*Saint Camber* 110)

## Sword Spells

What has killed Ariella, in the end, is the spell-powered blade that Alister Cullen threw at her with his dying energy. It may be a peculiarly Michaeline spell, because Jebediah uses a similar one involving a sword years later. Camber knows how to neutralize the residuals, though. Insulating his hand with a fold of

cloak wrapped several times around, he pulls the sword out of
Ariella's body.

> The weapon throbbed as he touched it, even through the
> layers of wool between his hand and the hilt, and it sang with
> a deep, thrumming note as he pulled it free.
> A low-voiced phrase, a stilling of all fear, and then he
> touched the sacred blade to his lips in salute. At once it was
> only a ruined sword. (*Saint Camber* 110–111)

Years later, as Camber and Jebediah fight their last battle,
both men use sword spells. Duplicating the real Alister Cullen's
last spell, Camber-Alister focuses all his remaining energy into
the sword that he hurls left-handed at his target, transfixing the
man and killing him instantly, with a burst of charring energy
as well as the physical wound. The sword's condition afterward,
with hilt blackened and twisted, is very similar to that of Cullen's sword at Iomaire.

Jebediah, on the other hand, employs a variation that he later
confesses is "grey around the edges." He does not throw his
sword but instead apparently launches a bolt of energy along the
blade. The clearing seems to erupt with light and a soundless
and unexpected shock that almost jolts Camber to his knees.
When the afterimage of the flash has faded sufficiently for Camber to see again, Jebediah is "slowly curling into a ball, an oddly
luminous sword sinking to the snow in his bloody fist" (*Camber
the Heretic* 476). The eyes of Jebediah's victim are "open and
staring, the face frozen in an expression of surprise and terror,"
and as Camber reaches out with his senses to investigate, he
feels "a residue of darkling magic" and suddenly knows its
source. As he scrambles toward the feebly moving Jebediah, he
sees the sword lying at the grand master's side in a blade-shaped
depression filled with melted snow and knows that if he touches
it, the blade will still be warm.

> "Good God, man, what did you do?" he whispered.
> Jebediah breathed in sharply through his teeth and rallied
> enough to look up at Camber with a tight little smile.
> "Don't tell me I've managed to come up with a magical
> application you don't know about," he murmured. "I'm afraid

it was a little grey around the edges, but your friend might have gotten you, otherwise.''

"A little grey? *What did you do?*"

"Just a little energy diversion. Never you mind." (*Camber the Heretic* 477)

"A little energy diversion," Jebediah calls it. But apparently he feels that this particular energy diversion might have offended Camber's moral scruples. Or perhaps it is Alister he is thinking of as his life slowly stains the snow, dying in the arms of the one who looks like his old friend—Alister, whose scruples might well have been offended by the use of what Camber probably would only call "expedient" magic. In this particular case, we may never know.

## The Forbidden Spell

We have already mentioned the so-called Forbidden Spell in passing—"a spell believed by most to be but merest legend." It is a spell to suspend life and keep it linked to the body. We have already speculated upon how it might be abused.

It is a spell that continues to haunt Camber, once he has seen evidence that Ariella actually tried to work it. By the time of "his" funeral, he thinks he knows why her last spell failed. We know that he continued to research the spell in the years to follow, scouring ancient records in the Grecotha collection, for by the time Rhys lies dying in his arms, he has puzzled it out, and the temptation to use the spell is very strong.

For a moment, hope flared. He knew why Ariella had failed, at least in theory. As surely as he now despaired for Rhys's life, he *knew*. Had Rhys been even remotely conscious, he could have fed the Healer the procedure and helped him work it, he was sure. The spell did not even depend on Healing function. He could have worried later about how to bring Rhys back from the spell's stasis. Again, he knew the theory. With another Healer close at hand, he felt certain he could have muddled through it somehow.

But Rhys was not conscious and might not have agreed to try so desperate a measure, even if he had been. The Healer was not as conservative as Joram, but there was an ethical question, nonetheless. Did Camber have the right to answer that for even one so close as Rhys? Dared he be another's conscience?

Almost, he decided to try it anyway. It was really little more than the stasis that could be put on bodies to prevent decay—well, perhaps a *little* more, to keep a soul bound to a suspended body. . . .

But while he argued with himself, and agonized, and even made a tentative probe to see whether he could work the spell on an unconscious subject, he realized that it was too late. Rhys was dead. (*Camber the Heretic* 411–412)

Camber does not allow death to stop him the next time he is faced with such a decision. After Jebediah has gone, reunited in death with the real Alister Cullen, the dying Camber finds himself thinking about those other deaths in the clearing at Iomaire, and Ariella in specific, "her fingers curved in death in the attitude of a spell which most men thought impossible."

She had failed, but Camber knew why. He had almost tried the spell on Rhys, confident that he could have made it work—but that would not have been proper, he knew now. No man had the right to make that choice for any other soul.

And yet, the matter of the spell would not be put aside. Time after time, his thinking made the same brief circuit—Jebediah, Alister, Ariella, the spell—and he could not seem to break the cycle.

Did one who mastered it indeed elude death? Or did one but gain access to that other sphere which now he twice had glimpsed? Somehow, simple yielding up to death, at least for now, did not contain the answer, though Camber had never feared to die—had always thought he would be ready, in his time. And close upon these musings came another question: had he been given these glimpses of that other sphere for a reason . . . ?

With sudden, blindingly obvious insight, he knew that reason—knew why Ariella's working of the spell had failed, knew a greater part of the Master Plan in which he was a keystone. He sensed, also, the reasons one might be granted such grace—not to die, for now, but instead to enter that other, twilight realm of spirit where one might serve both God and man in different ways—or were they different? And *he* had been given the knowledge whereby he might accept that challenge, might gird himself with the whole armor of God and labor on, in the service of the Light.

It was so simple. It was so beautiful. All he had to do was to reach out with his mind, just—so. . . . (*Camber the Heretic* 480-481)

Whether Camber actually succeeded in working the spell is the subject of much further speculation by Evaine and Joram. Evaine, not yet understanding the true nature of the spell, at first seeks merely to bring her father back and heal his wounds, releasing him "from that twilight state which was not death, yet not life as they had known" (*Camber the Heretic* 488). Only in the course of actually attempting that, willing to lay down her own life in the process, does she learn that the spell can be carried to another dimension.

Ponderously, Evaine tried to comprehend, only gradually coming to fathom just what her father had done. His spell had worked—to a point. Camber had bypassed Death, but only at a terrible cost. In exchange for the freedom to move occasionally between the worlds, continuing in spirit the work no longer possible in his damaged body, he had forfeited, at least for a time, the awesome ecstasy of union with the All High. Had he been more canny with his spellbinding, he might have won both, at once free to come and go in the Sacred Presence and to walk in both worlds as God's agent and emissary.

But Camber had not fully understood the spell he wove, in that moment of imminent death. Death had not bound him, no. But he was bound, nonetheless. By the fierce exercise of his extraordinary will, he had sometimes been able to break through to the world and make his presence felt, but those times were rare indeed, and costly on a level only comprehensible to those who have glimpsed the Face of God—or been denied that glimpse. And until the balance should be set right, by the selfless sacrifice of someone willing to pay in potent coin, that Face might remain forever hidden from Camber Kyriell MacRorie.

Evaine lingered hardly at all over her decision. She had guessed for some time that it would come to this. Bringing Camber back to life clearly was out of the question, and mere death would but set him back on the Wheel, to start again in another incarnation without benefit of any of the wisdom gained so dearly in this life—no insurmountable calamity for so advanced a soul as Camber, but a most untimely loss for human and Derynikind just now, whose cause he had served so faithfully and so long.

So she must release him to that joyful purpose beyond life, in which great adepts chose their work and eschewed the Great Return in preference for specialized assignments, teaching mankind to grow in the likeness of God. (*The Harrowing of Gwynedd* 412–413)

Heavy consequences, indeed, for working the Forbidden Spell; consequences that Camber obviously did not foresee. The circumstances go far beyond mere mortal morality into a realm all but incomprehensible to ordinary mortals. It is this kind of outcome that tends to reinforce human contention that Deryni magic is Dark. Even Evaine probably would agree that she deals with Shadow in her descent into the Underworld—though it is important to note that shadow does not necessarily conceal evil; it merely conceals. This is a perception that goes beyond ordinary human understanding and spirituality.

# CHAPTER NINETEEN

# Were-Deryni:
# The Haldane Subset and Others Who Do Not Fit the Usual Definitions

Occasionally, in the course of our peregrinations in the Eleven Kingdoms, we have come upon characters who apparently are not Deryni yet have powers very like those of the Deryni. We may divide these individuals into three general categories: Haldanes and those like them, who can assume or be given Deryni-like powers; descendants of Deryni who do not know what they are; and others, like Warin de Grey, whose abilities we cannot explain.

## The Haldane Subset

Since the time of the Haldane Restoration, it has been acknowledged among certain Deryni that the Royal House of Haldane comprises a special bloodline whose members have the potential ability to assume or be given Derynilike powers. This potential was first identified by Camber and his children in Cinhil Haldane, the first restored Haldane king, and for many years remained the exclusive province of the Haldane Royal House—which, outwardly at least, soon began to link the origins of its powers with the older precepts of divine right monarchy.

Well before the time of King Kelson, however, especially in

the East, the potential had begun to be observed in other individuals as well. Among certain eastern adepti, endowing political allies with quasi-Deryni powers came to be regarded as relatively commonplace, with the recipients of such power enjoying almost the same status as born Deryni. Charissa's Lord Ian and Lionel Duke of Arjenol are "made" Deryni, and Bran Coris likewise has limited Derynilike powers placed upon him.

Especially in the beginning, however, the process was anything but commonplace. Only desperation drove Camber and his kin to attempt it for the first time with Prince Cinhil Haldane; for only with Deryni powers could Cinhil hope to challenge and defeat the Deryni despot Imre and regain his ancestral throne. The first indication that something of this sort might be possible came from a chance observation of Rhys and then Camber that Cinhil seemed to generate an odd, discordant resonance during moments of extreme emotion coupled with great stress, specifically when he celebrated the Mass—a reaction to his grief at knowing he soon would be forced to set aside his cherished vocation as a priest. Furthermore, this resonance left a psychic residue over the altar where he celebrated—and Cinhil himself seemed to have developed some kind of strange, vestigial shields that activated during moments of extreme duress. Aspects of it all were very like things Deryni.

Camber was disinclined to use force where Cinhil was concerned, for forced cooperation would last only as long as active supervision. However, Evaine was able to observe another anomaly in Cinhil that led to a breakthrough. Persuaded to use a form of meditation taught him by Evaine, Cinhil proved able to make a *shiral* crystal glow—a feat hitherto thought possible only by Deryni. (Eventually, use of *shiral* crystals broadened to include detecting the power-assuming potential as well as mere Deryniness.)

Readers of *Camber of Culdi* are familiar with the process by which Cinhil gained his powers, so we will not reiterate that specific procedure in detail here (*Camber of Culdi* 260–268). Suffice it to say that at that time and for many years to come, those who guided the Haldanes—and the Haldanes themselves—came to believe that only Haldanes could have this done to them and that only the senior male representor of the line could hold the legacy at any given time. Whether this was true or not—and

it may have been fostered by Camber and his kin from the beginning, in an attempt to guard the rightful king from arcane
challenge by his sons or brothers—expectations certainly came
to be centered in the notion that only one Haldane at a time
could hold and wield the full range of Haldane powers. Well
into Kelson's reign, the Camberian Council (with the exception
of Tiercel de Claron) adamantly maintained this premise.

The question of whether a *female* of the Haldane line might
be able to hold and wield the power does not seem to have
arisen, perhaps because, in the less than two centuries docu-
mented thus far, the direct male line has not yet failed. Incidentally, there *have* been Haldane princesses over the years, just as
there have been princes in junior lines. The lineage charts included in the various appendixes show only direct Haldane descent in the reigning House. Collateral lines and descent through
Haldane females have been omitted in the interest of clarity.
(Which means that any or all of our Haldane princes and kings,
unless stated otherwise, might have sisters and/or daughters,
junior sons and/or brothers, who will show up only if there is a
reason for them to do so.) As just one example, Brion speaks of
a Haldane uncle, the childless Duke Richard Haldane, as his
heir in the early and little-circulated short story ''Swords Against
the Marluk,'' which takes place before Kelson is born. (The
material in this story and in another called ''Legacy'' eventually
will be expanded in the Childe Morgan Trilogy.)

It is unlikely that the Haldanes themselves were particularly
aware of the seniority restriction, once the immediate generation
of Cinhil's sons died out. Indeed, in the more than a century
and a half between the death of Cinhil's third son, Rhys Michael
Haldane, in 928, and the accession of Brion Haldane in 1095,
it is likely that many reigning Haldanes were not even aware of
their Deryni connections—or, if they came to recognize that
extraordinary Derynilike abilities did surface from time to time
in those of their royal line, they were taught to regard these
abilities as God-given adjuncts to their divine right as kings. It
was much safer, in an age when exhibiting such abilities might
be construed as sorcery and lead one to the stake. Furthermore,
it was in the interests of royal governors, regents, and courtiers
to protect their royal charges/masters from any contact with De-

ryni that might lead to contagion—and a lessening of their own influence.

Likewise, the identity of those Deryni charged with protecting and catalyzing the Haldane kings becomes increasingly obscured after Rhys Michael's death. In the beginning, at least until the death of Joram MacRorie, we know that responsibility rested with members of the MacRorie family, who were, almost by definition, members of the Camberian Council. We know of the potentializing of Cinhil's three sons and the accession of the eldest, and we can surmise that someone from the Council was able to assist Prince Javan when he eventually became king.

Just when this function shifted out of Council control is uncertain—perhaps when no one of MacRorie name any longer belonged to the Council. What *is* certain is that by the accession of Brion Haldane, himself only vaguely and uneasily aware of Deryni-Haldane connections, his empowering had been placed in the hands of a fourteen-year-old Deryni halfbreed, Alaric Morgan, who would not even become aware of the Camberian Council's existence until many years later, when Brion's son finally sat upon the throne of Gwynedd. Somehow, though, some vestige of Haldane potential and perhaps even occasional empowerment managed to survive the intervening years.

What, then, was really involved in this assumption of Haldane power? We know that the power-assuming potential was believed to be rare enough that its catalyzing could be confined to one family for many years. (We do not know when "making" Deryni became common in the East.) We also know that full power assumption has never been known to occur completely spontaneously—though certain individuals carrying the potential, such as Javan and Conall, have been known to develop varying degrees of Deryni-like talents through repeated contact with Deryni geared toward awakening such abilities. To a lesser extent, this had begun happening in Kelson as well, regarding Truth-Reading, possibly as a result of exposure to Morgan.

For full potential to be realized in an individual, however, the process must be triggered by the direct action and guidance of at least one Deryni well versed in the general principles of Deryni power utilization. In time, this function came to be linked directly with the right and duty of the Haldane sovereign to set the potential in his designated heir—or, occasionally, to delegate this responsibility. (Of necessity, Cinhil was empowered through the joint efforts of Rhys, Joram, Evaine, and Camber, but he set the potential in his own sons, in a manner of his own choosing, albeit with their help; we shall see how this practice generally persisted through subsequent generations of Haldanes.)

Regardless of the outward trappings that may surround the power assumption of any given individual, the actual process varies but little on the subject's inner levels. In practice, it falls rather naturally into two parts, the potentializing and the actual empowering, which may be (and ideally are) separated in time by many years. For immediate impact on the subject, the potentializing is by far the more dramatic of the two, for it must open up hitherto unused channels of energy flow in the subject's mind, often forcibly, usually in a manner that overwhelms the subject's previous abilities to perceive on paranormal levels. In a very real sense, it is a rite of passage, conferring a mystical initiation to a higher level of consciousness. The precise manner of doing this is decided by the person setting the potential. Almost without fail, the sensory overload that accompanies such an opening leads to loss of consciousness, at least for a short while.

Sometimes the process can be eased by the careful use of Deryni-specific drugs that help lower resistance. We are never told whether it is a drug that sifts from Camber's fingers above the cup from which Cinhil must drink—it may be only salt, as a symbol of Earth, since a drug presumably would have affected Camber, too, absorbed through his fingertips—but we know that Cinhil's sons were thoroughly medicated before even being brought into the ritual circle.

Under the supervision of Arilan (who presumably reflects the level of understanding of the process by "educated" Deryni at the time), later generations of Haldanes receive far less subtle treatment. Nigel absorbs a powerful psychic enhancer and sedative from an ointment that Arilan smears on his inner forearm. Perhaps its potency troubled Morgan and Duncan, for eleven months later, when it is Conall who must be potentialized and endowed, Arilan uses a much milder drug (or a milder dose of the same drug) in the oil with which he anoints Conall's head, breast, and hands—apparently harmless in small amounts, since he must absorb some of it on his own hands. He reinforces it with a second, presumably stronger substance on the clasp of the Lion brooch with which Conall must pierce his hand. The pain obviously is intended as a final trigger and focus here, much as it was for Kelson a few years before.

Or *was* pain the trigger for Kelson? Certainly he did not have the benefit of trained Deryni expertise to ease his ordeal. Morgan is operating partly on buried instruction from Brion, surfacing at need, and partly on ill-remembered recall of helping Brion himself come to power when Morgan was Kelson's age. The pain of the impalement is *part* of the trigger, serving to center Kelson for a drive toward the desired psychic unfolding; but before any ritual procedure is even contemplated, we are given the definite impression that use of the brooch alone would not have been sufficient to bring Kelson to his full potential. The Eye of Rom must be retrieved, even from the grave, and its mystical stone charged with Kelson's own blood.

Given the importance of both items, then, and knowing what we do of the energy required to open the appropriate pathways in a subject, we may postulate that perhaps energy stored in the Eye by Kelson's father fuels a resonance set up by the pain of impaling the hand—and it is this pain-fueled resonance that forces the opening of the necessary channels in Kelson's mind. Duncan identifies this element of the rite as "the obstacle, the barrier, the need for bravery" (*Deryni Rising* 161), which is a part of almost every rite of passage.

Later on, among the long-sequestered Servants of Saint Camber at Saint Kyriell's, Kelson encounters this theme of the need for an obstacle or trial in another context, when it becomes the means to prove his innocence upon his body. In this instance, Kelson must undergo "the *cruaidh-dheuchainn*, the *periculum*, the ordeal" (*The Quest for Saint Camber* 362), close cousin to the classic vision quest whereby ancient seers would seek communication with their gods by breathing narcotic fumes issuing from a rock fissure or, in Kelson's case, bubbling up through an underground spring. Like Arilan's drugs, the gas blurs normal perception and lowers resistance, opening psychic channels to receive input from other levels of consciousness. In all these cases, the esoteric principle is the same: that one must be willing to suffer to learn.

Learning is the key, then. For in all the instances we have mentioned of the ordeal, there *is* learning to be done. And in the potentializing and empowering of a Haldane, the learning involves establishing new patterns and pathways for energy flow—by a certain degree of force, no matter how willing the subject, and at greater speed and pressure than the virgin pathways are accustomed to carry. Small wonder that the experience is traumatic and the aftereffects staggering.

Nor is this the end for our would-be Haldane Deryni, for setting the potential has only *prepared* the candidate to carry the enormous power that awaits him; he does not yet have the power. The paths are established, and some few talents may begin to surface of their own accord, with the passage of time, but actual access to the power does not come until some final act is performed—and this only upon the death of one's predecessor. In Kelson's case, it involves stepping upon the seal of the Defender. For Cinhil, the power was conferred along with the potential, but access did not come until catalyzed by rage at seeing his firstborn son slain by magic.

Cinhil's heir assumes his powers with the placing of his father's ring on his finger—but he does not have the conscious knowledge to use it and is kept from any awakening of his powers by the constant sedation forced upon him by his regents. Conall's full empowering, first catalyzed by Tiercel's training and then augmented by his own assumption of forbidden knowledge, is confirmed rather than completed by the ordeal of the brooch. Nigel, though potentialized, never came to the full power of kingship and, further, had the mandate of his potential withdrawn when it was believed he could never reign. We have yet to see what will be the long-range effects of this later turn of events.

But the results are well worth any transient pain or discomfort or even terror. (Conall, before his discovery, would have said that they are worth the loss of honor, too.) The potentialized and empowered Haldane is the match for just about any Deryni, able to wield all of the ceremonial and practical magic of which the first empowerers were capable. This is not to say that wisdom, judgment, or experience are conferred along with power, but the tool is available, if the wielder has the common sense to use it wisely.

In conclusion, we must return to the earlier statement that not only Haldanes can have Deryni powers placed upon them. Charissa bestowed Deryni-like powers on Lord Ian. Wencit, though perhaps genuinely disappointed that Bran Coris was not himself Deryni, was able to give Bran enough of a semblance of Deryni powers to deem him a suitable teammate for a fourfold Duel Arcane with Kelson. Not even Lionel's powers are solely his own, though we may infer from the fact that Lionel married Wencit's sister that this was no longer deemed a stigma. Certainly Kelson is extremely wary of the ability of Lionel's younger brother, Mahael, whose powers must also be assumed.

All of which leads one to suspect that perhaps the ability to assume Deryni powers is not just an odd human trait but a very specialized subset of being Deryni—that some have the ability to take on full-blown powers at another's direction, without having to learn by conventional means, just as some Deryni have the ability to Heal—and some Healers can block. We might diagram the traits like this:

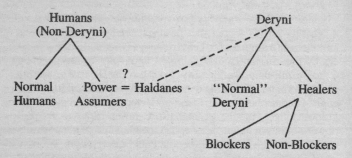

Finally, in this section, we should consider those humans (possibly not as rare as we might think) who apparently can learn to make limited use of Deryni techniques for meditation and concentration, who pick up these skills through repeated close contact with working Deryni. Javan and Conall both fit this category, but they both are Haldanes, and quite probably some odd sort of Deryni. Sean Lord Derry apparently is neither.

# Oddball Humans

Sean Seamus O'Flynn has always been something of an anomaly. We have no evidence that he comes from any of the human lines that can have Deryni powers placed upon them—Morgan is convinced that Derry is about as human as they come, though we know that his judgment may be impaired—yet Derry does perform rather better than we might expect. Part of what makes him so successful is that he trusts Morgan implicitly and wants to believe that Morgan can endow him with extra abilities and protection. (If he was resistant, Morgan's magic might not work half so well.) Derry learns to take Morgan's own skills mostly for granted, even to insisting that Morgan's Ward Cubes are really only an odd form of dice. He hardly bats an eye when, in Morgan's presence and certainly at his wish, a bully's whip coils in unexpected ways. Small wonder that, when asked by Morgan whether he would be willing to become involved in magic, Derry's immediate answer is "You know I would, sir!" (*Deryni Checkmate* 52).

That Morgan can store energy in the Saint Camber medal he gives Derry and then teach him a spell appropriate for tapping into that power, Derry accepts without question. Equally indicative of total trust is the fact that Derry readily goes into trance at Morgan's bidding—so readily that we must wonder whether Morgan does this often, even if Derry does not always remember what has been done.

And yet, Derry's delight at having Morgan speak directly into his mind suggests that the Deryni lord does not often involve him in his magic—even though we also get the impression that Derry has observed enough over the years of his service to Morgan that nothing particularly surprises him. He is totally nonplussed at the notion that he will be able to communicate with Morgan over the distance from Coroth to Fathane—"or farther, if necessary," as Morgan points out. Similarly, Derry does not question that Kelson adds his own protective ingredient to the medal before sending him out to hunt for Bethane, after the deaths of Bronwyn and Kevin.

Being aware of what the touch of a Deryni mind feels like, Derry also appears to possess at least some innate ability to resist such contact when Wencit captures him and sets about breaking his will. Whether this ability was always present or came about through close association with Morgan, we do not know. We do know that even with the protection of the Saint Camber medal taken away, Derry still is able to offer enough resistance that Wencit decides to add the reinforcement of drugs, some of them specific to Deryni in their action. This resistance puzzles Wencit greatly, for a mere human should not be able to stand up at all before a Deryni of his caliber and training.

It is not enough to save Derry, though. In the end, we know that his will *is* shattered and that he becomes a compliant tool in Wencit's hands, at least for a time. Bound by Wencit's spells and a ring that the sorcerer places on his finger, Derry is given the ability to form a communication link through an unconscious guard, the way Ian did, and to inform Wencit when the Portal may be activated to steal away Richenda's son. Light flares around his head in a very Deryni-like aura as he does so. Presumably he is carefully shielded, too, because Richenda senses nothing devious in his request to come to help the ailing Warin. Later, Derry actually tries to kill Morgan. Totally against his will, and helpless to prevent it, Derry has betrayed his lord, his king, and his own honor.

Morgan can blur the memory of that betrayal, after shattering the multileveled spell that bound Derry to Wencit's commands, but will that be enough? Does Derry still have some Deryni-like powers? What unknown damage has been done, and with what long-range consequences? Though Morgan states flatly that Derry will not have to live with the memory of what happened to him at *Esgair Ddu* because of the tinkering Morgan has done, he acknowledges in the very same breath that some of the horror of Derry's experience will be with him always.

How did that horror manifest itself in the weeks and months that followed? What further hells did Derry have to endure in the two years that pass between his rescue and the next time we see him, apprehensively informing Morgan that he has just escorted Richenda from Coroth to attend Christmas Court, knowing that Morgan has not authorized the visit? Now Morgan's lieutenant in Corwyn rather than his aide, Derry ostensibly has received a promotion. But is it a promotion or has he been quietly "kicked upstairs," away from the king and the court at Rhemuth, given a make-work kind of assignment to keep him safely out of harm's way—and away from the likelihood of doing harm? Is he, in fact, an unwitting exile in the Duchy of Corwyn? At such remove, one can hardly imagine that he still serves on Kelson's privy council with any regular frequency—or that this pleases him. Nor does he enjoy the day-to-day working relationship he once had with Morgan, since Morgan spends little time at Coroth.

On the other hand, not even Derry himself can deny that Morgan needs *someone* at Coroth to make certain that relations do not get out of hand between his wife and his household. It is clear from his remarks to Morgan that Derry is quite aware of the ongoing problems in that regard. Who better to be Morgan's agent than Derry, who possesses military and administrative acumen, undoubted charm and social polish, loyalty—and who can be watched by Richenda for any sign that the loyalty might be compromised again by residuals of Wencit's tampering? Given the ease with which he used to go into trance for Morgan, perhaps Richenda even utilizes this predilection in a therapeutic context, gradually digging away at the last vestiges of Wencit's old holds. (It may not occur to Derry that Richenda, as a Deryni, is at least as well equipped as Morgan to deal with any problems or potential problems that might arise out of Derry's ordeal with Wencit, and that in a sense, she is as much his keeper as he is hers.) In future works, perhaps we will get a further indication of the full price Wencit extracted from Sean Lord Derry, this human with the odd penchant for getting himself involved in the affairs of Deryni.

Finally, we should mention Revan, also a human who seems able to learn certain Deryni skills. Again, Revan has had ongoing contact with highly skilled and trained Deryni from a very early age and has come to accept the extraordinary as ordinary within that context. He trusts his Deryni lord and lady implicitly. When Evaine presents him with their plan for the Baptizer cult, he accepts his designated role without hesitation, once again offering his unreserved fealty—which includes the familiar process of opening his mind to fully learn her will.

"That's right," she murmured. "Relax and let me hold your mind, as we have done before. And for your own safety, remember nothing consciously of what we shall discuss unless you are with Rhys or me." (*Camber the Heretic* 160)

Presumably Evaine briefs him in detail on how he will make the transition from servant of a Deryni household to servant of Saint Willim, including the method for contact once his new identity has been established. In addition, we know that she and Rhys plant certain safeguards against casual probing by other Deryni—most probably selected memory blocks and limited shielding structures—for Rhys tests the limits of those safeguards when he and Evaine go to visit Revan in the Willimite camp.

Only when Revan begins building an actual working relationship with Tavis and Sylvan, however, do we see true Deryni-like talents coming into play with Revan. Indeed, as he learns how to manipulate the triggers that the two Healers preset in their subjects, Revan begins elaborating on the established routines and developing vestiges of new abilities on his own, all but indistinguishable from his own increasing personal charisma. Amplified with the power stored in the Willimite medallion Revan wears, and "reinforced by the laying on of hands and the expectations of his subjects, in conjunction with baptism, Revan could actually induce an effect ranging from disorientation and dizziness to near fainting" (*The Harrowing of Gwynedd* 218).

Nor is the working of Revan's new skills affected by *merasha*, except as the usual sedative effect of the drug in humans would slow him down and eventually put him to sleep, in high enough dose.

"Being neutral to *merasha* should be the clincher, when they eventually do question what you've been doing," Queron informed him. "The drug has been the great leveller for centuries, ever since its effect was first noted. Everyone who knows anything at all about Deryni knows that we're universally vulnerable to it. When you don't react, that will be the final confirmation that, whatever else you are, you aren't some new, insidious kind of Deryni." (*The Harrowing of Gwynedd* 218–219)

But if Revan is *not* some new, insidious kind of Deryni, what is he? Another genuine miracle-worker in the making, like

Warin? The human of the future? The prototype of the perfected human, who may attain to at least some of the mystical abilities of the Deryni? Only future explorations in the Eleven Kingdoms may give us further insight into the truth.

## Deryni in Hiding and Detection of Same

Occasionally we run across a character who turns out to be Deryni and did not know what he or she was. Generally, these individuals turn out to be descendants of Deryni who went into hiding during the times of the great persecutions, and who so thoroughly hid or suppressed what they were that even the memory of that identity faded after a few generations. After that, unless something happened forcibly to jar a potential talent into activity, or close contact with a Deryni catalyzed an awakening of those potentials, the individual's true identity might lie buried and untapped for untold generations.

Practically speaking, Deryni would have had a far easier time going into hiding or assimilating than many of the minority groups persecuted in our own earth history, for nothing in a Deryni's mere appearance would keep him or her from "passing" for human. Deryni did not have to contend with differences of skin color or hair texture or eye or nose shape, or even behavioral differences like the manner of religious observance. Deryni look like anybody else and partake of the same basic religious observances.

Unless a Deryni was tempted into self-betrayal, then, by using his or her forbidden powers in front of the wrong people, the danger of discovery could be minimized. Ways of actually ferreting out a determined Deryni were few and generally required a reason for suspicion—and by moving to another area, one could usually avoid the most immediate danger, of being recognized and denounced by former acquaintances. This danger decreased even more as the generations died out who had known Deryni firsthand.

The danger that did not decrease in the early days was to come under any kind of official scrutiny—for almost invariably, this entailed eventually coming to the attention of Deryni sniffers. Deryni themselves, and able to ferret out others of their kind, the services of these unfortunate individuals were secured by the upper echelons of the regency and its officers through the simple and brutal expedient of hostages. Collaboration meant life and limited privileges within the confines of the regents' service; refusal meant death, not only for the recruit himself (for they were always men) but for his family.

Many hostages and not a few potential sniffers were brutally slaughtered in the beginning, to secure the cooperation of a guarded few, but despite an ambitious beginning (from the regents' point of view), the use of Deryni sniffers lasted less than a decade. Few Deryni could live long with the knowledge that their collaboration was betraying their own people to their deaths, and many eventually chose death for themselves and even their families rather than continue as the ongoing instruments of other families' destruction.

Furthermore, as the collaborators chafed increasingly in their bonds, their human masters began to suspect and fear that anti-Deryni measures were not always being pursued with all the fervor desired. After all, how could a human confirm that a Deryni was telling the truth about whether an interrogation was yielding important information or not? Might not a Deryni sniffer conceal information that might be harmful to other Deryni, if he thought he would not be betrayed by another collaborator? What if the collaborators were conspiring among themselves to deceive their masters? Who would know? Best simply to phase them out—that is, to execute them and their families—though a few Healers were kept awhile longer, because of their obvious usefulness, probably safe enough to use as Healers because of the strength, thus far, of their vows.

Collaboration proved deadly, then, even for the collaborators, though it briefly may have eased the pressure on other Deryni, who might hope to bluff their way through an interrogation and win their freedom. Unfortunately, even as the use of Deryni sniffers was on the decline, a new instrument of Deryni detection was being developed that could be placed in the hands of more reliable humans. It hinged on the Deryni-specific drug *merasha.*

*Merasha,* as we have already established, is the one substance against which Deryni have no defense. All Deryni react to it. Even a small amount muddles the senses, inhibits concentration and the ability to think, and renders one incapable of using his or her magical powers. Humans merely get sleepy. Too much, for Deryni or humans, causes death. Deryni themselves developed the drug to control their own, and humans adopted its use for the same reason. (Morgan believed that Charissa developed the drug, but he obviously was misinformed on this point, as he has proven to be misinformed on many other things about the Deryni.)

Human utilization of the drug started out modestly. King Cinhil's men, continuing the policies of their Festillic predecessors—or perhaps at the initial suggestion of well-meaning battle surgeons reacting against the brutality of conventional incarceration and torture—used *merasha* increasingly to prevent Deryni prisoners from using their powers to escape or defend themselves. This continued and accelerated during the regency of Cinhil's son Alroy, when it also came to be used as a way of confirming the Deryni status of suspects about whom suspicions had already been aroused for other reasons. Inquisitors of the *Custodes Fidei*, founded specifically to ferret out Deryni, eventually adopted a bodkinlike device called a "Deryni pricker," with two or more needles set in the end, that could be dipped in *merasha* and then used to jab a suspected Deryni. (Later on, and *very* clandestinely, *merasha*-laced communion wine became the means by which the ecclesiastical authorities uncovered Deryni trying to infiltrate the priesthood.)

But most of the time, the average Deryni could avoid being dosed with *merasha* by keeping a low profile and not arousing suspicion in the first place. (And hardly a handful of men knew of the Church's limited use of the drug—and those who found out the hard way did not live to tell how they had been betrayed, if, indeed, they knew.) In later years, therefore, the greatest danger to Deryni came from themselves, when carelessness or pride allowed their magic to be observed by non-Deryni, or patience wore thin and someone lashed out with power, or someone merely slipped up.

How different individuals and groups went about hiding their identity largely determined how they fared several generations downstream. Some Deryni merely fled to other lands where their talents were still accepted to varying degrees, though the days of Deryni ascendancy in any land were largely past. Some, like the Saint Camber community at Saint Kyriell's, were able to make their way to places of safety within Gwynedd and shut themselves away from the rest of the world until sanity should return.

In the borders and highlands of the Purple March and Kheldour, more isolated than many other parts of Gwynedd, some Deryni managed to assimilate quietly into the clan structures, their talents gradually fusing and amalgamating with the more ancient notions of the border Second Sight until no one remembered when things had been any different. Everyone knew that borderers were good trackers, could move invisibly in the field, had a "knack" with animals, and so on. So Deryni blood might have been infused into Clan MacArdry, distantly descended from quiet, plain-spoken Deryni who withdrew to the borders, perhaps before the persecutions even reached very great proportions, to seek lives of peace.

In the lowlands, where hiding was more difficult, less-well-known Deryni sometimes became ardent supporters of the anti-Deryni regimes, as protective coloration. Some few, such as the Dukes of Corwyn (which at the time was an independent duchy, not yet a part of Gwynedd), developed precarious working relationships with human patrons in exchange for protection; it was difficult, without compromising one's honor or the safety of other Deryni, but it could be done.

Some simply denied what they were and built new identities for themselves, living out their lives in secret fear of being found out, waiting for the time when their children and their children's children should have forgotten who and what they were. Some were Deryni whose powers had been blocked by the Baptizers, during their short tenure around the capital area directly after the accession of King Alroy in 917.

The latter did not have to hide what they were, because for practical purposes they no longer *were* Deryni. They did not have access to their former powers. They did not react to *merasha* except as any human might. With the memories of their previous existence blurred and buried, even direct reading by another Deryni would not betray them. Given the suppositions reached by Camber and kin, the blocks placed on the powers of such Deryni would not pass to their children, but the potentials would—though in an atmosphere where being Deryni was apt to be deadly, it is likely that most children of such unions would have been actively discouraged from any interest in things Deryni. There is little incentive to uncover something about oneself that can get one killed. In addition, many children were blocked during the all-too-brief flourishing of the Baptizer cult, and *their* children would be of a generation with no reason to suspect or desire the stigma of being a Deryni. Hence, most of these descendants would have ended up the same as those of the Deryni who simply went into hiding, gradually losing track of what they were. Therefore, it is not at all unreasonable that we should discover "humans" from time to time who turn out to be Deryni.

## Deryni Who Aren't

Finally, we must consider those persons who, at least occasionally, appear to exhibit Deryni-like abilities but who are not Deryni, even in the sense that Haldanes might be. That is, they are not carriers of the potential for having Derynilike powers placed upon them. Thus far, Warin de Grey is the prime example we have seen of this sort of individual; for Warin, we really have only two possibilities. First, he *is* Deryni.

At first glance this would seem not to be possible, for both Morgan and Duncan agree that he is not. He does appear to heal as Deryni do, by the laying on of hands—but so do biblical healers. Derry observes him when he heals the injured Martin, in a tavern near the Sieur de Vali's estates. The injured man has had a lung pierced; back at the scene of battle, Derry had thought the man dead. Yet when Warin lays one hand on Martin's forehead and the other on the wound itself and prays, a misty blue-violet aura surrounds Warin's head—usually a certain clue that we are dealing with a Deryni (or a saint or deity). When the healed Martin stirs and sits up, his wound gone, one of Warin's men acclaims him as a new messiah—a notion that Warin does nothing to dispel, only raising his hand in benediction before departing.

Derry, who knows that the aura was no illusion (and who, we suspect, would be disinclined to acknowledge Warin as a saint), draws the more pragmatic conclusion that Warin must be Deryni, since he has done what Morgan can do and Morgan is

Deryni. Morgan argues that the conclusion may not necessarily follow, but concedes that if Warin *is* Deryni, he may not know it. Warin's later ignorance of *merasha* and its effects on Deryni, when Gorony proposes using the drug to incapacitate Morgan, does tend to bear out at least a stated ignorance of things Deryni, but does not prove Warin's own status one way or the other. The other possibility, which neither Morgan nor Duncan dismisses out of hand, is that Warin is a genuine miracle-worker, in the classic biblical sense.

> "The trouble is," Morgan said . . . "that Warin does the things saints and messiahs traditionally do. Unfortunately, those same deeds are not commonly attributed to Deryni, even though the deeds of many Christian saints may have their origin in Deryni powers." (*Deryni Checkmate* 140)

In other words, Warin could be a Deryni feigning saintlike abilities—which Camber certainly has done, if inadvertently. When Morgan and Duncan observe Warin's evangelical manner while healing Owen Mathisson's shattered legs, they believe this is probably the case. Only when Morgan has a chance to probe Warin deeply at first hand does he decide that Warin probably is *not* Deryni—an opinion also voiced by Duncan and Kelson.

Which, if Warin is *not* Deryni, leaves us with the supposition that perhaps he *is* a genuine miracle-worker.

*Or* perhaps Morgan and Duncan are mistaken. After all, they don't have the equivalent of a proper Deryni education between them, as Morgan reminds Kelson a few years later. And though we might expect Arilan to be able to tell for sure—might he not have had the opportunity to read Warin when they used him in the power link for establishing the field Portal at Llyndruth Meadows?—we also must note that it was Duncan who controlled Warin at that time. Given the urgency of opening a field Portal and making his contact with the Camberian Council, it is unlikely that Arilan would have thought to satisfy his curiosity in this regard. As he makes no mention of having done so, when Warin's name comes up in the Camberian Council (*The King's Justice* 63–64), we must gather that he did not. And since Warin has gone into hiding again, we simply do not know. Warin may, indeed, be Deryni. Or he may be a genuine miracle-worker.

# CHAPTER TWENTY

# Ritual I:
# Definitions and Physical Setup

There is nothing necessarily magical about ritual per se. A ritual is simply a way of putting oneself into an appropriate frame of mind for performing a specified task. Most people think of ritual in religious terms—and certainly, religious ritual helps set the stage for what is intended at any particular religious function, by using candles, incense, vestments, chanting, ritual movements, and the like to channel the devotee into the right "head space."

But we all perform less formal rituals every day, whether it is the rather prosaic ritual of putting bread in the toaster and waiting with knife poised above the butter, or checking to make sure all the doors and windows are secure before going to bed, or a more obvious ritual like the way you put the toothpaste on your toothbrush and whether you put the cap back on or not. All of these actions lead to an expectation of certain actions and results to follow. As a lady named Maxine Saunders once remarked of ritual, "When you lay out the tea things, the children know it's time for tea."

Deryni rely upon ritual settings for a number of religious and quasi-religious applications. We will examine specific examples of both sorts of application, but first we ought to define what makes a formal ritual in the Deryni sense. We can break a ritual into four basic parts: physical preparation and setup, defining and securing the working place, the operation itself, and closing down. (This presupposes, of course, that one had decided upon the end result required and the method for accomplishing that end result—that is, the plan of the ritual itself.)

## Physical Preparation and Setup

The physical aspect of preparing for a ritual includes selection of a suitable physical location, any necessary cleansing of the working site, (re)arrangement of any furniture items in a configuration appropriate to the physical movement anticipated, gathering of all physical items needed for the specific working to be carried out, and the setting out of those items in the working area, ready to begin the ritual. Wherever possible, symbolism meaningful to the participant(s) should be incorporated in the determination of what specific items to use in a given ritual. Any specifics of required or suggested attire would also fall under this heading, such as special robes or vestments. As examples, let us examine the preparations for five very different rituals in detail, three from the time of Camber and two from the time of Kelson.

## Cinhil's Empowering

The ritual for awakening Derynilike powers in Cinhil is one of the less formal rituals, partly because Camber and his kin are making it up as they go along, no one ever having done this before. What we see is filtered through Cinhil's own perceptions, heavily controlled by his Deryni mentors, but it is clear that great thought has gone into the process of setting the ritual framework in terms of familiar symbolism for the very orthodox Cinhil.

The physical setting is the octagonal chapel in the underground Michaeline sanctuary, already familiar to Cinhil and therefore apt to be at least a little reassuring. Outside, Jebediah fulfills the traditional function of guardian or tyler, standing watch before the door with sword in hand. We can surmise that special wards have been placed on the room for the night's work as well, for the Michaeline grand master touches a ''strangely glowing'' doorlatch to admit them.

Inside, the entranced Cinhil observes nothing to cause immediate apprehension. Ordinary white candles burn on the altar, and the lighted Presence Lamp suggests that whatever is to happen will not be offensive to the Sacred Presence thus symbolized. Plain beeswax candles in ordinary brass candlesticks mark the Quarters, and the unresisting Cinhil is made to stand in the center of the Kheldish carpet on which crowned him prince and witnessed his marriage vows. Joram wears surplice and stole over his cassock, familiar attire such as any priest might wear when performing a liturgical but non-Eucharistic function.

During the ritual, other accoutrements are brought into use as needed, including an ordinary thurible and familiar incense, the paraphernalia for piercing Cinhil's ear for the Eye of Rom, and a covered chalice very much like a Mass vessel, half filled with red wine. In addition, Camber sprinkles a white powder into the cup before Cinhil is made to drink of it—probably ordinary salt, as a symbol of Earth. All is as low-key and non-threatening as they can make it.

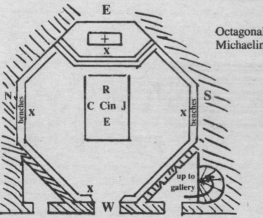

Octagonal Chapel,
Michaeline Sanctuary

## Scrying with the Haldana Necklace

A ritual of an entirely different sort, and far more likely to be at least somewhat "standard" (at least by Deryni reckoning), is that done by Camber in conjunction with scrying for information about Ariella's war preparations. Camber has never done this particular procedure before but works from instructions in the Protocols of Orin. Though he states a preference for consecrated ground as the place to do the working, he settles for the dressing room adjoining his quarters—a place he feels can be adequately warded and secured. Evaine is to bring a large silver bowl with a polished inside, Joram incense and something in which to burn it, and Alister Cullen is instructed to find an item of jewelry worn by Ariella. Camber himself must wear red.

In the dressing room itself, where they will work, Camber seals off outside openings and sets up a temporary altar in the center, covering it with a white cloth. On the table are a single lighted candle, glass flagon of water, a small, stoppered bottle, and four new tapers partially wrapped in a linen napkin. To these Camber adds the silver bowl, the necklace, and a small silver crucifix, while Joram sets out the thurible and incense.

## Setting Potential in Cinhil's Sons

The ritual of setting the Haldane Potential in Cinhil's sons takes place in Cinhil's private chapel, adjoining his sleeping chamber. After Mass on the morning of the ritual, Joram has the servants give the chamber a thorough cleaning. Later that afternoon and early evening, he and Evaine begin more specific preparations, whose effect Cinhil observes.

> It seemed almost stark compared to its usual appearance, dark but for the Presence Lamp and a single taper on a small table in the center of the room. After the servants had finished the general cleaning, Evaine and Rhys had removed everything except the heavy altar against the eastern wall and the thick Kheldish carpet which covered the tile at the foot of the altar steps. This last they had moved to the center of the chamber, and brought in a smaller one which they spread in the northeast corner. . . .
>
> New, fresh altar cloths and hangings had been laid in place next, the altar candles replaced with new ones, the sanctuary lamp replenished with oil. . . . Four candlesticks with colored glass shields in gold and red and blue and green now stood at the cardinal points of the room, very like those which had stood guard at his own rite so many years before, though all his had been white. (*Camber the Heretic* 71–72)

Various objects are assembled then. Jebediah brings Cinhil's sword of state, the jeweled belt wrapped loosely around the carved and gem-studded scabbard, and Camber-Alister lays it on the altar before lighting the altar candles with a taper kindled from the Presence Light. On the small table in the center of the chamber, which is covered by a floor-brushing white cloth, Evaine assembles smaller objects necessary for the ritual, similar to those used in Cinhil's own ritual: a thurible; a small, footed cup of white-glazed clay, filled with water; a slender silver dagger. (Cinhil notes that he has seen this dagger before, at Evaine's belt—an observation also made by Queron, at his induction into the Camberian Council. Its repeated use in ritual would seem to define it in the same general terms as an athame in our own world.)

In addition, several items have been assembled under the table: Rhys' medical kit, a pair of mismatched earrings made of twisted gold wire, and three small pieces of parchment that Cinhil himself has copied out earlier in the day, with inscriptions appropriate for each of his three sons. The one for the eldest reads:

> *I will decree the decree. The Lord hath said unto me, Thou art my Son: this day have I begotten thee. Ask of me, and I will give the heathen for thine inheritance, and the uttermost parts of the earth for thy possession.* (Camber the Heretic 79)

We may surmise that similar quotations were chosen for Javan and Rhys Michael.

Cinhil's three sons are brought in asleep, just before the ritual is to start. Alroy is laid on the carpet beside the center table, with Javan and Rhys Michael being left on the smaller carpet, outside what will be the actual place of working. Before the ritual actually begins, all three boys have their right earlobes pierced to receive one of the earrings. Alroy, as the immediate heir, is given the Eye of Rom; Javan and Rhys Michael receive lesser ornaments to hold the place, should they eventually inherit the Eye. Camber-Alister brings the Haldane sword into the center and slips it partially beneath the table. The stage is set.

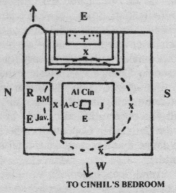

Cinhil's Chapel

## Setting the Haldane Potential in Nigel

Nigel's power-setting has certain similarities to the ritual described for Cinhil's sons, but there are major differences as well, not only because Nigel is a consenting adult, capable of active cooperation and at least somewhat aware of what he is about to undertake, but because it is hoped that he will be only a temporary heir. Some of the differences also can be ascribed to personal variations of style in those who set up the ritual—the manner of invoking the Quarters in this instance owes much to Richenda's eastern influence, for example. In addition, some of the differences almost certainly result from loss or transmutation of knowledge during the nearly two centuries of Deryni persecution between the time of Camber and the time of Kelson. We may assume that Denis Arilan, as a member of the Camberian Council of that time, has access to esoteric knowledge and theory at a very high level; but Kelson, Morgan, and Duncan have hardly any formal training and must rely on instinct tempered with what Arilan tells them. Still, the ritual has many of the stamps of classical and long-established procedure.

Nor should the importance of the candidate himself be overlooked. Nigel is no child like Cinhil's sons; he is the adult uncle of the king, only reluctantly drafted to function in the capacity of Haldane heir presumptive until Kelson sires a child. The decision to establish Nigel in this capacity, at this time, is precipitated by Sidana's murder in January of 1124 and Kelson's subsequent decision to go to war in the spring of that year, the two events separated by several months' time. As a consequence, we may infer that Nigel has rather more time than most candidates to prepare himself for his ordeal—which amounts to a magical initiation in the classic sense.

Holding Nigel's ritual in the tiny Saint Camber Chapel gives it a far more overtly Deryni context than for Cinhil's ritual. Duncan and Dhugal have charge of the physical preparation, which presumably would have included a thorough cleaning of the room. As further preparation—though this is done "as much to center and steady the participants as to cleanse a room long sanctified by its sacred use" (*The King's Justice* 34)—Duncan performs a formal censing and aspersing of the chapel while he

chants the verses and Dhugal makes the responses, in a classical
(and very orthodox) purification of the working area.

> *"Asperges me, Domine, hyssopo, et mundabor: lavabis me,
> et super nivem dealbabor."*
> "Amen."
> *"Pax huic domui."*
> *"Et omnibus habitantibus in ea."*
>
> (Sprinkle me, Lord, with hyssop, and I shall be cleansed;
> wash me, and I shall be whiter than snow. Amen. Peace to
> this house. And to all who dwell in it.) (*The King's Justice*
> 34)

We see the actual physical layout of the chapel through Nigel's
eyes and may contrast his perceptions, unfiltered by outside control, with those of Cinhil. Nigel is not particularly inclined toward formal religious observances, preferring to let his own
upright example witness for his faith, so the organizers of his
ritual endeavor to strip down the formalities to barest basics. It
is probably partially for this reason as well as sheer physical
expediency that formal attire is discarded before Nigel enters
the chapel, though the buildup of body heat in a confined space
is readily acknowledged by those accustomed to working ritual.

> The chamber beyond was dim and close—half the size of
> the room they had just left, and almost crowded even before
> they [Nigel and Duncan] entered. Arilan and Morgan stood
> against the walls to left and right, Richenda, all in white,
> immediately to his right against the back wall, but it was
> Kelson who caught and arrested his attention immediately.
> His nephew—no, *the king*—the king stood with his back to
> them in the precise center of the room, raven head flung back
> and hands hanging easily at his sides. . . . The object of his
> attention seemed to be a very ornate crucifix of ebony sus-
> pended above an altar set hard against the eastern wall—or
> perhaps it was the wall itself that held his gaze, painted all
> around the altar and above it like the midnight sky, spangled
> with bright-gilt stars that caught the light from six honey-
> colored tapers. The stars shimmered through the heat rising

from the candles, and the air tickled at Nigel's nostrils with the faint aroma of beeswax and incense.

"Come and stand beside me, Uncle," Kelson said softly, turning slightly to beckon with his right hand, quicksilver eyes drawing him even if the gesture had not. (*The King's Justice* 45)

On the altar are the Haldane sword, a small surgical kit for performing the lesser ritual of piercing Nigel's ear (this time, to be done after the circle is cast), a bowl of water for rinsing off blood, linen to dry same, a piece of parchment inscribed with all of Nigel's royal names, the ubiquitous thurible, and a thumb-size brass container containing a substance to lower Nigel's psychic resistance—Arilan's unique contribution.

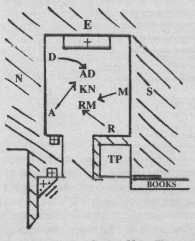

Saint Camber Chapel
Adjoining Duncan's Study

## Conall's Empowering

We may contrast the above preparations with those made for withdrawing the Haldane mandate from Nigel and passing it to Conall, when all the court believes Kelson to be dead and Nigel himself has been incapacitated, apparently permanently. Since such a situation has never arisen before, the team of Morgan, Duncan, and Arilan are forced to improvise—though we can note certain similarities to previous rituals as well as classical practices.

The ritual is to take place in Nigel's bedchamber, for they feel the necessity to have at least his comatose body present, as a physical symbol on which to focus their intent. For the first part of the ritual, before the circle is actually cast and Quarters invoked, Nigel's body in its canopied bed becomes, if not the altar itself, at least an altar focus, with a *prie-dieu* set at the foot of the bed and the unsheathed Haldane sword laid along the length of his body. Also at hand are a written declaration of the ritual's intent that Conall must sign, pen and ink for doing same, a bowl for burning the document after it is marked with both men's blood, Duncan's surgical kit, and a substitute for the Eye of Rom, since that is presumed lost with Kelson—this one, a blue star-sapphire in a mounting of twisted gold.

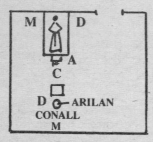

Nigel's Bedroom

For the second half, a small altar table is moved into the center of the room as is customary, with candles, an ampule of holy oil fortified with a substance to lower resistance and induce mild relaxation (Arilan's work again, we may assume), a linen cloth for Arilan's lap, and the heavy, fist-size Crimson Lion brooch, with its three inches of gleaming gold, the clasp prepared by Duncan with a drug to lower Conall's resistance to the forces about to be focused in him. A stool is also provided for Arilan's use while anointing Conall after the manner of kings.

These, then, are the physical preparations for a variety of different types of purely Deryni rituals. In the next chapter we shall examine the actual setting aside of the sacred space in which those rituals proceed: the casting of the circle and warding of the working place, also known as calling the Quarters.

# CHAPTER TWENTY-ONE

# Ritual II:
# Casting the Circle and Warding the Working Place

The purpose of casting a magical circle is threefold: to prepare and set aside the sacred space in which the ritual is to be performed; to contain the power to be raised in the course of the ritual; and to prevent the interference of outside forces that might be detrimental to the intended work.

In very general terms, formal casting of a magical circle usually involves three circuits of the area to be included within the circle. In Deryni tradition, all movement in the circle begins and ends in the East, acknowledging the source of Light, and proceeds clockwise—or deosil, or sun-wise, or *jesh*-wise (an old Cornish term)—with reference to the center, even if this sometimes means going "the long way around" for some participants at some times.

Paths of Various Officers of the Ritual
when Casting from South, West, and North

Counterclockwise movement is avoided in most instances because it is performed by turning to the left, which is associated with negative energies and intentions—the "Left-hand Path," and so on—though there are specific and generally advanced operations in which this type of symbolism might be appropriate.

The first two circuits in the casting of the circle generally are seen in a purificatory context as well as one of defining physical space. In a general way, by what is used in the circuits, they also are meant to begin establishing connections with the Elemental Forces, whose attributes will be amplified later in the ritual, when the Quarters actually are set.

The usual order is to *asperse* first with holy water—which always contains a pinch of salt, thus embodying the elements of Water and Earth—then to *cense*, adding the symbolic presence of Fire and Air, and finally to *cast* with the sword (or dagger, or athame, or first two fingers of the right hand).

Variations are not only possible but common. The casting with the sword sometimes is taken to include the unifying aspect of Spirit as a fifth element as well, binding together and balancing the four physical ones. Sometimes the preliminary minor ritual of carrying fire around the circle to light the quarter candles replaces the aspersing circuit or functions as a fourth circuit to work in symbolism of four rather than three (or five rather than four). The form is entirely up to those working the ritual, according to what seems appropriate to them, as is the formal calling of the Quarters, which constitutes the major outward designator of warding.

## Warding the Circle: Invoking the Quarters

Warding can take many forms, and the elemental Guardians of the Quarters can be conceptualized in many ways. The Deryni almost invariably prefer the biblical symbolism of Archangels. Some traditions in our own world invoke Sylphs, Salamanders, Undines, and Gnomes as embodying the elemental attributes of Air, Fire, Water, and Earth, and others personify these in the Elemental Kings called Paralda, Djinn, Niksa, and Ghob. Still others invoke the four Holy Creatures associated with the Gospels: the Man of Saint Matthew, the Lion of Saint Mark, the

Eagle of Saint John, and the Bull of Saint Luke. The suit-symbols of the Tarot deck are equally appropriate: Swords, Wands, Cups, and Pentacles. So long as the system is consistent, it matters little which specific forms are used.

Whatever system is used, repeated visualization and conceptualization does build up specific images. Through centuries of envisioning the elemental forces as great Archangels, Deryni probably do tend to See them as distinct beings, with very definite attributes, appearances, and even personality traits. Indeed, certain "trademarks" have become quite well established, if only as convenient psychic shorthand, so that the common symbolism provides a continuity to bridge many centuries of magical endeavor.

The Quarters are called in succession, beginning in the East. Though one person *may* Call all the Quarters, the more usual practice, as far as possible, is to have a different individual represent each Quarter, assignments being made on the basis of particular affinity for the element represented. Raphael, for example, will always be represented by a Healer, if one is available. Michael will be represented by a warrior, and Gabriel, because of association with the Virgin Mary, by a woman. One of Uriel's attributes is the wisdom of age, so an elder adept usually will take the North.

In the examples cited, we can see clear demonstrations of both casting and warding principles. Again, we must expect some variety because of personal style and source of training. Contrasts may be more readily apparent if we extract the bare bones of the castings and wardings and set them out in the form of working scripts.

## Cinhil's Empowering

To minimize the possibly non-Christian elements of what Camber and his kin intend to do, and to avoid upsetting Cinhil any more than necessary, the casting and warding are done as unobtrusively as possible. Through Cinhil's admittedly fogged senses, we see Evaine light the quarter candles (probably in substitute for aspersing) and Joram cense the circle and participants, to the accompaniment of the Twenty-third Psalm—which would have been of some comfort to the traditionalist Cinhil.

We do not see a specific casting of the circle with the sword, but we know that Cinhil's attention drifted while preparations were being carried out, so it is likely that (probably) Joram did this as well, and Cinhil simply was not aware.

As for formal setting of wards: Given the context of the rest of the ritual, it is likely that some rudimentary form of warding and calling Quarters was carried out before Cinhil was brought in, probably in conjunction with setting up the wards that Jebediah temporarily released so Cinhil's party could enter the chapel. Evaine's invocation after the casting reinforces what will become a familiar "trademark" of the future Camberian Council and serves as a transition into the ritual per se.

> We stand outside time, in a place not of earth. As our ancestors before us bade, we join together and are One. . . . By Thy Blessed Apostles, Matthew, Mark, Luke, and John; by all Thy Holy Angels; by all Powers of Light and Shadow, we call Thee to guard and defend us from all perils, O Most High. Thus it is and has ever been, thus it will be for all times to come. *Per omnia saecula saeculorum.* (*Camber of Culdi* 266)

The preliminary warding then is reiterated by the preparation of the cup, in words that echo previous Quarter calls and whose general form gives the shape for Quarter calls to come. Note how each exhortation reinforces the attributes of the Archangel associated with that element and then specifies the particular elemental attribute to be instilled into the wine. Note also the "cap" for each exhortation: *Fiat voluntas mea*—Let it be done according to *my* will.

RHYS: I call the mighty Archangel Raphael, the Healer, Guardian of Wind and Tempest. As the Holy Spirit didst brood upon the waters, so instill thou life into this cup, that he who drinks thereof may justly bid the forces of the Air. *Fiat, fiat, fiat voluntas mea.*

JORAM: I call the mighty Archangel Michael, the Defender, Keeper of the Gates of Eden. As thy fiery sword guards the Lord of Heaven, so lend thy protection to this cup, that he who drinks thereof may justly forge the might of Fire. *Fiat, fiat, fiat voluntas mea.*

EVAINE: I call the mighty Archangel Gabriel, the Herald, who didst bring glad tidings to Our Blessed Lady. Send thou thy wisdom into this cup, that he who drinks thereof may justly guide the knowledge of the Water. *Fiat, fiat, fiat voluntas mea.*
CAMBER: I call the mighty Archangel Uriel, Angel of Death, who bringest all souls at last to the Nether Shore. Herewith I charge this cup, that he who drinks may justly bind the forces of the Earth. *Fiat, fiat, fiat voluntas mea.* (*Camber of Culdi* 266–267)

## Scrying with the Haldana Necklace

No actual circle is cast for this working, for it falls into the realm of rituals intended to function primarily on an inner level. Warding is felt to be sufficient protection. Compare these warding invocations with those used in the preceding ritual—a close parallel, but tailored to the specific intent of this working.

RHYS: I call the mighty Archangel Raphael, the Healer, Guardian of Wind and Tempest. May thy winds blow cool and sweet this night, to send us that which we must know. *Fiat, fiat, fiat voluntas mea.*
JORAM: I call the mighty Archangel Michael, the Defender, Keeper of the Gates of Eden. Lend thou thy fiery sword as protection this night, that naught may keep us from that which we must know. *Fiat, fiat, fiat voluntas mea.*
EVAINE: I call the mighty Archangel Gabriel, the Herald, who didst bring glad tidings to Our Blessed Lady. As we are born of water, so let knowledge be born of water here tonight, that we may learn what we must know. *Fiat, fiat, fiat voluntas mea.*
ALISTER: I call the mighty Archangel Uriel, Angel of Death, who bringest all souls at last to the Nether Shore. Mayest thou pass us by this night, and bring instead that thing which we must know. *Fiat, fiat, fiat voluntas mea.*
CAMBER (lifting the fifth candle): Air, Fire, Water, Earth—and Spirit: the unity of Man. All are joined in One within the circle. (*Saint Camber* 45–46)

# Setting Potential in Cinhil's Sons

Camber and his kin have allowed Cinhil himself to set the form of the central part of this ritual, but they construct the setting as seems most appropriate to them. They begin a low-key casting of the circle, but Cinhil himself completes it. The component parts are:

1. Evaine lights the charcoal in the thurible, then takes a taper and, beginning in the East and proceeding clockwise, lights the quarter candles.
2. Joram censes the circle while reciting the Psalm of the Shepherd (Psalm 23), also censing all the participants inside the circle, including the sleeping Prince Alroy. The incense smoke hangs on the air, apparently contained by the circle being built. When Joram has finished, himself being censed by Camber-Alister, he replaces the censer on the center table and takes up the Haldane sword, which he draws partially from its scabbard and offers to Cinhil.
3. While Cinhil casts the circle with the sword, he also begins the calling of Quarters, stopping at each Quarter to salute with the sword while he recites the appropriate invocation. Note well that invoking the Quarters while casting with the sword is not the usual sequence—but it is what Cinhil has chosen to do. (Later we see that Cinhil chooses to augment this initial summoning of the Quarters by the form in which he charges the cup from which his sons will drink.)

CINHIL: Saint Raphael, Healer, Guardian of Wind and Tempest, may we be guarded and healed in mind and soul and body this night.

(tracing to the South.)

CINHIL: Saint Michael, Defender, Guardian of Eden, protect us in our hour of need.

(tracing to the West.)

CINHIL: Saint Gabriel, Heavenly Herald, carry our supplications to Our Lady.

(tracing to the North.)

CINHIL: Saint Uriel, Dark Angel, come gently, if you must, and let all fear die here within this place. (*Camber the Heretic* 77)

When Cinhil has traced back to the East to complete the circle, saluting and laying the sword along the northeast arc of the circle, Evaine repeats the invocation she used in Cinhil's own power ritual, to seal what has been done so far and to anchor the ritual back in a more familiar framework.

EVAINE: We stand outside time, in a place not of earth. As our ancestors before us bade, we join together and are One. By Thy blessed Apostles, Matthew, Mark, Luke, and John; by all Powers of Light and Shadow, we call Thee to guard and defend us from all perils, O Most High. Thus it is and has always been, thus it will be for all times to come. *Per omnia saecula saeculorum.* (*Camber the Heretic* 77)

## Setting Nigel's Potential

The casting of the circle for the setting of Nigel's Haldane potential follows more formal and classical lines, probably because of Arilan's influence, though the aspersing and censing are reversed. (In fact, they are conducted almost simultaneously, Arilan censing and Duncan sprinkling.) After Morgan has cast the third circuit with the Haldane sword, Arilan recites the first half of what we now recognize as the standard invocation developed by the Camberian Council at the time of Camber, probably sprung from even earlier roots. But he omits the reference to the four Apostles, perhaps in deference to the shift in tradition when Richenda calls *all* the Quarters, according to a more eastern emphasis.

ARILAN: We stand outside time, in a place not of earth. As our ancestors before us bade, we join together and are One.
RESPONSE: Amen.
RICHENDA (raising right hand to trace a circle in the East): Before us . . . *Ra-fa-el* . . . God has healed.
RESPONSE: God has healed.
                    (All face South.)
RICHENDA (setting a red-glowing triangle in the South): Before us . . . *Mi-ka-il* . . . Who is like God.
RESPONSE: Who is like God.
                    (All face West).

RICHENDA (tracing a crescent of white in the West): Before us . . . *Ji-bra-il* . . . God is my strength.
RESPONSE: God is my strength.

(All face North.)

RICHENDA (tracing a golden square in the North): Before us . . . *Au-ri-el* . . . Fire of God.
RESPONSE: Fire of God.

(All face toward center as Richenda
spreads both hands at waist level.)

RICHENDA: At our center and foundation is Spirit—that which endures.

(As Richenda moves hands apart and tilts them slightly down, a violet star materializes and floats to floor. She lifts palms heavenward.)

RICHENDA: Above us, the circled cross: defining and containing, unity of all contained within One.

(A green circled cross appears
and floats toward the ceiling.)

(*The King's Justice* 47–49)

When Richenda has finished her invocation of the Quarters, Arilan picks up again with another formula traditional within the Camberian Council, adding a more ecclesiastical phrase that probably comes from his own particular training. In fact, it has a distinctly Gabrilite flavor to it, perhaps passed down through successive generations to those who gave Arilan his training in high magic. The same may be said of the biblical phrase Kelson gives in response, certainly gained from coaching by Arilan.

ARILAN: Now we are met. Now we are One with the Light. Regard the ancient ways. We shall not walk this path again. *Augeatur in nobis, quaesumus, Domine, tuae operatio. . . .* (May the working of Thy power, O Lord, be intensified within us. . . .)
RICHENDA: So be it. Selah. Amen.
KELSON (signing himself with a cross): *Lumen Christi gloriose resurgentis sissipet tenebras cordis et mentis.* (May the light of Christ rising in glory scatter the darkness of our hearts and minds.) (*The King's Justice* 49)

Immediately afterward, Kelson remarks that the warding was drawn "partly from the tradition Richenda grew up in. Other than the Moorish elements that have crept in over the years, it's supposed to be fairly close to the form Camber might have used. Not that we'll ever know for certain, I suppose."

*Some* of the material undoubtedly *has* been passed down more or less intact since Camber's time—we can recognize some of it from our omniscient perspective, knowing many things about Camber and his times that are not known by Kelson's time—but other material probably has experienced what we might call "ritual drift," in which scribal errors and memory aberrations have garbled or at least subtly altered the transmission of information. Knowing Arilan's high-handedness, we can assume that he contributed what *he* felt to be authentic and ancient tradition. However, his input can have been only as good as his sources; and we know that the Camberian Council has changed a great deal since Camber's time, not always for the better.

## Conall's Empowering

New elements as well as interesting variations on old ones appear in the ritual to empower Conall—which really includes a preliminary ritual as well, to withdraw the Haldane potential from Nigel. Because of the sheer logistics of ritually managing everything that must be done, the preliminary takes place *before* the casting of the circle, and the calling of the Quarters is moved to a transitory position between the two.

In the preliminary, three things happen:

1. Morgan asks Conall formally whether he is willing to place himself unreservedly into the hands of his initiators, body and soul—to which Conall replies in the affirmative. (This is always understood in any initiatory ritual, even if not stated.)
2. Duncan reads out a formal declaration withdrawing the Haldane mandate from the incapacitated Nigel and bestowing it on Conall, stating the authority of himself, Morgan, and Arilan to do so. (This focuses the ritual intent of the working.)
3. The document is signed and witnessed by the participants and sealed in blood by the two principals, after which Conall is invested with a blue star-sapphire earring to replace the

lost Eye of Rom. (The business with the document seals the
ritual intent; the earring, in this case, probably can be regarded mainly as stage dressing, since it does not have the
potency associated with the Eye of Rom.)

For the transition, after Conall himself is exhorted, the Quarters are invoked to witness the actual withdrawing of the mandate from Nigel. Note how Morgan's style has evolved, after a
few years' exposure to trained Deryni like Richenda and Arilan—crossing his arms on his breast in a classic esoteric pose of
attentive receptivity (sometimes called the Osiris pose) and
chanting the Archangel names to a sung *Amen*.

MORGAN (arms crossed on breast): I now charge and require
you, Conall Blaine Cluim Uthyr, as the true-born heir of Nigel
Cluim Gwydion Rhys, to witness the lawful withdrawing of the
Haldane mandate from this Nigel Cluim Gwydion Rhys.
                 (Closing his eyes, Morgan raises
                 open palms to shoulder level.)
MORGAN: To that end, I now summon, stir, and call up invisible
witnesses to approve and ratify this act. May we be protected
from all dangers and adversity approaching from the East, in
the name of Ra-pha-el.
RESPONSE (sung): Amen.
MORGAN: So, likewise, may we be protected from all dangers
and adversity approaching from the South, in the name of Mic-
cha-el.
RESPONSE (sung): Amen.
MORGAN: May we also be protected from all dangers and adversity approaching from the West, in the name of Ga-bri-el.
RESPONSE (sung): Amen.
MORGAN: Finally, may we be protected from all dangers and
adversity approaching from the North, in the name of Au-ri-el.
RESPONSE: Amen, Amen, Amen, and with open hearts may we
proceed. (*The Quest for Saint Camber* 296–297)

Next Arilan summons the power lying dormant in Nigel,
drawing it into focus, using a variation on a formula we have
seen twice before: used by Camber in its near-original context
(ordinarily, it is used to bless the Paschal candle) to bless the

water he is about to use for scrying and also by members of the Camberian Council, when setting the boundaries for the Duel Arcane between Kelson and Wencit.

ARILAN (with right hand, tracing a cross the length of Nigel's body & across shoulders):
Blessed be the Creator, Yesterday and Today,
the Beginning and the End, the Alpha and the Omega.
    (Traces Greek letters at Nigel's head and feet,
        symbols of elements in angles of cross.)
His are the seasons and the ages,
to Him glory and dominion
through all the ages of eternity.
Blessed be the Lord. Blessed be His Holy Name.
(*The Quest for Saint Camber* 297)

After Morgan and Duncan have visualized the withdrawal of power from Nigel, focusing the energy into the Haldane blade, the protective circle finally is cast in a near-classic manner:

1. Morgan takes the Haldane sword into the center of the room.
2. Arilan asperses the perimeter, beginning and ending in the East.
3. Duncan (*a*) lights the candles on the central altar; (*b*) burns the withdrawal document, sealed with both Nigel's and Conall's blood, as a blood offering; and (*c*) invokes a blessing on the incense with which he then censes the perimeter.
4. Morgan traces the circle a third time with the sword, finishing in the East and then returning to the center, where he raises the sword horizontally above his head, tip resting against his left hand. Arilan's familiar words intersperse with Morgan's actions for the completion of this part of the rite.

ARILAN: Now we are met.
(Morgan sweeps his arms wide to either side and downward, describing an arc that closes the circle above their heads and downward to floor level at their feet.)
ARILAN (bowing his head): Now we are One with the Light. Regard the ancient ways. We shall not walk this path again.
DUNCAN: *Augeatur in nobis, quaesumus, Domine, tua virtutis*

*operatio.* (May the workings of Thy power, O Lord, be intensified within us.)

MORGAN: So be it. Selah. Amen.

ARILAN (raising his hand in blessing, as Morgan and Duncan bless themselves): *Ex mentis nostri tenebras, gratia tuae visitationis, illustra, Qui vivus. Amen.* (By the grace of Thy coming, light up the darkness of our minds, Thou Who Art.) (*The Quest for Saint Camber* 299)

Having examined the physical preparations for a ritual, the casting of the circle, and the setting of the wards by calling the Quarters, we logically would next take a closer look at specific intentions of rituals—but those have received ample illustration in the various books. Suffice it to say that each will vary according to the particular intent of the ritual. Hence, we will not linger on analyses here but move, instead, to how the ritual ends—an all-too-often overlooked aspect of magic that is as important as any other part of the ritual, if the operator hopes to enjoy positive fruits of his or her labor.

# CHAPTER TWENTY-TWO

# Ritual III:
# Ending the Ritual and Summary

Ending a ritual properly is a formality that many operators tend to take for granted once the ritual intent is accomplished, but the well-trained occultist knows that endings are is just as important as the rest. Authors tend to gloss over or segue past endings of rituals because too much detail can drag at the pacing of the story, and the detail of endings tends not to be as flashy as what went before.

Unfortunately, skipping tedious details tends to reinforce the impression that a ritual simply ends. The former may be a very good literary device, but the latter is *not* good magic. Closing down a ritual too quickly, or without observing the due forms, can leave potent energies out of balance. There are reasons for due forms, after all. The end effect can range from a vague sense of uneasiness that something is not quite right, to nagging headaches for one or more participants, to unexpected phenomena in the ritual area after everyone and everything is supposed to be dispersed, to outright disaster.

We have seen the result of one such premature ending, verging on disaster, when the passage of Cinhil's soul through a circle gate without sufficient preparation utterly shatters the fabric of the circle's dome (*Camber the Heretic* 96). In effect, the abrupt transition of Cinhil's soul from mortal dimensions to those of the Nether World, ringed close by the cosmic balance of

Elemental Forces, creates a cosmic void of imbalance that tries to fill simultaneously as the formerly bound energies suddenly are released. The end result is an instantaneous dispersal of all the considerable energy that went into the building of the circle, with a force so powerful that Camber becomes convinced that only the countering energy of the consecrated Hosts in the ciborium at his elbow has saved him from immortal peril.

This is an extreme example, to be sure, but it graphically illustrates the very real danger that may await even the wary. Camber and his children are all highly experienced ceremonialists, and *they* were taken by surprise. What Camber does, by instinctively shielding under the umbrella of energy associated with the Reserved Sacrament, is to mediate single-handedly the energies that should have been mediated by the group together in the course of closing down the circle.

Almost of necessity, the unexpected mediation of so much energy is uneven—which is why the circle shatters. Had Camber not been able to pull this off, Cinhil Haldane might not have been the only casualty of the night's work. At very least, Camber might have spent hours or even days stunned unconscious by the blast-shock of the circle's dispersal. In retrospect, one suspects that he would have been better advised to close down the circle and *then* allow Cinhil to pass into the escort of the waiting Archangels—but then, hindsight usually is 20/20. In this case as in most, the failure to balance was inadvertent, but the consequence was nonetheless notable and real.

Fortunately, inadequate grounding of residual energy usually does not have such dire or dramatic results. Especially during the early stages of esoteric training, when the student's newly opening power-shunting centers are not yet functioning to full capacity, the student may well misgauge his or her abilities and try to take shortcuts or overdo. Mild headaches the morning after or sometimes just a vague, general malaise for a few days are not at all uncommon, even in our own universe. Such residual effects generally diminish and disappear altogether with experience, as the process of mediation and grounding becomes second nature—at least for lesser functions—but until the lesson is learned, headaches like the ones suffered by Conall after intensive sessions with Tiercel can be the norm. In nearly all instances, natural sleep is the best prescription.

Happily, in a properly managed ritual situation, responsibility for the grounding process and shut-down can be spread among all the participants, so that by following certain prescribed procedures, all the excess energy ends up properly dispersed. Again, the inner components of what actually happens are couched in the symbolism and mnemonics of the outward ritual, comprising three basic parts: consciously mediating any extra energy raised, dismissing the Quarters, and cutting the circle.

## Mediating the Energy

Mediating the energy may seem a fairly nebulous term, but roughly it means to disperse in a controlled manner any residual energy that has not been put to the intent of the ritual. Energy is always produced and contained in the circle during a magical working, sometimes as the ritual's particular intent and sometimes as a by-product of some other operation. If all of it is used in the course of accomplishing the ritual's intent, well and good. If not, or if the power was a by-product, then the excess must be dissipated in an appropriate manner, rather than allowing it to discharge all at once or at random, with possibly undesirable results—as Camber has cause to know full well.

The methods for doing this are many and varied. One of the simplest and most common forms has all the participants link hands and shepherd the remaining energy into a flow or "current" around the circle, usually clockwise, leveling out the excess energy among them. They then may focus and direct, or "launch," that energy toward a specific goal, possibly in a classic "cone of power," as decided by the group and directed by the Master (or Mistress) of the ritual; they may simply allow each member to tap what he or she needs to recharge psychic resources; or they may elect merely to earth the energy through the feet, for the betterment of the planet. A specific working might contain elements of all three applications.

Whatever the specific method of mediating the excess energy, the end result should be to diminish the power levels in the circle to only that energy required to maintain the circle. A commonly used visualization of this result is the impression that the circle's dome is slowly collapsing like a giant, iridescent soap bubble, until all one can See is the faintly glowing ring of the line the sword projected during the third circuit of the casting. Another image is to See the glow of the circle's dome (which is the "visible" manifestation of the energy that binds it) gradually shrink from the center top, down the curve of the sides, and into the ground, like a giant iris opening. (One suspects that Camber's circle might have come down that way, if under control, rather than having the shattered fragments slide down the fading energy containment of the circle's dome.)

The *right* image, in the end, is the one that works for the operator(s). Once any excess energy has been earthed, however much there is of that and however it is done, the circle essentially has been defused, and the circle's Quarter Guardians now can be safely dismissed.

## Dismissing the Quarters

In fact, the term dismissing the Quarters is a misnomer, since a mere mortal really should not presume to "dismiss" such potent beings as Elemental Lords. When one summons these entities, in the personae of the four great Archangels, one is not really commanding them to attend; one is inviting—yea, entreating—them. One *requests* their attendance for a specific purpose—whether to guard and protect, witness, assist, ratify—whatever. Then one builds as strong a visualization of their real presence as possible—and they do attend. (Interestingly enough, just as an infinite God is sufficiently indivisible to be present in all places all at once without diminution, so those aspects of elemental force that we personify as Archangels have the capacity to be present at an infinite number of magical workings simultaneously. In short, one doesn't get a busy signal when requesting a house call by Archangels.)

However, because it is a convenient human convention to think of these elemental archetypes as individuals, with specific characteristics peculiar to the elements they represent, whose expected presence is real in a way that goes beyond mere permeance of any given place, it is only good manners to let them know when their attendance has served its purpose, to thank them for their assistance, and then to bid them hail and farewell before they return to more accustomed climes. The formula used generally will be a variation on the words used to summon, and each one should be acknowledged separately, in the order originally invoked. For example, if Raphael was summoned thus—"I call the mighty Archangel Raphael, the Healer, Guardian of Wind and Tempest. Be with us, we beseech thee, thou Lord of Air, to guard our circle and witness this rite"— then Raphael's dismissal might go something like this, the speaker facing in the appropriate direction and with right hand raised in salute:

"Hail, mighty Raphael, Archangel of the Air, Healer and Guardian of Wind and Tempest. We thank thee for thine attendance and protection here tonight, and before thou departest for thine airy realms, we bid thee hail and farewell!"

To which the rest of the participants, also with right hands raised in salute, would echo, "Hail and farewell," and all bow with right hands to hearts. (If this manner of dismissal strikes familiar chords for some readers, that is hardly surprising. Many different traditions honor the concept of Archangels of the Quarters/Elemental Lords/Watchtowers, and basic courtesy crosses many different disciplines without difficulty.)

The above process would be repeated for each of the remaining three Archangels, substituting appropriate names and attributes, each one addressed by the individual who summoned and all participants facing the appropriate direction, with all turning at last to salute the East a final time. By the time this is completed, the last residuals of energy in the circle itself have been stepped down another level, by the intent of the operator(s), so that all that remains is the final dispersal of the circle.

## Cutting the Circle

Finally, whoever cast the circle the third and final time with the sword (usually the designated Master of the ritual) takes that sword to the East, salutes, then makes an X-shaped cutting motion with the blade, symbolic of severing the last energy connections. This is repeated in the South, the West, and the North, finally returning to the East for a final salute toward the source of Light.

As a side note, some traditions prefer to cut the circle during a counterclockwise or widdershins circuit, reinforcing the imagery of undoing or dismantling or unwinding the circle, but the circuit still goes from East to East—via North, West, and South. Another common reinforcement, if a cord has been used to delineate the physical boundaries of the circle, is to physically wind the cord back onto a spindle, proceeding counterclockwise, while focusing on the inner process associated with the outward action. This usually would be done just after the Master cuts the circle but before his final dismissal.

After the final salute in the East, whatever variations may have been introduced, the Master grounds his blade and turns to face the center to announce "This rite is ended. Go in peace," to which the others respond, "Amen." Variations on this ending are not only possible but likely, but the above is a typical general form.

## Creating a Ritual Framework

So. Drawing upon the background we have established, we now can piece together what might be a general form for creating the basic framework of a "generic" Deryni ritual. Details will vary according to the intent, the setting, the available "props," and the tastes and training of the participants, but the following constitute basics.

## Physical Setting

Four candles or votive lights are required for designating the location of the Quarters. To review, the Deryni convention (at least in the West) for assigning colors to the Archangels of the Quarters is as follows:

> East (Raphael)—Yellow or gold
> South (Michael)—Red
> West (Gabriel)—Blue
> North (Uriel)—Green

The colors can be indicated by glass around the flames, by the candleholders themselves, or even by the color of candles. Any additional lights, such as altar candles, generally will be white or the pale, neutral cream of natural beeswax. (For that matter, the quarter candles *can* be white, too, but why make life difficult? Any occultist worth his or her salt will tell you that a good magician *can* work High Magic naked in the middle of a desert, with no physical accoutrements whatsoever—the trained mind and will should be sufficient—but he or she will also tell you that color is an excellent *aide de memoire* for noting and holding the correct mental set for the elemental orientations. One has more important things than color correspondences to keep actively in mind when one is performing a ritual.)

An altar table, covered with a white cloth, usually occupies the center of the area to be included in the circle. Unless designated otherwise, for a very specific purpose, it is not a Christian altar of Sacrifice but solely a focal point for the ritual to be worked, separate and distinct from any other altar that may be in the room. (The altar table sometimes is omitted if the planned ritual is to be entirely an inner working, as in Evaine's attempt to free her father.) If the ritual is to be held in a church or chapel, to gain the benefits of working in a previously consecrated space and the protection conferred by the Presence of the Reserved Sacrament, the circle usually is laid out to include the room's Christian altar at the eastern perimeter or just outside it, as in Cinhil's power assumption. In this case, at least two white candles are lighted on the altar.

Like a Christian altar, the altar table is always oriented toward the East, the source of Light, as indeed all movement in the circle begins and ends in the East, proceeding clockwise. At least two white candles generally are lighted on the altar table, and other items may be added as needed. Other colors of candles may be substituted or added to enhance particular symbolism appropriate to the intent. Extra accoutrements needed for the ritual tend to be gathered beneath the table, hidden by the altar cloth until needed, since the clutter of superfluous items can be a distraction.

## Attire

Special ceremonial robes as such do not seem to be a particular factor for Deryni practitioners of ritual, except that priests do favor appropriate clerical attire when functioning in a clergy capacity within a magical working. (One gets the impression that the formal robes worn by the Camberian Council in Arilan's time are more a statement of membership than a ceremonial requisite, though distinctive ceremonial dress *is* worn when the Council arbitrates the Wencit-Kelson Duel Arcane.)

At least during Camber's time, however, cleanliness and practicality seem to be more important than any specific style or color, though garments with particular associations may help to establish a desired atmosphere in some instances. Distinctive garments, such as Healer's mantles, Gabrilite habits, or anything of Michaeline blue tend to evoke very precise and very different emotional responses. (So does the braided cincture of Haldane crimson and gold worn by the black-habited *Custodes Fidei*.) Robes, cloaks, or mantles with hoods are useful because the hoods can help shut out distractions during meditations and preparatory rites. Within these kinds of parameters, attire is chosen to fit the occasion.

Thus Morgan, though not a priest, chooses to wear a black cassock when he, Duncan, and Arilan withdraw the Haldane mandate from Nigel and set it in Conall instead. The black is a neutral background for the things he must do; and since he is designated Master of the rite, he also may have been thinking of the imagery of priestly authority that the garment might conjure in Conall. Camber wears a scarlet velvet gown for his scrying attempt, because the rubric specifically says he ought to, but such particular instruction is rare.

The main color constant that we observe in ritual attire is that Rhys nearly always wears Healer's green in the circle to underline his function in that capacity. Priests such as Joram, Queron, and Duncan wear monastic habits or other clergy attire without fail—Michaeline blue, white, or black. Bishop Arilan wears purple. Evaine is one of the few women we have seen work in a ritual capacity so far, and she tends to wear plain, neutral gowns that will not distract, if she dresses purposefully at all. The one time we see Richenda in such a setting, when Nigel's potential is set, she wears only a long white shift—again, a stark, neutral sort of garment; her male counterparts discard layers, open collars, and generally strip down to basics—for physical discomfort can distract the most disciplined concentration. In conclusion, Deryni wear whatever seems most appropriate for the situation.

## Assignment of Roles

Assignment of participants to specific ritual functions in the circle will be determined partly by their real-world vocations. If available, a Michaeline will always take the Southern Quarter and generally (though not always) is the one to wield the sword. If a Healer is present, he generally will stand in the East, for Raphael is the Archangel of healing, despite the fact that the greatest Healing order has Gabriel for its patron. Gabrilites prefer to work from the West for that reason, though a Gabrilite will defer to a woman, if one is present, since the West is associated with the Annunciation and the Virgin. A senior adept such as Camber tends to officiate from the North.

## Casting the Circle

Holy water is required to cast the circle, which may be prepared beforehand or as a part of the ritual. (In the course of the preparation, the water is exorcised—banished of negative influences—and blessed, usually by a priest. A small amount of pure salt is then blessed and added to the water, giving the finished product the purifying attributes of both Water and Earth.)

The holy water is sprinkled around the boundaries of the circle with a traditional aspergillum or else dipped from a bowl and scattered with a tuft of greenery or even the fingertips, with the intent to purify by Water and Earth. The person who does this—ideally a woman, since Water and Earth are feminine attributes—is called the asperser. The Twenty-third Psalm, also known as the Psalm of the Shepherd, is a favorite recitation while walking the circle, partly because of the protective atmosphere it reinforces (usually first established in childhood) and partly because of its accessibility by way of being familiar. Another favorite is the traditional Asperges that precedes the Mass on a Sunday, the passage beginning "Thou shalt sprinkle me with hyssop, O Lord, and I shall be cleansed; Thou shalt wash me, and I shall be whiter than snow." However, any other suitable meditation might be substituted with similar effect, and silence is an equally appropriate accompaniment. The crucial focus is the intent to purify.

Holding this in mind, the asperser walks the first circuit, pausing at each Quarter to salute with an extra sprinkle and a bow, starting and finishing in the East. Before putting the implements aside, he or she usually sprinkles each of the other participants to purify them and is purified by one of them in turn.

Incense is required, and something to burn it in. It may be in a proper thurible, hanging from chains, or simply a fireproof container to hold a charcoal block on which the incense may be sprinkled. (Stick incense was not known to the Deryni but would be better than no incense at all.) For calling up associations, the sense of smell is extremely potent. Just a hint of a familiar aroma can release a flood of memories and associations and images, all of which can be used to reinforce a desired mental set. The sharp, clean smell of cedar oil conjured almost overwhelming memories for Camber-Alister, and the rich, pungent scent of church incense is one never to be forgotten, once experienced, recalling all the soaring splendor of time-hallowed places of worship: the hushed, tranquil mystery of candlelit altars and snowy altar linens, the vibrant jewel-tones of silken vestments rustling in the silence, the reverent expectation of golden chalices raised to receive the Presence that descends, voices blending in harmonies as sweet as the tendrils of smoke that spiral upward with thoughts and prayers. . . . Powerful images for one little smell, aren't they?)

The person who carries the incense is called a thurifer and is usually a man, since he consecrates by Fire and Air, which are male attributes. Like the asperser, he proceeds clockwise from East to East, saluting at each Quarter and bowing, censing the other participants (and being censed) when he has finished his circuit. He may also recite a psalm or other meditation.

A sword generally is used to cast the final circuit of the magical circle, though a dagger or other ceremonial blade may be used (the traditional *athame*), or even the first two fingers of the right hand, directed like a blade. (If the sword is used, it almost always is wielded by a man.) The tip of the sword generally does not touch the ground or floor, but points to the perimeter of the circle (previously established by the first two circuits) and projects a quasi-visible beam of energy, usually bluish violet in color, to hover at the circle's boundary. Actual physical visibility of the circle boundary will vary, depending on the psychic sensitivity of the observers.

Note that a circle *can* be made visible to physical sight, as when protective circles are erected to protect outsiders from a Duel Arcane, but in the usual ritual context, a human generally will not be able to see anything—or, at best, he or she may sense a vague impression of—*something* out of the corner of the eye. Trained practitioners will See the circle with another sense besides physical sight, though convenience generally leads one to interpret what one perceives through Sight as a more familiar visual image. Describing the color of a magical circle as bluish violet is as convenient a way as any to identify a color that does not exist in the visual spectrum.

The *intent* of the casting with the sword is to finalize and seal the delineation of the boundaries. After the third circuit, the operator generally expands the hovering circle of ''light'' to delineate the circle's dome, using the sword or hands to direct the energy. It should always be understood, even if not noted specifically, that the dome extends below ground level as well, so that the warded area actually is spherical.

## Invocation of Quarters

Since this aspect of Deryni ritual already has been examined in depth (see Chapter 21), we need not reiterate here except to note that its usual order falls after the circle is cast. A statement of the ritual's intent often is incorporated with the setting of Quarters, or may constitute a separate part. The protection of the Deity usually is invoked at some point as well. The working that follows, unless it is a set procedure for accomplishing a particular end result, will be designed specifically to accommodate the participants and their goals, using as much outward symbolism as possible to reinforce, in terms of sight, sound, smells, and ritual gestures.

## Opening and Closing Gates

Finally, a few words about opening and closing gates in the circle, since this may be necessary in the course of a ritual working. Though this should be minimized where possible, by planning ahead—leaving the circle to fetch forgotten paraphernalia is a poor excuse—opening a gate sometimes is unavoidable. The very nature of the ritual to potentialize Cinhil's sons required that Joram open the circle several times so that the boys could be rotated in and out in turn; and Gregory had to open the circle in the *keeill* to admit Queron for his induction into the Camberian Council. As a side note, we may recall the heavy cord used to physically delineate the *keeill* circle (*The Harrowing of Gwynedd* 73), with the ends being knotted and unknotted to reinforce the symbolism of closing and opening a gate.

Gates also may be required to permit the passage of nonphysical entities—to depart, as when Joram opened a gate for Cinhil's soul to pass, or to enter, as when Kelson opened a gate to allow the approach of Saint Camber. However, as may be inferred from what happened in Cinhil's case, opening a gate does create a structural weakness in the circle. Hence it is important to minimize the opening of gates at all, to open them only for as long as is necessary, and to close and seal them completely. The more powerful the working intended, the more important this becomes.

We have seen several examples of opening and closing gates. Most often this is done with whatever magical weapon was used to cast the final circuit of the circle, usually the sword. If the need for a gate has been anticipated, the sword usually will have been laid along the arc of the circle where the gate will be cut, after the third circuit is cast, as Cinhil did in the ritual for his sons (*Camber the Heretic* 84–96).

Taking up the magical weapon, the operator usually salutes the area of the circle where the gate is to be opened, often by kissing the blade—or the first two fingers, if his hand is to be used. The purpose of the salute is to recollect one's attention for the work to be done, to set the coming intention apart from what has just gone on—a transition, if you will.

Facing where the gate will be, the operator touches the tip of the blade to the circle on the floor at his left, then sweeps upward, to the right, and downward, in a narrow arc large enough for a person to pass, all the while willing his intent that a door should open. To trained perceptions, the area within the arc of the doorway becomes clear when compared with the "material" of the circle-dome still surrounding the opening. The description of Kelson opening a gate for the approach of Saint Camber shows this change in the fabric of the actual doorway quite clearly.

His pulse was pounding as he traced the outline of the opening, using the edge of his hand like the blade of a sacred sword to cut the energies and seal them at the edges. And as the outline was complete, Kelson's hand moved again to dissipate the energy bound within the outline and open the gate. (*The Quest for Saint Camber* 382)

Occasionally, especially if a hand or the shorter blade of dagger or *athame* is to be used in tracing the outline of the opening itself, the operator will draw the hand or blade across the edge of the circle at either side of the intended doorway, symbolic of actually cutting a segment out of the circle at that point. Once the opening has appeared, whichever way it has been cut, the operator normally stands aside, the sword still grounded from cutting the opening, and keeps psychic watch at the gate while necessary physical passage is made.

If the operator himself must leave the circle, with no one to take his place as guardian, he lays the sword across the opening just outside the circle, taking it up again on his return. If the gate must be left open while the operator is occupied in another part of the circle, sometimes the blade is laid to the left of the opening with the point at the edge of the doorway and the hilt toward the center of the circle, symbolic of the magical sword still being poised to deny entry to those who have no right to pass.

Closing the gate also can take several forms. Most often the tip of the sword is merely drawn across the threshold of the doorway from left to right, retracing that part of the circle while firmly envisioning the closure, though some practitioners trace the line three times, to symbolize the three original circuits that were cut to open the gate.

The premier thing to remember in all of the above operations is that the outward actions only reinforce inner processes, the latter of which are the important ones. A true adept can cast a circle, summon Quarter protection, accomplish his ritual intent, and take care of all the little housekeeping details of mediating

the excess energies, releasing the Quarters, and winding down
the circle without raising a physical finger.

## Summary of Ritual Structure

In this chapter, we have gone into some detail about the physical
requirements common to most Deryni rituals. In conclusion, let
us summarize the basic structure of the ritual itself. We can
isolate ten elements common to nearly every formal ritual. All
else really is embellishment, for one reason or another.

1. Lighting of the quarter candles (may also constitute a preliminary walking of the circle perimeter with fire).
2. Exorcism of water and blessing of salt, if this has not already been done—and if needed for aspersing.
3. Casting the circle: aspersing, censing, tracing with the
   sword.
4. Invocation of the Quarters: East, South, West, and North.
5. Statement of Intent (may be incorporated with 4. above)
6. Invocation of the Deity for guidance, protection, and so on.
7. The Working.
8. Mediation of excess power.
9. Dismissal of the Quarters.
10. Cutting of the circle.

# CHAPTER TWENTY-THREE

# Ritual IV:
# Applications

Most of what the Deryni call magical "work" (usually distinguished from simple telefunctions or utility spells) involves ritual application of their power. We have already established that ritual is simply a convenient framework or context in which to place a procedure. Its particular use lies in establishing a mental set suitable for accomplishing the desired end and reinforcing that mental set by repeating the same outward actions and physical settings for similar workings. As above, so below; as without, so within. Interior reality may be mirrored in the exterior.

In addition, specific rituals repeated over a period of time in a particular way with a particular intent accumulate an esoteric "weight" greater than the sum of any single working, that facilitates and enhances further workings of those rituals. In the same way that travel over a particular route through a field gradually establishes and keeps open a path that enables others to pass without the necessity to clear the way each time with a machete, so repeated enactment of a ritual can open and strengthen the circuits for making the connections with Other. Furthermore, not having to reinvent the wheel for every single ritual means that more energy can go into the actual working.

Ritual also provides a common ground of symbolism and focus if two or more people are attempting to work together. Were it not for the unifying nature of ritual, coordinating the energies and mental sets of multiple operators might prove an insurmountable obstacle.

Having reviewed the nature of ritual, we may consider that most of the nonecclesiastical ritual we have seen in a Deryni context falls roughly into three general classifications. *Protective* rituals include all wardings and rites designed to concentrate power for the protection or defense of a subject. Sometimes the ritual is very precise and almost mechanistic, such as the procedure for activating Ward Cubes—itself a shorthand ritual to call up function, based on the far more elaborate and disciplined outpouring of psychic energy that went into charging the set of cubes when new, making of them Ward Cubes rather than four pairs of odd, blank dice. Circle wardings also fall into the protective ritual category, though their conduct can vary widely according to the tastes and training of the operator(s).

In fact, protective magic does not have to involve much ritual at all. Sometimes it can be as simple as Morgan concentrating power in the Saint Camber medal that Derry wears (though Morgan undoubtedly has already done some work on the medal from his own wearing of it), or Tiercel setting limited memory blocks to protect Conall from casual reading by others.

*Initiatory* rituals tend to be far more formal and always involve opening the candidate to a higher level of awareness and understanding. The Haldane potentializing ritual is initiatory in nature, as is the induction of Camberian Council members. Not only the Christian faith regards priestly ordination as an esoteric initiation; adding Deryni elements only makes it more so. The sacrament of Christian initiation, more commonly called Baptism, is another example, and when combined with a Healer's dedication, as in "Healer's Song," it gains added mystical character. Eventually we will see that the formal commissioning and consecration of an accredited Healer was an initiatory rite as well.

The third general area of Deryni ritual work falls into what broadly might be called *contemplative* or meditative or inner-growth techniques. In the Deryni context, such techniques often tend to be associated with more conventional religious practices and devotions, though their content and orientation are not necessarily exclusively Christian. Using a *shiral* crystal as the physical focus for meditation might be considered a secular Deryni application of the same kind of meditative technique used in praying the Christian rosary, the term rosary defining both the devotion and the beads used to count the prayers. (The rosary as we know it did not come into popular use until the mid-1400s, which is after the equivalent period in the history of Gwynedd, but the concept of using stones or beads to count prayers is ancient and appears in many different cultures. In the Eastern Church, prayers sometimes are counted on rosaries made of knotted cord—one suspects that the Deryni cording lore might adapt readily to such a use—and if Deryni *did* use rosaries, one might consider the possible enhancement of the devotion by using a rosary made with *shiral* crystals for beads.)

In general, Deryni tend to be far more open than humans to the esoteric dimensions of religious practice. Or perhaps it is that Deryni have more ready access to these esoteric dimensions—which, as we have already suggested, may partially account for the hostility of the institutional Church, whose guardians both fear and covet what they do not understand or possess. Cinhil's grief at the expectation of having to give up his priesthood provides poignant contrast with his spiritual ecstasy during celebration of the Mass, and his defense of his priestly vocation is an almost textbook example of classic mystical experience.

> "How can I make you understand what it's like to be able to live a life totally committed to God? . . . It's as though you're shielded in a soft, golden light, floating about a handspan off the ground, and you're safe from anything that might try to harm you, because you know that He is there, all around you. It's as though—you reach out with your mind and grasp a beam of sunlight, yet even as you grasp it, it's all around you. . . ." (*Camber of Culdi* 226)

Intellectually, Camber certainly can commiserate with Cinhil at the time—though not enough to be swayed from what he and his kin have planned for the prince. One suspects, however, that it is not until Camber's own priestly ordination that he truly understands what Cinhil is talking about. We have already looked at his ordination in regard to the extra dimensions experienced by a Deryni, but his perception of the actual mystical experience bears reexamination.

. . . A subtle pressure grew inside his mind, a gradual filling and expanding with Something which was so powerful,
so awesome, that no corner of his being escaped Its insistent
touch.

His hearing went first, and he knew that his vision also was
gone—though he could not, to save his mortal life, have
opened his eyes to test that knowledge.

Then all awareness of having a body at all began to fade.
He was pure consciousness and more, centered in a bright,
shining point, bathed and immersed in a golden brilliance,
cool and fascinating, which was unlike anything he had ever
experienced or imagined experiencing.

He was no longer frightened; he was engulfed in an emotion of peace and joy and total oneness with all that was and
would be and once had been. He stretched and soared on
rainbow wings, exulting in the certainty that there was far
more to being than a mere mortal body and lifetime—that
even when this human body died, whatever guise it wore, he—
the essence of him—would continue, would grow, would move
on to the fullness of eternity.

In a sparkling instant, he saw his past, and other pasts, in
shimmering, quicksilver glimpses, immediately lost to memory; and then his present experience, as though observing his
own body from above, silver-gilt head bowed unflinching beneath consecrated hands whose touch was both delicate and
relentless.

The thought whisked across his consciousness that perhaps
he was fantasizing all of this; and a rational part of himself
agreed. But another part of him banished that notion almost
before it could take definite form.

What did it matter, at this point, whether he was experiencing true reality or one created, born of his own emotional
need and reaching? No mere mortal could hope to experience
the Godhead in *all* Its many facets. Man the finite could but
glimpse the filmy shadow-trails of the Infinite, and that only
if he were very fortunate.

But in his present mode, given all the weaknesses and
strengths both of human and Deryni resources, was this not
as close as he had ever brushed the Power which governed
the wheeling of the Universe? (*Saint Camber* 265–266)

Arilan also experiences a mystical enlightenment at his ordination, but not during the rite itself. It is during the Mass that follows, when he unreservedly has given himself over to God's will, accepting that he will die if there is *merasha* in the chalice, that Denis Arilan learns the true power of his faith.

The wine was sweet and heady, lighter than he remembered, igniting a gentle but growing tingle that spread from his stomach, up his spinal column, and out to the tips of his fingers and toes, to explode at the back of his head in a starburst of warmth and light and love—and it was not *merasha*.

Light seemed to fountain from the vessels still on the altar, from the tabernacle on the credence shelf behind it, from the chalice de Nore carried back to the altar, and Denis sensed a similar energy pulsing through the bodies of all those assembled to assist. Benjamin and Melwas, kneeling reverently to either side of him, had the same glow; and the ciborium de Nore set solemnly in his hands a few minutes later throbbed gently with a rhythm that was the heartbeat of the universe, silvery radiance spilling from the cup to bathe his hands in light that apparently only he could see.

He felt as if he was floating a handspan off the ground as he rose to go down to the communion rail where his brother waited with the other members of the new priests' families to receive the Sacrament. Indeed, he made certain he was *not* floating, for the way he felt—his Deryni powers not only intact but apparently enhanced—he thought he could have, given even a whit more provocation. The intimacy of the moment in which, a priest at last, he gave his brother Holy Communion for the first time, was almost too much joy to contain, the awe and wonder on Jamyl's face a sight he would cherish until the day he died. (*The Deryni Archives* 153–154)

As a further confirmation that something Other touched Denis Arilan that day, he later learns that he *did* drink *merasha*. That he was not affected he can ascribe only to direct Divine intervention. "He knew that he had experienced as much of a miracle as any man could hope for—and that he would spend the rest of his life trying to serve the purpose of the One Who had spared him." (*The Deryni Archives* 156)

*Did* Arilan experience a miracle? If his survival was *not* a miracle, then we must search for some "rational" explanation. So far as we know, no Deryni before or since has done what Denis Arilan did on his ordination day. Shall we say that he somehow neutralized the *merasha* in his body, that he transmuted it into some harmless substance that would not betray him? From a purely rational perspective, this obviously is what must have happened. Yet this, too, is a miraculous occurrence, since we can no more explain how Arilan did it than we can fathom how God might have worked such a transmutation directly.

Nor are such moments of spiritual transport confined to ecclesiastical contexts. Several times now, in a variety of basically secular settings, we have observed a most extraordinary phenomenon at the moment certain individuals pass into the Nether World.

When Cinhil lies dying, after setting the Haldane potential in his three sons, Camber tries to ease his passing. His Deryni senses are fully open, his true identity as Camber-Alister offered up for Cinhil's knowledge, as Cinhil offered up the knowledge of his secret priesthood to Alister so many years before—for there may be no subterfuge between the two in this final moment.

With a weary nod, Camber closed his eyes and let his thoughts cease, let himself open along the old, familiar link which the Alister part of him had formed with the king so long ago. He felt Cinhil's presence, somehow refined and *different* from what it had been before. And then, gradually, his mind began to fill with what he could only describe as sound, though he knew it was not that—a light, hollowly resounding tinkle as if of tiny bells mingled with the hush of many voices chanting a single Word on tones which blended in indescribable harmony.

*The music of the spheres,* a part of him thought sluggishly— *or perhaps the voices of the heavenly hosts—or both—or neither.*

For a moment, there was a swirl of foggy, opalescent color, a feeling of disjointure—and then he seemed to be looking down at Cinhil through eyes somehow more perceptive, though objectively he knew that his physical eyes were still closed.

With his Sight which was not sight, he Saw the years melt away from Cinhil's face, knew Cinhil's awe as the king gazed up at the form which was no longer quite the Alister Cullen whom he had seen and known for the past twelve years. Whatever was happening had stripped away the facade, leaving his psychic form naked, for Cinhil to see in all its many facets.

*Camber?* came the king's tentative query, somehow past shock or anger or fear.

*And Alister, in part,* came Camber's meekly tendered answer.

And with that, he offered up the rest of the story to Cinhil's clearing consciousness, leaving out no detail—for he could conceal nothing in this dreamlike, awesome realm in which they both hovered now. In an immeasurable stretch of time, the deed was done, the tale told; and Cinhil's awed expression had changed to one of beatific acceptance. (*Camber the Heretic* 93–94)

We may be assured that Camber is in a highly altered state of consciousness as he cradles the king's failing body in his arms and bids Joram open a gate in the circle for Cinhil's soul to pass. To Camber's hyperextended perception, a renewed and rejuvenated Cinhil seems to rise up out of the mortal body to pass into the escort of the four guardian Archangels themselves. So concrete a visualization of these Elemental Guardians is not achieved often, even by Deryni of Camber's caliber, and it is impossible to say whether the shattering of the circle's dome at the instant of Cinhil's passage beyond the gate is actually caused by the archangelic blowing of a spectral horn or merely by the abrupt change of energy levels as Cinhil passes into another dimension.

Then Cinhil was moving through the gateway, his face transformed by a shining light which grew around him. Dimly, past the slowly receding Cinhil, Camber thought he could see others standing and reaching out to Cinhil—a beautiful young woman with hair the color of ripe wheat, two young boys who were Cinhil's image, others whom Camber could not identify.

In a rush of wind and the illogical impression of wings,

four Presences seemed to converge around Cinhil then—*Be-*
*ings* with vague shadow-forms and sweeping pinions of raw
power which somehow sheltered rather than threatened.
(*Camber the Heretic* 95–96)

We have already dealt with the appearance of the four great
Archangels in some detail in another chapter. The key here is
the transformation of Cinhil as he rises up out of his spent body
and the images of Cinhil's loved ones waiting for him—his dead
wife and sons, and others unknown to Camber, probably from
Cinhil's former monastic life, before he became king.

Jebediah, too, is renewed at the moment of his passing—and
is greeted by one who has gone on before. Again it is Camber
who Sees, his perceptions preternaturally sharpened this time
by his own impending death.

Again he felt the ethereal, detached sensation as the silver
cord began to unravel and the ties of earth-binding were
loosed. Even though they were not in a magic circle this time,
as he turned his Sight outward he could See the vague, insub-
stantial image of a younger Jebediah superimposing itself over
the failing body in his arms, a Jebediah restored to vigorous,
vibrant youth.

Jebediah was not looking at him, though—not any more.
Instead, his face was turned toward the little shrine across the
clearing, which blazed in Camber's Sight like a friendly beacon of cool, silver light. From it a familiar form in Michaeline
blue seemed to grow out of a pinpoint of light, drifting slowly
toward them, booted feet never quite touching the new snow.
A wide smile was on his face—the same face which had looked
back at Camber in his mirror for many years now, though
younger—and he held out his arms in welcome to the man
who was now rising out of the spent shell which once had
housed Jebediah.

Forgetting to breathe, Camber watched as a new and young
Jebediah rose from the ground at his knees and went to join
the specter, the two men embracing like long-parted brothers
in a joy which brimmed and overflowed even as far as Camber. They drew apart to turn and gaze at him then, first Jebediah and then the other stretching out their arms as though

inviting him to join them. The lure was appealing, but even
as Camber wavered on the verge of accepting, pain jarred the
vision and shook his concentration. When he tried to look for
them again, he could not See them. (*Camber the Heretic* 478–
479)

*Could* Camber have joined Jebediah and Alister? Certainly
his body was mortally wounded, physical life ebbing slowly but
inexorably as his blood seeped onto the snow. Yet Camber eventually comes to believe that it is not yet time to yield himself up
to death, and the absence of any of *his* close loved ones with
Jebediah and Alister tends to confirm that he has made the decision intended. Rhys was recently dead, after all, and very
close to Camber; we surely would have expected he would be
there. Likewise, we might have anticipated the shade of the
murdered Cathan, or Camber's departed wife, Jocelyn. We know
little of her, for she has been dead for some seven years before
we meet Camber for the first time, but given the man, one would
expect that he probably had a close and loving relationship with
her. That none of these loved ones were present may be significant.

Such a passing into the Nether World is no less dramatic when
seen from the perspective of the one who passes—though
Evaine's experience leaves us just short of the actual transition
beyond the Gates of Death.

For just an instant, she gained one final sensory impression: an overwhelming visual image of her father, all his
wounds healed and a semblance of youth restored, opening
his eyes to smile up at her in love, compassion, understanding, and even forgiveness and gratitude for the inestimable
price she had paid for his release.

Then he was simply gone, and she was turning her face to
the gateway in the circle, where a dearly beloved man with
unruly red hair and laughter in his amber eyes beckoned to
her with one outstretched hand, a giggling nine-year-old
perched precariously astride the green-mantled shoulders. She
gave no further thought to the body she left behind, as it
collapsed softly into Queron's arms like a spent set of sails.
She had eyes only for the man, the boy—and then the great

Light that beckoned from beyond the shadows as she passed outside, caught up in a flutter of green-black wings. (*The Harrowing of Gwynedd* 415)

Not miracles, perhaps, but certainly beyond the usual ken of ordinary mortals. For someone besides the principal to sense what is happening at the moment of transition probably is a distinctly Deryni ability and one limited to exceedingly advanced Deryni at that. But many of the images tally with reports of individuals in our own world who have had near-death experiences and come back to tell of them. Details vary, but certain common elements recur again and again: the great Light beckoning from the distance, the vision of loved ones already gone on, things receding in a point of light, the overwhelming sensation of a great, overwhelming, enfolding Love. All of these strike familiar chords. Perhaps we are more Deryni than we think. Or perhaps the Deryni are more human than *they* think.

## Meditation in the Deryni Context

The distinctive feature of most meditative techniques, whether human or Deryni, is the ability of the subject to shift into an alternate state of consciousness whereby insights and understanding are gained that might not be accessible to normal waking consciousness. This usually is done in a religious or quasi-religious context, because contemplation of issues of importance tends to be associated with loftier concepts than the mundane activities that occupy so many of our waking hours. In normal human practice, the subject generally fixes on or through a point of focus, often a flame or point of reflection or some other distinctive object separate from the surroundings, or else closes his or her eyes and does the same thing with a mental image. In either case, the attention is then directed, with varying degrees of activity, toward a particular idea or concept or general aim. Sometimes the purpose is active enlightenment; sometimes it is sufficient for the subject merely to "rest in the Grace" for a time, basking in the regenerative energies that often accompany closer contact with one's higher self (or God).

Deryni generally do the same kinds of things, except that their powers of concentration and ability to move more readily between levels of the mind may give more concrete results more quickly. If the Deryni uses a *shiral* crystal as a focus for meditation, the stone can act as a kind of biofeedback device, visually confirming that the subject has achieved an interior balance and receptiveness to allow further work to be done. One may surmise that some inner awareness of this change of level accompanies the visual verification, though detecting this awareness may be difficult until one gains working experience.

When Cinhil chances upon Evaine meditating in the chapel, he becomes aware of such a look of peace upon her, "such tranquil oneness with the universe," that he nearly kneels in awe of it himself. A "glow of pure radiance" and a "sanctity" are other terms he uses to describe it. When Cinhil gathers the courage to ask whether Evaine's *shiral* crystal had anything to do with the look he saw on her face, she concedes that it did not cause it but that it may, perhaps, have enhanced it. We see numerous examples of particular meditations and devotions used by Deryni in a wide variety of contexts. Some aspects of the contemplative life lie at the foundations of most highly trained Deryni, even if they live totally in the world, but the Deryni religious orders perhaps epitomize the ideal.

## The Deryni Religious Orders: Their Distinctive Meditative Practices

Deryni religious orders, or those orders whose membership is predominantly Deryni, tend to have distinctive meditative and devotional practices of their own. This is a natural outgrowth of the spiritual discipline practiced by any religious order, enhanced by superior abilities of perception and the close bonds arising out of living and worshipping as a community.

The *Order of Saint Michael* has a reputation for being militant, well educated, and close-mouthed about its internal affairs. We might think of it as a Gwynedd-equivalent of a Templar-Jesuit cross, combining the military prowess, courage, and fiscal-administrative acumen of the Knights Templar with the discipline, razor-sharp intellectual training, and zeal of the Society of Jesus. (Interestingly enough, both real-world orders have or had secret devotional practices and disciplines that contributed to their success—and downfalls. Imagine what they might have done with Deryni powers.)

We have not yet been shown a great deal about Michaeline practices that differs from other orders. We know that Michaeline Knights, as soldiers of the Church Militant, are dispensed from the injunction against killing that binds most other religious. We know that they celebrate the Eucharist under both species; that is, they offer the Chalice as well as the Host to communicants—which was unusual both for Gwynedd and in our own Middle Ages.

We know, too, that the Michaelines had a meditation involving a sword. For private devotions, it is likely that this consisted mainly of the Michaeline Knight kneeling with his sword held like a cross before him, cross-quillons up, the point resting against the ground, while he recited certain prayers. Perhaps he was instructed to make visual focus on a relic in the pommel or under a boss at the crossing, where the quillons met the hilt. With appropriate concentration and intent, underlined by Michaeline spiritual discipline, fixing on such a point should have made it easy enough for even a human Knight to ease into an altered state of consciousness—a trance, if you will. From there, the individual's own predilections would carry him on to appropriate insights or revelations. Modern Knights Templar have a meditation very like this.

In Chapter, as a group exercise, it is likely that the Michaeline Meditation of the Sword took on added dimensions, for the Deryni members of the order could carry the human ones along with them in the meditation. Probably the exercise was accompanied by some kind of guided meditation led by the Grand Master or some other designated officer, directing the appropriate visualization and the desired end result. Camber recalls that Michaelines were trained to focus on a flame or the Sword of Saint Michael for their special workings (*Camber the Heretic* 173)—a tantalizing snippet of information that seems to have come from his Alister memories rather than his own experience, for no further detail emerges. Perhaps the sword was set upright in a slot in a stone altar like the bluestone cube in the Gabrilite chapter house, with the flame burning in a hollow before it. Perhaps the flame actually was handfire. We can gather that energy ended up being stored in some way, for Camber recognizes a similarity between the Gabrilite cube and the feel of the Michaeline workings, and senses a further connection with the black and white cube altar under Grecotha, which he *knows* is a power nexus. As for *why* the Michaelines performed this particular meditation, we simply do not know. Not yet, at any rate.

The *Order of Saint Gabriel* presents even more of a mystery than the Michaelines, in some respects. Since *all* Gabrilites were Deryni, they had no need to accommodate the lowest common denominator of human inability among them. *All* Gabrilites were adepts or adepts in training. Accordingly, their practices were always more openly magical than those of the Michaelines, though both orders were careful to guard their inner workings from outsiders, whether human or Deryni.

We have already mentioned the bluestone cube in the Gabrilite chapter house. Camber recognizes it as a power focus, but that is the extent of his knowledge. Nor can Rhys offer much enlightenment, only then sensing as somehow familiar a perception he had not known how to recognize when last he had been at Saint Neot's as a student.

He would have known something about the chapter house itself, of course. Aside from sharing occasionally in the duties of cleaning it, as did all inhabitants—ordained priest and Healer as well as novice, apprentice, and student—he would have stood before the Chapter for examinations and in matters of discipline. Not being a member of the Order, however, he would not have been privy to what went on at Chapter meetings or during the devotions of the senior brethren.

And if Rhys *did* see or hear anything he should not have done, by the knack students often have for picking up odd bits and pieces about their mentors and stringing them together to form correct but undesired conclusions, might not his masters have taken gentle measures to ensure that such information did not leave Saint Neot's walls? Master Healers, entrusted with the training of Healer students, would have had regular and deep access to those students' minds. Gently defusing information that might have reflected undesirably on the order would have been a simple matter for such adepts.

We see indications of the Order's hidden roots all around us at Saint Neot's. Outside the chapter house, on the tiles of the blue faience domes, Camber notes the distinctive Gabrilite crosses, ''equal arms touching a solar ring at the four quarters, the arms flaring slightly at the ends.''

That motif and others which seemed somewhat familiar were repeated in the carving of the heavy bronze doors framing the entry portico of the chapter house—subtle, but there for those who knew what to look for. The overall impression rather confirmed his suspicion that the origins of the Gabrilites, like the Deryni themselves, stretched back much farther in history than most folk assumed. While it was much discussed, especially among the more orthodox clergy, those who studied such things were well aware that many faiths besides Christianity had contributed to the body of knowledge which was the legacy of Deryni magic. (*Camber the Heretic* 171)

Part of this legacy shows up fairly openly in Gabrilite usage. We see it when Camber-Alister goes to Saint Neot's on Christmas Eve of 917 to warn the Gabrilites that they soon will be attacked by regents' men. Dom Emrys' back is to Camber, a pure silver light streaming from behind him to illuminate the filled rows of choir stalls to either side and beyond him.

The Office in progress was Compline, which closed the canonical hours for the day, and in two orderly lines, the Gabrilite brethren, priests, Healers, and a few older students were filing out of their stalls and up the center aisle to make a reverence before their abbot and then conjure handfire symbolically from the light in his hands. As Camber and Joram watched, each man took his light back to his place in the choir and knelt, the silver glows gradually taking on individual tints of color as each man merged his own meditations with the spark which the abbot had given. (*Camber the Heretic* 366)

It *is* a uniquely Deryni devotion, as Camber observes. It also is a Deryni adaptation of a Benedictine practice, in which members of the community come forward at the end of Compline to have the abbot or abbess trace a cross on each person's forehead with holy water dipped from a filled scallop shell. Deryni might do that, too, especially Gabrilites, for the water-filled seashell is a potent visual link with the Blessed Virgin as Star of the Sea—and we know the Gabrilites have a special devotion to Our Lady. Perhaps the Gabrilites are Deryni Benedictines. Both orders keep Perpetual Adoration/Vigil, the Benedictines before the Blessed Sacrament, the Gabrilites before the shrine of Saint Gabriel and the Lady—which shrine would also house the Reserved Sacrament. That is where Jaffray knew he would find Emrys, keeping the midnight vigil as the week turned to the Sabbath, when he was set the task of arranging a meeting among Emrys, Queron, Rhys, and Camber.

That meeting—or rather, what Camber experienced just at the beginning of that meeting—points up another distinctively Gabrilite practice that seems to have no other Gwynedd parallel; the science of sound and musical harmonies. It has long been understood in our own world that certain sounds, certain frequencies, certain combinations of frequencies, produce definite physiological responses in humans. Music is not only a matter of aesthetic taste, but certain kinds of melodies and rhythms affect the way we feel. (Elevator music, or what one hears in the dentist's waiting room, inspires very different feelings from Mozart or hard rock.)

The ancient Celts had a profound understanding of the effects different sounds could have on the listener. Major and minor keys produced quite different responses. Certain harmonies were irresistible. A master harper had a repertoire of songs for everything from inducing sleep or healing, to stirring men to war, to awakening love. The harp was the bard's instrument of choice—one well able to mimic the human voice—so it should not be surprising that the Gabrilites, coming from a parallel Celtic stock, learned to utilize some of the same principles, turning the principles of harmonics, in particular, to the enhancement of their chants and hymns— enhancements that would convey multidimensional meanings to a Deryni listener. Camber had heard the *Adsum Domine* sung once before, when Rhys dedicated his infant son Tieg as a future Healer, but hearing it sung solo does not compare with having it sung in full choir the way he hears it that day, from behind the altar at Saint Neot's, as the Healer-priests chant it antiphonally in the nave beyond.

The hymn was the ancient and haunting *Adsum Domine*, heartstone of the ethical precepts which had governed the conduct of lay and ecclesiastical Healers for nearly as long as there had been Healers among the Deryni. Only once before had Camber heard it sung, though he had read the words a dozen times or more, and knew them all by heart. . . .

Now the voices of the Healer-priests wove spine-tingling harmonics which touched at deeper chords within his being, seeking but never quite finding in Camber those differences which made some men Healers and some not. (*Camber the Heretic* 168–169)

This particular hymn is intended primarily for Healers, then, though it has the power to set up resonances in some non-Healer adepts as well. We might liken the process to a television not quite able to pull in a signal, drifting in and out of focus, catching occasional ghost images and snatches of dialogue, but not quite able to lock in. Given the poignancy awakened in Camber by his experience, we can imagine what it must have been like for a Healer, who *could* catch all the nuances. One must wonder whether the Gabrilites had other such hymns for other purposes. One suspects they might well have done.

Two additional Gabrilite practices have come to light in *The Harrowing of Gwynedd*, the full implications of which are apparent only to very senior Gabrilites, it seems. Queron Kinevan describes a piece of ritual that the "Master" used to do, several times a year, at morning meditations in the chapter house. (Who the Master is, is not clear. If it was the abbot, it seems like Queron would have said so. The abbot headed an advisory council of twelve Elders and presumably was an Elder himself, but were the abbot and the Master one and the same? One must wonder whether the Master fulfilled some other, more esoteric role.)

"We were always taught that it was symbolic—exactly what the symbol was, was never made quite clear—and I never questioned that," Queron tells Evaine and Joram, speaking of Ward Cubes arranged like a cube altar on the cube altar in the *keeill*.

". . . what the Master used to do was to set up this configuration in the proper sequence, then recite a particular prayer while he held his hands over the checkered cube—sort of cupped, as if he were consecrating the Eucharistic elements. After a while, energy washed outward from the cube, all the way to the edge of the altar. . . . Actually, I suppose I always thought the working was to purify the altar. But now that I think about it, he only ever did it on the cubical altar in our Chapter House—never the oblong one in the sanctuary—and the cubical altar was only ever used for meditation.'' (*The Harrowing of Gwynedd* 273–274)

We learn, of course, that the ritual was not one of purification—or not one *exclusively* of purification, at any rate—just as we discover that the carved wood catafalque used in the funeral of Gabrilite Elders disguised a secret correspondence to Orin's bier of four white and four black cubes arranged like the Pillars of the Temple laid on their side, so that the deceased rested, in symbol and in fact, in balance between the twin Pillars of Severity and Mercy—classic images of Cabalistic symbolism.

"It was made of eight hollow, wooden cubes that bolted together to make a shape like this—and came apart for ease of storage and assembly, I'd always assumed. The top surfaces were plain, stained wood—yew, I think—and the sides were carved with the symbols of our Order and our Faith, as one might expect. The surfaces that butted together were blank.'' He ran a fingertip along the join of black and white cubes.

"But the insides of the cubes were painted, some black and some white—something I only found out when I was a very senior brother in the Gabrilites, when I was poking around in the storeroom where the cubes were kept, looking for something else. It never occurred to me to ask about it, but when they were bolted together, the cubes with the black insides would have been lined up along the left side and the white ones along the right. . . .

"Brother Sacristan always supervised the preparations for an Elder's funeral. Not only that, I don't recall ever being asked to help assemble the bier, though the cubes must have been very heavy, and someone would have had to bring them into the church from storage. Novices and junior brethren handled most of the other preparations, but the bier was always in place when we began.''

"And I'll bet that Brother Sacristan was always an Elder, correct?" Joram asked.

"Always."

"What you've been describing suggests that there may have been a—an Order within an Order," Evaine ventured, after a few seconds. "Obviously, some practices had lost at least part of their original meanings from older times—like the purification ritual—but is it possible that a very select inner Order were attempting to perpetuate old Airsid traditions?" (*The Harrowing of Gwynedd* 298–299)

It has been noted that Dom Emrys had received his earliest training in an esoteric tradition that was neither Gabrilite nor Michaeline, which preferred the symbolism of sandalwood to cedar oil for polishing the wood in its sacred precincts. Perhaps this was a remnant of an ancient Airsid school. Perhaps the Gabrilite Council of Elders also constituted an Inner Order who were the last keepers of that ancient lore from which the Deryni's esoteric roots spring. Hopefully, we shall find many more such remnants, as the Deryni endeavor to reclaim their lost inheritance and use it to forge a peaceful coexistence with their human neighbors.

# APPENDIX I

# DIOCESES OF GWYNEDD AND SURROUNDS

VALORET—northeastern half of Haldane, excluding Dhassa; area north of river to Saint Jarlath's.

RHEMUTH—southwestern half of Haldane and bounded by the major rivers.

DHASSA—the free holy city and the Lendour Mountains east to Jennan Vale and north to Kingslake.

GRECOTHA—northeastern half of the Gwynedd plain.

COROTH—Carthmoor and Duchy of Corwyn north to Jennan Vale.

CARBURY—the area around the city; amalgamated with Grecotha and abolished in 1122.

CULDI—southwestern half of Gwynedd plain, bounded on south by line between Rhemuth and Cùilteine.

MARBURY—Earldom of Marley.

STAVENHAM—Claibourne, Kheldish Riding, and Rhendall lake region.

MEARA—Old Meara, which is Meara and Kierney.

CASHIEN—north of Llannedd along river, bounded northerly by a line between Rhemuth and Cùilteine and westerly by the mountains.

CARDOSA—Eastmarch south to Kingslake.

BALLYMAR—Cassan.

The kingdoms of Howicce, Llannedd, and the Connait have their own hierarchies, not yet integrated into the central Gwynedd administration.

# APPENDIX II

# VARIOUS BISHOPS OF GWYNEDD

## Bishops of Gwynedd, c. 905 (temp. I Cinhil)

VALORET—Archbishop Anscom of Trevas [Deryni] [891–906]
   Archbishop Jaffray of Carbury, Order of Saint Gabriel
    [Deryni] [906–917]
   Auxiliary—Bishop Roland [d. 906]
   Auxiliary—not named [906–916]
RHEMUTH—vacant "for some time" in 905
    Archbishop Robert Oriss, *Ordo Verbi Dei* [905- ]
    Auxiliary—not named
DHASSA—Bishop Niallan Trey, Order of Saint Michael [Deryni]
GRECOTHA—vacant "for more than 5 years" in 905
   Bishop Alister Cullen, Order of Saint Michael [Deryni]
[905–917]
NYFORD—Bishop Ulliam ap Lugh
CASHIEN—Bishop Dermot O'Beirne
Itinerant Bishops: 8 (includes 2 auxiliaries)
   Bishop Kai Descantor [Deryni]
   Bishop Eustace of Fairleigh
   Bishop Davet Nevan
   Bishop Turlough
   2 not named

By February 2, 917, with the accession of King Alroy, the complement had changed little. During the previous year, Ailin MacGregor and Hubert MacInnis had been elected Auxiliary Bishops of Valoret and Rhemuth, respectively. Soon after King Alroy's accession, four new itinerant bishops were appointed, bringing the total to twelve.

## Bishops of Gwynedd, 917
### (temp. I Alroy)

VALORET—Archbishop Jaffray of Carbury, Order of Saint Gabriel
[Deryni] [906–917]
  Auxiliary—Bishop Ailin MacGregor [916– ]
RHEMUTH—Archbishop Robert Oriss, *Ordo Verbi Dei* [905– ]
  Auxiliary—Bishop Hubert MacInnis [916– ]
DHASSA—Bishop Niallan Trey, Order of Saint Michael [Deryni]
GRECOTHA—Bishop Alister Cullen, Order of Saint Michael
          [Deryni] [905–917]
NYFORD—Bishop Ulliam ap Lugh
CASHIEN—Bishop Dermot O'Beirne
Itinerant Bishops: 12 (includes 2 auxiliaries)
  Bishop Kai Descantor [Deryni]
  Bishop Eustace of Fairleigh
  Bishop Davet Nevan
  Bishop Turlough
  Bishop Zephram of Lorda, *Ordo Verbi Dei*—former Vicar
    General of *Ordo Verbi Dei*
  Bishop Archer of Arrand, *Ordo Verbi Dei*—theologian
  Bishop Alfred of Woodbourne—Royal Confessor
  Bishop Paulin of Ramos—stepson of Tammaron
  2 not named

In November of 917, following the death of Archbishop Jaffray of Carbury, two itinerant bishops were translated to new titular sees: Bishop Turlough for the Diocese of Marbury and Bishop Paulin for the Diocese of Stavenham. On December 24, following extensive debate and despite strong opposition from the regents, Alister Cullen was elected Jaffray's successor as Archbishop of Valoret. Though legally enthroned on December 25, he was deposed and ousted by the regents on the same date and forced to flee, taking Bishops Niallan Trey and Dermot O'Beirne with him. Bishop Davet Nevan died in the accompanying civil disorder, as did Bishop Kai Descantor, the last remaining Deryni bishop.

The next morning, the remaining five bishops bolstered their depleted ranks by appointing six new itinerant bishops, Hubert's twenty-year-old bachelor nephew Edward among them. A carefully managed election that afternoon led to Hubert's enthronement as Archbishop of Valoret and Primate of All Gwynedd on the morning of December 27. Immediately following, Hubert opened the Council of Ramos, with the following holding episcopal office:

# Bishops of Gwynedd, Spring 918 (temp. 2 Alroy)

VALORET—Archbishop Hubert John William Valerian MacInnis, Regent
      Auxiliary—Bishop Ailin McGregor

RHEMUTH—Archbishop Robert Oriss
      Auxiliary—Bishop Alfred of Woodbourne

DHASSA—Bishop Archer of Arrand

GRECOTHA—Bishop Edward MacInnis of Arnham, nephew of Hubert

NYFORD—Bishop Ulliam ap Lugh

CASHIEN—Bishop Zephram of Lorda

MARBURY (new)—Bishop Turlough

STAVENHAM (new)—Bishop Paulin of Ramos (mid-November 917 to February 2, 918, until he resigned to head the *Ordo Custodem Fidei*)

Once the dust had settled, only Eustace of Fairleigh remained from the ten itinerant bishops previously holding office (not counting the two auxiliary bishops). Five replacements were appointed in the next fortnight to bring the complement to six, with an additional four selected in the next six months.

We may assume that the General Synod continued to evolve in the next two hundred years, but it will remain for future works to elucidate specifics. Suffice it to say that, by the time of King Kelson's accession in November of 1121, the complement stood at ten titled bishops (two of them archbishops) and twelve itinerant bishops (including two auxiliary bishops).

# Bishops of Gwynedd, 1121
## (temp. 1 Kelson)

VALORET—Archbishop Edmund Loris
    Auxiliary—not named
RHEMUTH—Archbishop Patrick Corrigan
    Auxiliary—Bishop Denis Arilan
DHASSA—Bishop Thomas Cardiel
GRECOTHA—Bishop Bradene
COROTH—Bishop Ralf Tolliver
CARBURY—Bishop Creoda
MARBURY—Bishop Ifor
STAVENHAM—Bishop de Lacey
MEARA—Bishop Carsten
CASHIEN—Bishop Belden of Erne
Itinerant Bishops: 12 (includes 2 auxiliaries)
    Siward
    Gilbert Desmond
    Wolfram de Blanet
    Henry Istelyn
    Conlan
    Morris
    Richard of Nyford
    3 unnamed

By 1122, offices had shuffled. Loris had been deprived of office and imprisoned, a number of men had died (Patrick Corrigan in 1121, of a heart attack; Richard of Nyford, executed with Duke Jared in 1121; de Lacey in 1122, of pneumonia; and Morris, date and cause unspecified). In addition, the new sees of Ballymar and Cardosa had been activated, and the see of Carbury had gone into abeyance.

# Bishops of Gwynedd, 1122
## (temp. 2 Kelson)

VALORET—Archbishop Bradene of Grecotha
    Auxiliary—Bishop Henry Istelyn
RHEMUTH—Archbishop Thomas Cardiel
    Auxiliary—Bishop Duncan McLain
DHASSA—Bishop Denis Arilan

GRECOTHA—Bishop Wolfram de Blanet
COROTH—Bishop Ralf Tolliver
CULDI—Bishop Creoda of Carbury
MARBURY—Bishop Ifor
STAVENHAM—Bishop Conlan
MEARA—Bishop Carsten
CASHIEN—Bishop Belden of Erne
CARDOSA—Bishop Siward
BALLYMAR—Bishop Lachlan de Quarles
Itinerant bishops: 12 (plus two auxiliaries)

| | |
|---|---|
| Gilbert Desmond | Nevan d'Estrelldas |
| James MacKenzie | Corbet Mathiesen |
| Hugh de Berry | John Fitz-Padriac |
| Mir de Kierney | Amaury of Rhelledd |
| Raymer de Valence | Edward of Cloome |
| Bevan de Torigny | Calder of Sheele |
| | (Dhugal's uncle) |

At the Synod of Meara in fall of 1123, following the death of Carsten of Meara, Henry Istelyn was nominated as the royal candidate for Bishop of Meara, duly elected, and installed. Shortly thereafter, former Archbishop Edmund Loris escaped from his incarceration at Saint Iveagh's, deposed Istelyn and connived at his judicial murder, took the style of Primate of Meara for himself, and named Judhael of Meara as Bishop of Ratharkin, which titles persisted until the capture and execution of the two by Kelson in the summer of 1124. As part of the resolution of this episode, several bishops who had supported Loris and Judhael were imprisoned or deprived of office, necessitating yet another shuffle of bishoprics.

## Bishops of Gwynedd, 1125
## (temp. 5 Kelson)

VALORET—Archbishop Bradene of Grecotha
          Auxiliary—Bishop Benoit d'Evering
RHEMUTH—Archbishop Thomas Cardiel
          Auxiliary—Bishop Duncan McLain
DHASSA—Bishop Denis Arilan
GRECOTHA—Bishop Wolfram de Blanet
COROTH—Bishop Ralf Tolliver

CULDI—Bishop Bevan de Torigny
MARBURY—Bishop Ifor of Marley
STAVENHAM—Bishop Conlan
MEARA—Bishop John Fitz-Padriac
CASHIEN—Bishop James MacKenzie
BALLYMAR—Bishop Hugh de Berry
CARDOSA—Bishop Siward
Itinerant bishops: 12

>Corbet Matheisen
>Amaury of Rhelledd
>Edward of Cloome
>Jodoc d'Armagne
>8 not named

Suspended and imprisoned for life:

>Belden of Erne
>Lachlan de Quarles
>Creoda of Carbury

Deprived of rank but still allowed to function as priests, under supervision:

>Gilbert Desmond
>Mir de Kierney
>Raymer de Valence
>Calder of Sheele
>Nevan d'Estrelldas

# APPENDIX III

# RELIGIOUS ORDERS IN GWYNEDD

*The Order of Saint Michael (Michaelines—OSM), priests and knights, mostly Deryni; suppressed in Gwynedd and dispersed in 917.

    Vicar General: Alister Cullen; then, Crevan Allyn

    Grand Master: Lord Jebediah of Alcara, KSM

    Michaeline Houses:

> Cheltham (Commanderie pre-905)
>
> Haut Eirial
>
> Mollingford
>
> Argoed (Commanderie 905–917)
>
> Cùilteine (Meara/Gwynedd border)
>
> Saint Liam's Abbey (School)
>
> Djellarda (Original Mother House and Commanderie, Anvil of the Lord)

    Saint Elderon (coastal Torenth, near Eastmarch)

    Brustarkia (House-Minor in Arjenol)

    Saint Michael's Sanctuary

    Habit: Priests—dark blue monastic robe or cassock, red cincture or fringed red sash, dark blue mantle with full Michaeline device on left shoulder; small, token tonsure, size of coin.

    Knights—dark blue surcoat with full Michaeline device on front and back, white belt or fringed white sash or white belt, same dark blue mantle as priests; small, token tonsure, size of coin.

    Device: *azure*, a cross moline fitchy *argent* issuing from a flame *gules* fimbriated *or*. (Lay brethren and military sergeants wear the badge of a plain white cross moline-fitchy.)

*The Order of Saint Gabriel (Gabrilites—OSG), all-Deryni, mostly
Healers and teachers of Healers; suppressed and dispersed
917.
Abbot: Dom Emrys
Habit: cowled white robe, white cincture, white mantle; no
tonsure; uncut hair worn in single braid.
Badge of the order: a circled cross with flared ends, usually
white or pale blue.
Gabrilite Healer's badge—a couped right hand *vert* pierced
in the palm by a white star of eight points (reverse of
secular Healer's badge)
Mother House: Saint Neot's Abbey (south Lendour Mountains)

*The *Ordo Verbi Dei* (Order of the Word of God—OVP), semi-
cloistered contemplatives, originally known as the Order of
Saint Jarlath.
Vicar General: Father Robert Oriss; then Zephram of Lorda.
Mother House: Saint Jarlath's Abbey (north Lendour moun-
tains)
Abbot: Father Gregory of Arden
Habit: abbot—burgundy; monks—deep grey; lay
brothers—brown.
Saint Piran's Priory (near Valoret)
Prior: Father Stephen
Habit: prior—white; lay brothers—grey; novices—
black.
Saint Foillan's Abbey (Lendour highlands)
Abbot: Father Zephram of Lorda
Prior: Father Patrick
Habit: abbot—white; brothers—white; lay broth-
ers—grey.
Saint Ultan's Priory (southwest Mooryn)
Saint Illtyd's Priory (near Nyford)

The Little Brothers of Saint Ercon
Founder: Father Paulin (Sinclair) of Ramos, stepson of Earl
Tammaron

The Willimites—lay order devoted to Saint Willim (younger brother
of Saint Ercon), an early martyr to Deryni ill use.

*The *Ordo Custodem Fidei* (Order of the Guardians of the Faith—OCF), founded in 918 as a human answer to the Michaelines; warriors and teachers, especially in seminaries.

Founder: Archbishop Hubert MacInnis

First Vicar General: The Very Reverend Paulin (Sinclair) of Ramos (former Bishop of Stavenham)

Chancellor General: Father Marcus Concannon, in charge of seminaries

Inquisitor General: Brother Serafin; Father Lior, assistant

Habit: brothers—black cassocks, braided cincture of Haldane crimson and gold, black mantles faced with crimson.

Device: *gules*, a winged golden lion *sejant guardant*, its head ennobled with a halo, holding in its dexter paw an upraised sword.

Chapters associated with all cathedrals in Gwynedd.

Principal Seminary: *Arx Fidei* (Citadel of Faith), in central Gwynedd near Valoret; Abbey Church of the Paraclete.

*Equites Custodum Fidei* (Knights of the Guardians of the Faith)

First Grand Master: Lord Albertus (elder brother of Paulin, formerly Earl of Tarleton)

Commanderies sited at all cathedral cities; priories scattered.

Habit: black surcoats bearing red moline cross charged with haloed lion's head, white sash fringed with red, braided cincture worn as cordon around left shoulder, black mantles faced with scarlet.

*Fratri Silentii* (Brothers of Silence)—Saint Iveagh's Abbey

Habit: sea-blue robes

*Ordo Vox Dei* (Order of the Voice of God—OVD)

Habit: black robe with blue girdle

*Brotherhood of Saint Joric

The Varnarites—Canons of the Varnarite School, separated from the cathedral chapter at Grecotha late in the eighth century and coexisted as a Deryni teaching order and school until shortly after the Haldane Restoration. Ultra-conservative Varnarites split off earlier and eventually became the Gabrilites. Earlier esoteric threads contributed to both traditions.

*Templum Archangelorum*—long-destroyed abbey with ancient esoteric antecedents; the seal on Jodotha's dower coin.

The heads of the great religious orders, generally mitred abbots (which are indicated by an \*), enjoy rank equivalent to that of a bishop, and may be called upon to sit in an advisory capacity to the General Synod.

# APPENDIX IV

# PORTAL LOCATIONS IN GWYNEDD

## Ecclesiastical Portal Network
### (confirmed Portals indicated by an asterisk * )

Cathedral of Saint George, Rhemuth:
>   *Sacristy
>   *Priest's study, Saint Hilary's Basilica-within-the-Walls

Cathedral of All Saints, Valoret:
>   *Sacristy
>   *Oratory, archbishop's apartments

Cathedral of Saint Senan, Dhassa:
>   Sacristy (presumed)
>   *North transept, private chapel of bishop's residence

Grecotha Cathedral:
>   Sacristy (presumed)
>   *Several other Portals in bishop's residence
>   *Tower-top at bishop's residence (specialized Portal, presumed closed with death of Camber-Allister)
>   *In ruins beneath bishop's palace

Nyford Cathedral:
>   Sacristy (presumed)

Cashien Cathedral:
>   Sacristy (presumed)

Cathedral of Saint Uriel and All Angels, Ratharkin, Diocese of Meara:
>   Sacristy (presumed)

# Gabrilite and Michaeline Portals

The Order of Saint Gabriel:
  *Saint Neot's—sacristy; at least one other probable
The Order of Saint Michael:

|  | Sites given over to other orders at suppression of Michaelines, but Portals still open and operational 12-24-917, when Jebediah went to warn new orders. |
|---|---|
| Haut Eirial | |
| Mollingford | |

Cheltham (Main Commanderie in 904, when destroyed):
  *Impression that this Portal was in the Vicar General's quarters or chapter house, rather than a sacristy; Probably a secondary Portal as well, perhaps in sacristy.
Argoed (Commanderie 905–917): (presumed)
Cuilteine (Meara/Gwynedd border): (presumed)
Saint Liam's Abbey (School): (presumed)
Djellarda (Original Mother House and Commanderie, Anvil of the Lord): (presumed)
Saint Elderon (coastal Torenth, near Eastmarch): (presumed)
Brustarkia (House-Minor in Arjenol): (presumed)
Saint Michael's Sanctuary

  *Portal separate from chapel/sacristy, but nearby

# Other Presumed Institutional Portals

Llenteith, near the Connait—a Deryni school there was warned of impending dissolution in October 917; Portal was disguised and Deryni left.
Nyford Schola—partially rebuilt after being burned out in summer of 916; warned of return engagement in October 917; Portal closed and site abandoned.

# Private Portals

*VALORET—beneath King's Tower, disguised as a garderobe.
*CAERRORIE—in corner of Camber's study; *second one off underground passage leading away from castle (how Ansel got to Camberian Council after death of Davin)

cor culdi—secondary MacRorie holding; inconceivable that Camber would not have had an additional Portal here.

*sheele—in Rhys' study; later, closed to all but those of Thuryn or MacRorie blood.

*trevalga—Gregory's new stronghold in the Connait. (Presumably he had no Portal at Ebor, or else Rhys would have had Camber-Alister and Joram use it when Gregory was injured.)

*rhemuth—chamber adjacent to Brion's library, with a Portal in the center of the room. Originally a guest chamber, quite probably the one occupied by Ian on the night before Kelson's coronation (both rooms are described as having their Portals in the center of the room—fairly unusual for residential Portals), it almost certainly was the means by which Charissa gained access to the library that night. By the time of Kelson's knighting, the room had been made an annex of the library, its corridor door sealed off and a doorway cut through the common wall, the passageway guarded by a Haldane-specific ward, as Tiercel explains.

> "Kelson and his friends set up that very specific ward to permit my fellow Councilors to use the library resources, but to keep us out of the rest of the castle unannounced. After Charissa, one can certainly understand his reasoning. In any case, the only way I could have left that room was the way we did or else for you to take me through under your shields. It isn't a foolproof situation, but it serves the purpose." (*The Quest for Saint Camber* 130)

## Private Portals—Camberian Council

In addition, members of the Camberian Council certainly have access to private Portals in their residences or other personal retreats. Specifically mentioned are those of Thorne Hagen, Denis Arilan, and the Arilan family Portal in the ritual chamber at Tre-Arilan (which may be the same as the one where Denis Arilan takes Cardiel).

## Non-Portal Locations

Locations that specifically do *not* have Portals include Trurill (because Camber's sister did not marry a Deryni) and Coroth, at least by the summer of 1121. (There may *be* a Portal or two at Coroth, for Deryni dukes have held the duchy for many years, but Morgan does not know of them and to date has not had time to assemble the necessary personnel to establish one of his own.)

# THE *ADSUM DOMINE*:
# THE HEALER'S INVOCATION

Here am I, Lord:
>Thou hast granted me the grace to Heal men's bodies.

Here am I, Lord:
>Thou hast blessed me with the Sight to See men's souls.

Here am I, Lord:
>Thou hast given me the might to bend the will of others.

O Lord, grant strength and wisdom to wield all these gifts
>only as Thy will wouldst have me serve.

The Lord of Light said unto me: Behold!
Thou art my chosen child, My gift to man.
Before the daystar, long before thou wast in mother-womb,
thy soul was sealed to Me for all time out of mind.
Thou art My Healing hand upon this world,
Mine instrument of life and Healing might.
To thee I give the breath of Healing power,
the awesome, darkling secrets of the wood and vale and earth.
I give thee all these gifts that thou mayst know My love.
Use all in service of the ease of man and beast.
Be cleansing fire to purify corruption,
a pool of sleep to bring surcease from pain.
Keep close within thy heart all secrets given,
as safe as said in shriving and as sacred.
Nor shall thy Sight be used for revelation,
unless the other's mind be freely offered.
With consecrated hands, make whole the broken.
With consecrated soul, reach out and give My peace.

Here am I, Lord: All my talents at Thy feet I lay.
Here am I, Lord: Thou art the One Creator of all things.
Thou art the Omnipartite One Who ruleth Light and Shade,
Giver of Life and Gift of Life Thyself.
Here am I, Lord: All my being sealed unto Thy will.
Here am I, Lord: Sealed unto Thy service,
  girt with strength to save or slay.
Guide and guard Thy servant, Lord, from all temptation,
that honor may be spotless and my gift unstained.


Adsum, Domine:
    Me gratiam corpora hominum sanare concessisti.
Adsum, Domine:
    Me Visu animas hominum Videre benedixisti.
Adsum, Domine:
    Me potentiam dedisti voluntate aliorum intendere.
Da, Domine, vires et prudentiam omnis haec dona tractare
    solum ut voluntas tua me ministraret.


Dominus lucis me dixit, Ecce:
Tu es infans electum meam, donum meam ad hominem.
Ante luciferum, multi ante in utero matris eras,
anima tuam me sancitur aetatis ex mente.
Tu es manus sanatio mea super hoc mundo,
instrumentum meum vitae et potestatis sanationiae.
Te spiritum potentiae sanationiae do,
res arcanas reverentias et obscuras sylvae et luci et terrae.
Te omnis haec dona do, ita ut scias caritatem meam.
Haec utere in ministerio mitigationis viri et pecoris.
Ignis purgationis esto corruptio purificare,
lacuna somno esto mitigatio de dolor ferre.
In pectore tuo cela onmi secreta dabantur,
quam tutus confessione dictus, et quam sacrosanctus.
Visus tuus pro revelatia non uteor,
nisi mens aliae sponte offertur.
Cum manibus consecratus, fractum restitude.
Cum anima consecrata, tende et pacem meam da.

Adsum, Domine: Totus ingenibus meis ad pedes tuos proponeo.
Adsum, Domine: Tu es Creator Unius de rerum totum.
Tu es Unus Omnipartus, Qui Lucem et Umbram regit,
Donator Vitae et Ipse Donum Vitae.
Adsum, Domine: Omnis existentia mea ad voluntatem tuam ligatur.
Adsum, Domine: Ad ministerio tuum consecratur,
     cum viribus conservare aut interficiere cingitur.
Duce et regere servum tui, Domine, ab omnibus tentationem,
     ita ut honor purus et donum meum incontaminatus sit.

# APPENDIX VI

# DERYNI ESOTERIC TEXTS

The *Annales* of Sulien of R'Kassi—ancient Deryni adept.

The *Codex Orini*—bound with violet cord; commentaries and working notes of the great Orin.

> "Holding Off Death"
> "Conversation with the Holy Guardian Angel"
> "Preserving Life Beyond Death
>   and Bringing Life Back Out of Death."

"The Ghosting of Ardal l'Etrange," by Eamonn MacDara—Mearan poet, flourished ca. 700; alludes to a spell for defying death.

*Haut Arcanum*, by Dom Edouard—Gabrilite philosopher.

*History of Kheldour* by Mahael.

*Lays of the Lord Llewellyn*, died ca. 850; great bard and troubadour.

The *Liber Fati Caeriesse*—collected prophesies of Nesta a 6th century Deryni Seeress.

The *Liber Ricae* of The Book of the Veil—extremely rare.

The *Liber Sancti Ruadan*, by Ruadan of Dhassa—Deryni mystic text.

*Principia Magica*, by Kitron—parts coded.

*The Protocols of Orin*

> The Black Protocol:
> > "Placing Another Shape on the Dead"
> > "Re Animating the Dead"
> > "Calling Up Creatures"
> The Vermillion Protocol:
> > "Setting Wards"
> > "Scrying"
> > "Construction of Portals" (including Trap Portals)
> The Golden-Yellow Protocol:
> > "Taking a Dead Man's Shape"
> > "Reading Memories of the Dead"
> > "Assimilation of Memories of Another"
> The Green Protocol: a Healing text

The Royal Blue Protocol: (the Fifth Protocol, "The Scroll
         of Daring")
       "On Staring Patterns"
       "Moon-Scrying"
       "Blocking of Power in Those of Magical Inheri-
         tance"

# Other Deryni Authors

Jokal of Tyndour—poetic work with healing passages; Rhys was
  surprised by some of the procedures.
Jorevin of Cashel—Deryni mystic.
Leutiern—Deryni mystic.
Nesta—Deryni seeress who foretold the doom of Caeriesse.
Pargan Howiccan—ca. 800; Deryni epic poet; classic epic sagas of
  the old gods.

# APPENDIX VII

# MEMBERS OF THE CAMBERIAN COUNCIL THROUGH 918

The Camberian Council (though not yet called that) was founded in 909 by:

> Lord Camber MacRorie (as Bishop Alister Cullen)
> Father Joram MacRorie, Order of Saint Michael
> Lady Evaine MacRorie Thuryn
> Lord Rhys Thuryn
> Lord Jebediah of Alcara

On December 21, 910, the five founders added:

> Archbishop Jaffray of Carbury, Order of Saint Gabriel
> Gregory, Earl of Ebor
> Dom Turstane, Order of Saint Gabriel

Shortly thereafter, Jaffray coined the name the Camberian Council, which stuck. The Council began surveillance of Deryni abuses, discipline of same, and codification of practices such as the Duel Arcane.

In the spring of 916, Dom Turstane died in a fall. When his seat was not immediately filled, Jebediah began calling it Saint Camber's Siege, in which form it remained unfilled. Though Davin MacRorie was being considered for admission, he was killed on September 28, 917, before a decision could be reached.

Less than a month later, in mid- to late October, Archbishop Jaffray was killed, further reducing the Council to six. Ansel MacRorie was selected to replace Jaffray, but before he could be formally inducted, three more deaths reduced the Council's ranks still further: Rhys, on December 25, and Jebediah and Camber-Alister on January 6, 918.

With only Joram, Evaine, and Gregory remaining, Ansel MacRorie was inducted with reduced formality sometime during the period of January 7–9. Gregory's son Jesse and Dom

Queron Kinevan followed, on the 10th and 11th respectively. Queron's induction brought the complement back to six: Joram, Evaine, Gregory, Ansel, Jesse, and Queron. Tavis O'Neill was added in the spring of 918, followed by Bishop Niallan Trey, Order of Saint Michael. Evaine's death on August 1, 918, reduced the Council to seven once more.

# APPENDIX VIII

# GLOSSARY OF DERYNI TERMS

Airsid, the—ancient esoteric fraternity.

*cognomen*—the name of a pairing of Ward Cubes, i.e., *Prime + Quinte = Primus* (plural, *cognomena*)

*cruaidh-dheuchainn*—the ordeal, the *periculum*.

*g'dula*—the single braid of four strands worn by professed brethren of the Order of Saint Gabriel; later, a general term for a single braid or clout worn at the nape of the neck, as the border braid (plural *g'dulae*).

*keeill*—chapel or sanctuary; specifically, the ritual chamber underneath the Camberian Council chamber.

*merasha*—Deryni-specific mind-muddling drug; in humans, it has only a sedative effect.

*nomen*—the particular name of a Ward Cube in a set of Wards Major (plural *nomena*).

*phrasa*—the phrase that names and activates a switched pair of Ward Cubes (plural *phrasae*).

*salutus*—the Reverence to the Four, e.g., *Primus est Deus* . . . (plural *saluti*).

*shiral*—a psi-sensitive stone similar to amber, found in streambeds and on seashores.

*talicil*—antipyretic drug, similar in effect to aspirin.

# INDEX OF MAGIC

AIRSID—built *keeill* and Camberian Council chamber: *Camber the Heretic* 243; unknown whether celebrated Mass as Camberian Council knows it: *Camber the Heretic* 322.

ANIMALS, magical—Stenrects: *Deryni Rising* 67–69, 70–71, 262; caradots: *High Deryni* 151; lyfangs: *Deryni Checkmate* 49.

ANIMALS, rapport with—Morgan "can charm deer": *Deryni Rising* 4; "could call [the fish] and they would come": *Deryni Checkmate* 36; Bronwyn can call birds to her hands: *Deryni Checkmate* 145; Dhugal good with: *The Bishop's Heir* 22, 85, 174, 177–178; Dhugal uses horse as physical link to Ciard: *The King's Justice* 213–215; Dhugal controls horse: *The King's Justice* 243; Dhugal with cheetah: *The Quest for Saint Camber* 64, 69–70; Dhugal catches eyeless fish: *The Quest for Saint Camber* 264; Rhys good with, like most Deryni: *The Deryni Archives* 15, 18; Morgan gentles wounded horse: *The Deryni Archives* 181.

ASSUMPTION of power, Haldane—potential first glimpsed in Cinhil: *Camber of Culdi* 217–219; Evaine's followup: *Camber of Culdi* 250–260; Cinhil's: *Camber of Culdi* 260–268; Cinhil's power catalyzed by son's death: *Camber of Culdi* 274; Cinhil's sons potentialized: *Camber the Heretic* 70–90; Alroy's (in theory): *Camber the Heretic* 105; Kelson's first mentioned: *Deryni Rising* 43–45, 61, 63; Kelson's: *Deryni Rising* 156–174; re: *Deryni Rising* 192–193; re Kelson's magic: *The Bishop's Heir* 71–72, *The King's Justice* 44–56; Nigel potentialized: *The King's Justice* 42–55; Conall empowered: *The Quest for Saint Camber* 293–305.

ASSUMPTION of power, other—Ian's powers assumed from Charissa: *Deryni Rising* 202, 246; Hort of Orsal's line has assumed power like Haldanes: *Deryni Checkmate* 123; Derry not of known assumptive line, but could be taught some spells: *Deryni Checkmate* 123; Bran's assumed powers, via Wencit:

*Deryni* 186; Arilan's, during Portal setting: *High Deryni* 294; around Derry's head (connected with communication link): *High Deryni* 316; Duncan's, at consecration: *The Bishop's Heir* 238; Arilan's, as reveals self to Jehana: *The King's Justice* 264; Kelson's, at Mearan capitulation: *The King's Justice* 297, 304 (and Morgan and Duncan); Duncan's, with sword, at Dhugal's knighting: *The Quest for Saint Camber* 58–59 (and Dhugal's); Al Rasoul's: *The Quest for Saint Camber* 63; Kelson's and Dhugal's: *The Quest for Saint Camber* 345, 349, 350; Conall's, blazing white light, actually a ward of some sort: *The Quest for Saint Camber* 418; Barrett's emerald green (shields also): *The Deryni Archives* 85; Darrell's golden: *The Deryni Archives* 88; Hogan Gwernach's: *The Deryni Archives* 168–169.

AUTOMATIC WRITING—Camber, of Ariella's plans: *Saint Camber* 52–53; Joram, of Grecotha plans: *The Harrowing of Gwynedd* 226–227.

BAPTIZER CULT—first discussion of possibility: *Camber the Heretic* 145, 151–154; approaching Revan: *Camber the Heretic* 156–160; building Revan's cover: *Camber the Heretic* 186–187; regarding Rhys teaming with Revan: *Camber the Heretic* 235; Revan and Willimites: *Camber the Heretic* 273–279; Tavis to join: *Camber the Heretic* 467.

BINDING of soul to dead body—Brion's: *Deryni Rising* 154; Alister's: *Saint Camber* 108–109, 112, 116.

BLOCKING of powers (and unblocking)—Rhys, first time, on Gregory: *Camber the Heretic* 13–14, 31–32; of Gregory, as demonstration for Camberian Council: *Camber the Heretic* 122; regarding theory: *Camber the Heretic* 123–129; testing on Jeb, Evaine, etc.: *Camber the Heretic* 133–140; regarding talent: *Camber the Heretic* 148; information to Queron: *Camber the Heretic* 177–186; regarding blocking Tavis: *Camber the Heretic* 235–236; blocks Davin before shape-changing: *Camber the Heretic* 249; Tavis discovers, while reading Rhys: *Camber the Heretic* 384; Tavis blocks Rhys: *Camber the Heretic* 390; Tavis unblocks Rhys: *Camber the Heretic* 395; Tavis, of Niallan: *Camber the Heretic* 426; Tavis, of Queron: *The Harrowing of Gwynedd* 45–46; Tavis, of Jamie and Elinor: *The Harrowing of Gwynedd* 94–95; Tavis, of Ansel: *The Harrowing of Gwynedd* 99; Tavis, of Aurelian and Sylvan: *The Harrowing of Gwynedd* 106–107; Tieg, of Evaine: *The Harrowing of Gwynedd* 113; Tavis

over: *The Quest for Saint Camber* 37; Conall drugs Dhugal's flask: *The Quest for Saint Camber* 181; Kelson drinks: *The Quest for Saint Camber* 199–201; re: *The Quest for Saint Camber* 202, 290; Dhugal doses Conall with: *The Quest for Saint Camber* 427; to screen Deryni candidates for priesthood: *The Deryni Archives* 111, 112, 138–141, 153–156.

DRUGS, sedative—to Cinhil, on road: *Camber of Culdi* 195; to Guaire and Johannes, before Camber appearance: once *Saint Camber* 216–217 (plus drug to make Guaire more susceptible to Camber's intervention); to Gregory: *Camber the Heretic* 7–9; to Cinhil's sons, as tonic (= cinquefoil, poppy extract, wolfbane, anhalon, and *merasha*): *Camber the Heretic* 61–62, 65–69, 126; to Alroy: *Camber the Heretic* 122; to Queron, before blocking: *Camber the Heretic* 185; to Alroy and Rhys Michael: *Camber the Heretic* 211; to Tavis: *Camber the Heretic* 212; to Alroy, in tonic (subtle): *Camber the Heretic* 256; to Queron, in melted snow: *The Harrowing of Gwynedd* 15; to Tieg, in vapor and vial: *The Harrowing of Gwynedd* 118–119; to Lionel and men: *High Deryni* 34–38; to Dhugal, at his order: *The Bishop's Heir* 132–136; to Istelyn, to make compliant: *The Bishop's Heir* 168; to Kelson, hot wine posset with sedative, after Sidana's murder: *The King's Justice* 30; to Nigel, with psychic enhancer, by Arilan: *The King's Justice* 52–56; to Janniver, by Lael: *The King's Justice* 107; to Conall's squire, by Conall: *The King's Justice* 125; to Tiercel: *The King's Justice* 132–133; to Liam, by Richenda: *The King's Justice* 199; to Morgan: *The Deryni Archives* 97; to Denis Arilan: *The Deryni Archives* 141.

DRUGS, other—anhalon, cinquefoil, poppy extract, wolfbane (with *merasha*) to Cinhil's sons, as "physic against colds," before power assumption: *Camber the Heretic* 61–62, 65–69; bélas, works as truth drug on drunken humans: *Deryni Checkmate* 96, 101–103; drug with effect similar to *merasha*, but slow poison (and partial antidote) at Duel Arcane: *High Deryni* 335–341; bluish-grey powder for wounds (probably penicillinlike mold): *The Bishop's Heir* 24; sphangum moss for binding wounds: *The Bishop's Heir* 26; psychic enhancer to Nigel, by Arilan: *The King's Justice* 52–56; psychic enhancer with sedative, to Conall, by Tiercel: *The King's Justice* 132–133; holy oil with psychic enhancer to lower resistance and mild relaxant, to Conall, by Arilan: *The Quest for Saint Camber* 300; second drug to reinforce first, on shaft of brooch: *The Quest for Saint Camber* 301; Conall knows drugs from work with Tiercel: *The Quest for Saint Camber* 303; grain with hallucinogenic mold: *The Quest for Saint Camber* 329; psychic enhancer, to make more vulnerable, with sedative, to Guaire, by Camber: *Saint Camber* 216–217; reference to drugs Tavis can use to help Javan: *Camber the Heretic* 383; *merasha* plus, to Rhys, by Tavis: *Camber the Heretic* 376–378, 379–380; drugs to counteract ones given to Rhys by Tavis: *Camber the Heretic* 395–396; remedy for nausea, with slight minty taste: *Camber the Heretic* 389; *talicil* to break fever: *Camber the Heretic* 376; poison, attempted by Bethane, to Morgan: *The Deryni Archives* 92–93.

DUEL ARCANE—Cinhil versus Humphrey: *Camber of Culdi* 274–277; Cinhil versus Imre: *Camber of Culdi* 292–294; Camberian Council begins codifying rules of: *Camber the Heretic* 117; Ulric slays Novice Master in: *Camber the Heretic* 234–235; Kelson versus Charissa: *Deryni Rising* 241–267; Kelson et al. versus Wencit et al.: *High Deryni* 286–289, 297–304, 326–327, 329–346; Kelson versus Conall: *The Quest for Saint Camber* 421–427; Brion versus Marluk: *The Deryni Archives* 170.

FATIGUE-BANISHING—Cathan, words of Deryni charm to banish fatigue: *Camber of Culdi* 61; Camber, relaxation technique: *Saint Camber* 39; Queron's, after re-creating Guaire's "vision": *Saint Camber* 374; Morgan's: *Deryni Rising* 120; Duncan's: *Deryni Checkmate* 289; Morgan's, in cathedral: *High Deryni* 149; Duncan's, applied to Morgan: *High Deryni* 155; on Morgan, after Portal setting (implied): *High Deryni* 295; Morgan, after treating Duncan: *The Bishop's Heir* 39–40; Kelson may have helped Nigel with: *The King's Justice* 68; Morgan, too much, after contact with Duncan (reaction buildup): *The King's Justice* 97; Arilan: *The King's Justice* 260–261; Conall and Tiercel, regarding: *The Quest for Saint Camber* 128; Duncan's: *The Quest for Saint Camber* 163–164, 165; Morgan's: *The Quest for Saint Camber* 274, 275; Dhugal's: *The Quest for Saint Camber* 336; Denis, after ordination: *The Deryni Archives* 155.

FIRE, conjuring—Camber does *not* do: *Saint Camber* 248; candle lighting at Camber's ordination: *Saint Camber* 260; Camber vaporizes wax in bare hand: *Saint Camber* 271; extinguishes candles: *Saint Camber* 273; for funeral pyre: *Camber the Heretic* 455; Queron's pillar of fire: *The Harrowing of Gwy-*

*nedd* 278; Morgan lights torch (though says used flint and steel): *High Deryni* 8; Thorne lights candles: *High Deryni* 63; fire on hearth to life: *High Deryni* 181; Arilan lights candles and torches in Camberian Council with gesture: *High Deryni* 296; candles dim and flare in Richenda's tent: *High Deryni* 313, 314; Morgan lights candles: *The Bishop's Heir* 245; Morgan lights fire: *The Bishop's Heir* 248; Tiercel lights candles: *The Quest for Saint Camber* 129; Wencit douses wall torches with gesture: *The Deryni Archives* 166.

FIREBALLS—Duncan's (green) knocks out guard: *Deryni Rising* 179; Charissa's (blue) becomes armored blue knight: *Deryni Rising* 258.

*G'DULA*—Queron's: *The Harrowing of Gwynedd* 17–19, 21, 30, 48; Kelson's: *The Quest for Saint Camber* 370.

HANDFIRE—Joram conjures: *Camber of Culdi* 185; Camber's: *Saint Camber* 108, 110, 273, 303, 304, 305; Camber's in *keeill*: *Camber the Heretic* 314, 322; Jebediah's is crimson: *Camber the Heretic* 314; use in Gabrilite Compline service: *Camber the Heretic* 366–367; Evaine's: *The Harrowing of Gwynedd* 1, 229; Ansel's: *The Harrowing of Gwynedd* 172; Tavis': *The Harrowing of Gwynedd* 216; Queron's: *The Harrowing of Gwynedd* 242, 283; Joram's: *The Harrowing of Gwynedd* 282; Arilan's: *High Deryni* 119; Morgan's: *High Deryni* 175, 176, 177 (glow sphere), 178, 180; Morgan's: *The Bishop's Heir* 244; Arilan: *The Bishop's Heir* 252, *The King's Justice* 264 (a child's trick); Kelson: *The King's Justice* 37, 38, *The Quest for Saint Camber* 27; Tiercel's (silver): *The Quest for Saint Camber* 121, 123, 125, 126, 127, 129, 134; Conall's (red): *The Quest for Saint Camber* 135; Duncan's silvery: *The Quest for Saint Camber* 157; Dhugal's silver and Kelson's crimson, in flooded crypt: *The Quest for Saint Camber* 174–175; Dhugal's, at riverside: *The Quest for Saint Camber* 194, 203; Arilan's, in study Portal: *The Quest for Saint Camber* 218; Dhugal's as high as he can make it go: *The Quest for Saint Camber* 266; Conall's, after ritual: *The Quest for Saint Camber* 306–307; Dhugal's, takes energy: *The Quest for Saint Camber* 314, 315, 316, 321; Dhugal temporarily loses ability to maintain: *The Quest for Saint Camber* 329; Dhugal's: *The Quest for Saint Camber* 338; Kelson's: *The Quest for Saint Camber* 350; Jamyl and Denis: *The Deryni Archives* 128.

descript dust tones: *Camber the Heretic* 272; Emrys and Kenric conjure cobwebs and mire to slow attackers: *Camber the Heretic* 370; Derry taught to see through: *Deryni Checkmate* 135.

INTERROGATION—Tavis, of Deryni suspects, leading to Dafydd's suicide: *Camber the Heretic* 259–261; Tavis questions suspects after assassination attempt: *Camber the Heretic* 300–302; Oriel questions: *Camber the Heretic* 302–307; Nigel et al., of assassins: *The King's Justice* 200, 260; Morgan, of Nevan: *The Bishop's Heir* 147–149. See Truth-Reading, forced.

LEGISLATION, anti-Deryni (Ramos)—*Camber the Heretic* 466.

LOCKS, unlocking and locking—Joram, using blade: *Camber of Culdi* 181; Joram: *Camber of Culdi* 183; strangely glowing door latch on chapel door, which Alister Cullen touches to open: *Camber of Culdi* 262; Duncan, green-glowing doorway: *High Deryni* 187; compartment with scrolls, opened by mental syllables unlikely to be articulated by chance: *Saint Camber* 152; Camber, of door to archbishop's quarters: *Camber the Heretic* 118; Morgan, gate of crypt: *Deryni Rising* 145–146; Duncan, door under Saint Torin's: *Deryni Checkmate* 222–223, 224; regarding: *High Deryni* 114–115.

MANUSCRIPTS, Deryni—Protocols of Orin: *Saint Camber* 153–156, *The Harrowing of Gwynedd* 26, 224, 293–294, 371; the *Liber Sancti Ruadan*: *The Harrowing of Gwynedd* 26, 267; *Haut Arcanum*: *The Harrowing of Gwynedd* 224, 239; the *Liber Ricae* or Book of the Veil: 224, 245, 246, 268; *Principia Magica*: *The Harrowing of Gwynedd* 246; the *Codex Orini*: *The Harrowing of Gwynedd* 294, 372, 378; "The Ghosting of Ardal l'Etrange": *The Harrowing of Gwynedd* 224.

MEDITATION—Camber, preparation for scrying: *Saint Camber* 39–40; Camber, about asking for ordination and memorizing rite: *Saint Camber* 257; Evaine and rings: *The Harrowing of Gwynedd* 373–374; Javan at Mass: *The Harrowing of Gwynedd* 349; Evaine's final: *The Harrowing of Gwynedd* 407–416.

MEMORY—Duncan's precise Deryni memory: *Deryni Checkmate* 203; Dom Emrys' "perfect memory": *Saint Camber* 193.

MEMORY assumption—*see* Death Reading.

MEMORY erasing/alteration—Coel, of two watchmen: *Cam-*

on Camber: *Camber the Heretic* 485; Camber-Alister change: *The Harrowing of Gwynedd* 231; Brion's body: *Deryni Rising* 153–154; Rhydon to Coram: *High Deryni* 339; Coram as Camber: *High Deryni* 339.

SHIELDS—Cinhil's unexpected: *Camber of Culdi* 91, 185–186, 194, 195–196, 218, 250; Cinhil's set back in place by spells loosing Haldane potential: *Camber of Culdi* 269; Imre's: *Camber of Culdi* 290; Cinhil sure he is shielded: *Saint Camber* 33; Ariella's men: *Saint Camber* 101; Cinhil's: *Saint Camber* 428–429; Tavis', in place: *Camber the Heretic* 68; Tavis senses in assailants: *Camber the Heretic* 206, 208; Tavis and Javan about: *Camber the Heretic* 225–227; regarding Tavis' shields, and Ulric: *Camber the Heretic* 234–235; Tavis, re Javan's: *Camber the Heretic* 262; Davin, about avoiding Tavis': *Camber the Heretic* 289; faint snap of shields being raised: *Camber the Heretic* 290; Davin's, against Tavis: *Camber the Heretic* 295–296; Prisoners', hazy and confused from drugs: *Camber the Heretic* 298; clash of Niallan's and Kai's: *Camber the Heretic* 345; Rhys' fall from drugs and interrogation: *Camber the Heretic* 379; Tavis lowers, for Camber: *Camber the Heretic* 431–436; Sylvan's, testing Javan: *The Harrowing of Gwynedd* 195; Revan's, lie: *The Harrowing of Gwynedd* 342; Dhugal has: *The Bishop's Heir* 83–85, 140, 210–212, 234, 245; Dhugal's waver: *The Bishop's Heir* 248, 321; Dhugal lowers for Kelson: *The King's Justice* 61; King Liam has: *The King's Justice* 76; Rothana's: *The King's Justice* 104–105; Liam's, Richenda Reading: *The King's Justice* 123–124; Conall's: *The King's Justice* 130–132; Jehana's: *The King's Justice* 147; Azim's: *The King's Justice* 152; Conall's secondary: *The King's Justice* 167; Arilan makes his transparent, to fool Jehana: *The King's Justice* 262; reveals: *The King's Justice* 264; Tiercel's: *The Quest for Saint Camber* xvi; Al Rasoul's: *The Quest for Saint Camber* 62, 68 (and Kelson's), 71; Duncan's and Arilan's: *The Quest for Saint Camber* 97, 98, 104, 105; Conall's, with Tiercel: *The Quest for Saint Camber* 123, 125, 127, 128, 131–132; Tiercel's: *The Quest for Saint Camber* 136; Duncan's, at Mass: *The Quest for Saint Camber* 161; Kelson's, after injury: *The Quest for Saint Camber* 197, 213; Nivard's: *The Quest for Saint Camber* 220–222; Morgan's, with Richenda: *The Quest for Saint Camber* 228; Dhugal, regarding Kelson's: *The Quest for Saint Camber* 240; Conall's, with Arilan: *The Quest for*

*Deryni Archives* 166; staring patterns in dust: *The Deryni Archives* 169.

STARING PATTERNS—on door of *keeill*: *The Harrowing of Gwynedd* 70–71; Tiercel's, scratched in earth: *The King's Justice* 165–166; Raif, with Hoag: *The King's Justice* 269; in sand: *The Quest for Saint Camber* 434–435; the Marluk's, in dust: *The Deryni Archives*.

SUICIDE—Daffyd Leslie (voluntary, rather than betray friends): *Camber the Heretic* 260; pact among prisoners, to set death-triggers (Denzil Carmichael): *Camber the Heretic* 301–302; Oriel triggers: *Camber the Heretic* 304–305; Declan's: *The Harrowing of Gwynedd* 310–314; Aislinn might have willed own death in preference to being murdered: *Camber the Heretic* 454; Ian forces Edgar: *Deryni Rising* 185; Andrew, by poison: *Deryni Checkmate* 111–112; Wencit threatens to make Derry commit: *High Deryni* 241–242; Derry attempts: *High Deryni* 243–245; Coram, by poison: *High Deryni* 338–341.

SUSPENSION SPELL—Ariella tried: *Saint Camber* 110; why Ariella's failed: *Saint Camber* 203; Camber tempted to use on Rhys: *Camber the Heretic* 411–412; Camber tries: *Camber the Heretic* 480–481; Evaine, regarding Camber's attempt: *Camber the Heretic* 485–490, *The Harrowing of Gwynedd* 4–5.

SWORD magic—Alister's, to slay Ariella: *Saint Camber* 104, 110–111; Jebediah's, to protect Camber-Alister: *Camber the Heretic* 476.

SYMPATHETIC magic—Ariella's weather magic: *Saint Camber* 2; regarding: *Saint Camber* 5, 49; reference to Charissa stopping Brion's heart with: *High Deryni* 342; Kelson learns to use: *High Deryni* 344; Rothana's feared, re Sidana's ring: *The Quest for Saint Camber* 247–246.

TELEKINESIS—Gregory smashes crockery and so on: *Camber the Heretic* 9–10; Camber tries to lift Rhys' depressed fracture: *Camber the Heretic* 410; Morgan and whip: *Deryni Rising* 39; Charissa makes gauntlet return to hand: *Deryni Rising* 255; Kelson and Morgan with arrows: *The King's Justice* 10–12; Conall ties knot in blade of grass; *The King's Justice* 168; Kelson diverts arrows: *The King's Justice* 240–241; Morgan takes over: *The King's Justice* 242; Dhugal unlocks Duncan's shackles: *The King's Justice* 245; Duncan unlocks tabernacle at wedding: *The Quest for Saint Camber* 16; Arilan makes cups float to him: *The Quest for Saint Camber* 29; Dhugal lifts skull fracture: *The Quest for Saint Camber* 211–213; Dhugal moves bar on door: *The Quest for Saint Camber* 325–326, 331; Dhugal loosens knots: *The Quest for Saint Camber* 338; Rhys moves game piece: *The Deryni Archives* 11; Joram moves game piece: *The Deryni Archives* 12. See Locks.

TELEPATHY—Queron to Jesse, via medallion: *The Harrowing of Gwynedd* 186–188; Morgan sends burst of strength and confidence to Kelson: *Deryni Rising* 180; Morgan sets up link with Derry: *Deryni Checkmate* 55; link with Derry: *Deryni Checkmate* 99, 100–102; Bronwyn once did mind-link with Kevin: *Deryni Checkmate* 145, 151; vision of Saint Camber at Saint Neot's, to Morgan and Duncan: *High Deryni* 82; Morgan calls Duncan and Kelson: *High Deryni* 179; Arilan calls Camberian Council: *High Deryni* 296; Duncan's mental scream, caught by Morgan: *The Bishop's Heir* 37; Morgan will try to reach Kelson in sleep: *The Bishop's Heir* 44; does try: *The Bishop's Heir* 75–78, 79; link established: *The Bishop's Heir* 81–82; Morgan and Kelson, during Duncan's consecration: *The Bishop's Heir* 236, 239; Morgan and Duncan during consecration: *The Bishop's Heir* 240; Morgan and Richenda: *The Bishop's Heir* 272; Morgan and Kelson, at procession: *The Bishop's Heir* 328–329; Kelson's mind screams for Morgan and Duncan to save Sidana: *The Bishop's Heir* 339; Laran to Barrett: *The King's Justice* xvii; Kelson to Morgan, re Liam: *The King's Justice* 76; Morgan and Duncan, at distance: *The King's Justice* 95–96; Morgan to Kelson: *The King's Justice* 105; theory of how to contact Morgan out of hours: *The King's Justice* 144, 204; Richenda to Rothana: *The King's Justice* 147; Richenda, Rothana, and Azim: *The King's Justice* 152; Kelson to Morgan: *The King's Justice* 169; Jehana releases Ambros' memory: *The King's Justice* 176; Nigel feels Richenda's touch: *The King's Justice* 187; Duncan orders Dhugal to escape: *The King's Justice* 202; Morgan to Kelson: *The King's Justice* 240; Sofiana's link to Raif: *The King's Justice* 268; Kelson to Dhugal, greeting before knighting: *The Quest for Saint Camber* 52; Kelson to Duncan, at Dhugal's knighting: *The Quest for Saint Camber* 58; Duncan to Kelson: *The Quest for Saint Camber* 59; Dhugal to Kelson: *The Quest for Saint Camber* 64; Kelson to Dhugal: *The Quest for Saint Camber* 87; Duncan to Morgan: *The Quest for*

# PARTIAL LINEAGE OF
# THE HALDANE KINGS

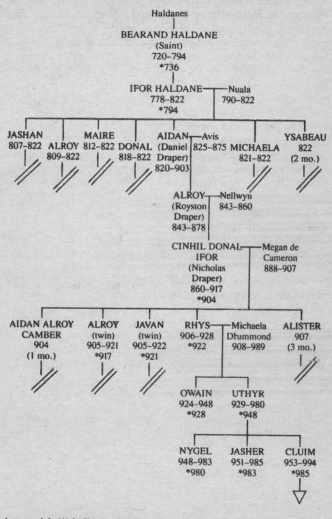

Haldanes

BEARAND HALDANE
(Saint)
720–794
*736

IFOR HALDANE——Nuala
778–822      790–822
*794

JASHAN      MAIRE      AIDAN—Avis         YSABEAU
807–822  ALROY  812–822  DONAL  (Daniel  825–875  MICHAELA  822
         809–822      818–822  Draper)      821–822  (2 mo.)
                             820–903

ALROY—Nellwyn
(Royston  843–860
Draper)
843–878

CINHIL DONAL——Megan de
IFOR         Cameron
(Nicholas    888–907
Draper)
860–917
*904

AIDAN ALROY   ALROY   JAVAN   RHYS—Michaela   ALISTER
CAMBER        (twin)  (twin)  906–928  Drummond  907
904           905–921  905–922  *922    908–989   (3 mo.)
(1 mo.)       *917     *921

OWAIN      UTHYR
924–948    929–980
*928       *948

NYGEL      JASHER     CLUIM
948–983    951–985    953–994
*980       *983       *985

An asterisk (*) indicates the date of the beginning of each king's reign.

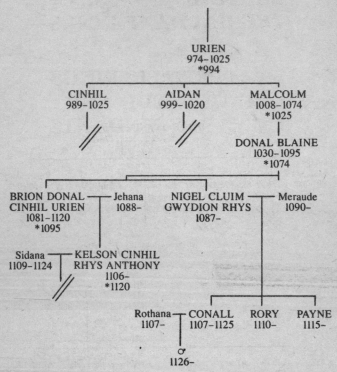

URIEN
974–1025
*994

CINHIL
989–1025

AIDAN
999–1020

MALCOLM
1008–1074
*1025

DONAL BLAINE
1030–1095
*1074

BRION DONAL
CINHIL URIEN
1081–1120
*1095 — Jehana
1088–

NIGEL CLUIM
GWYDION RHYS
1087– — Meraude
1090–

Sidana
1109–1124 — KELSON CINHIL
RHYS ANTHONY
1106–
*1120

Rothana
1107– — CONALL
1107–1125

RORY
1110–

PAYNE
1115–

♂
1126–

# THE FESTILLIC KINGS OF GWYNEDD AND THEIR DESCENDANTS

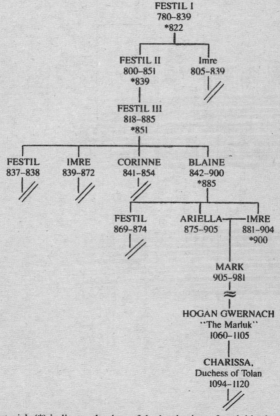

An asterisk (*) indicates the date of the beginning of each king's reign.

# PARTIAL LINEAGE OF THE MacRORIES

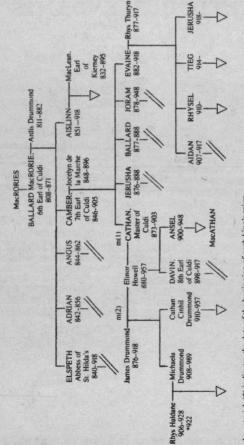

An asterisk (*) indicates the date of the beginning of each king's reign.

# ABOUT THE AUTHOR

Katherine Kurtz was born in Coral Gables, Florida, during a hurricane and has led a whirlwind existence ever since. She holds a Bachelor of Science degree in chemistry from the University of Miami, Florida, and a Master of Arts degree in English history from UCLA. She studied medicine before deciding that she would rather write, and is an Ericksonian-trained hypnotist. Her scholarly background also includes extensive research in religious history, magical systems, and other esoteric subjects.

Katherine Kurtz's literary works include the well-known *Deryni*, *Camber*, and *Kelson* trilogies of fantasy fiction, an occult thriller set in World War II England, and a number of Deryni-related short stories. At least three more trilogies are planned in the Deryni universe, and several additional mainstream thrillers are also currently in development.

Ms. Kurtz lives in Ireland with her husband and son in a Victorian gothic-revival house that looks like Toad Hall.

# KATHERINE KURTZ *The first lady of legend, fantasy and romance!*

*"A great new talent in the field of fantasy!"*